AF575098

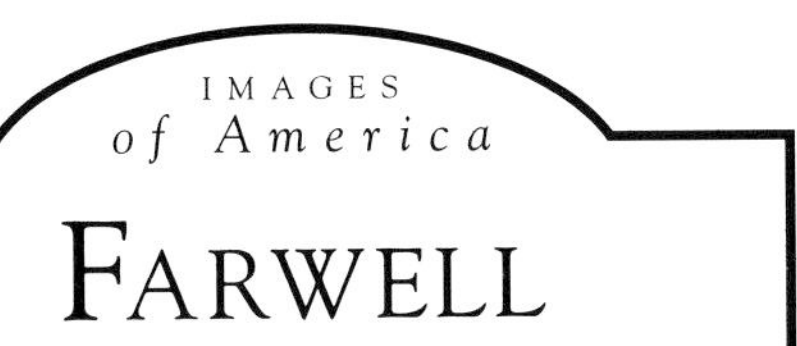
IMAGES
of America
FARWELL

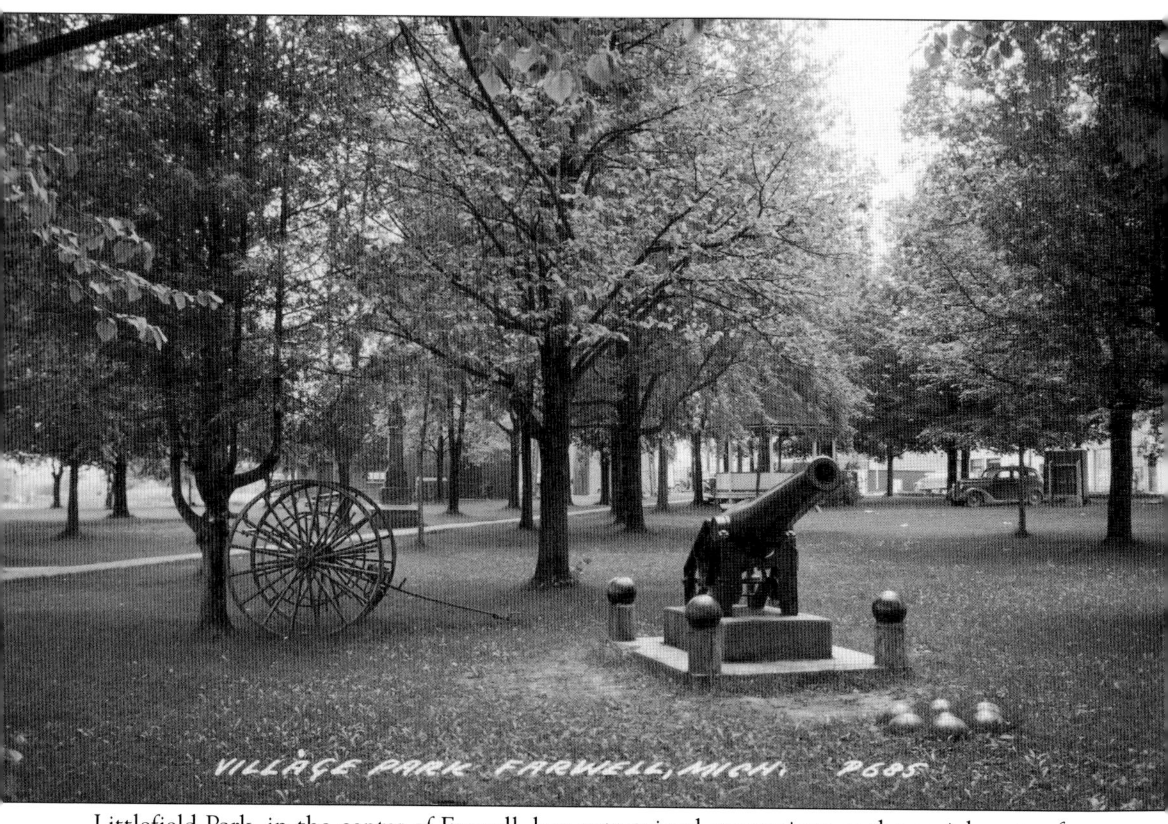

Littlefield Park, in the center of Farwell, has entertained generations as the social center for memorial services, festivals, reunions, and photo opportunities on the Civil War cannon. This photo postcard shows a view of the GAR monument, the cannon, and the gazebo. (Courtesy of the Harrison District Library.)

On the Cover: The Farwell City Band was founded by C.F. Lyon in 1886 and taken over in 1887 by Eugene "Dutch" Eager, who led it for over 38 years. The band performed in parades, at school functions, and at every important event in the community. They were the pride of the community in their gold braided green suits. The band even drew audiences for their practices at Littlefield Park. (Courtesy of the Farwell Area Historical Museum.)

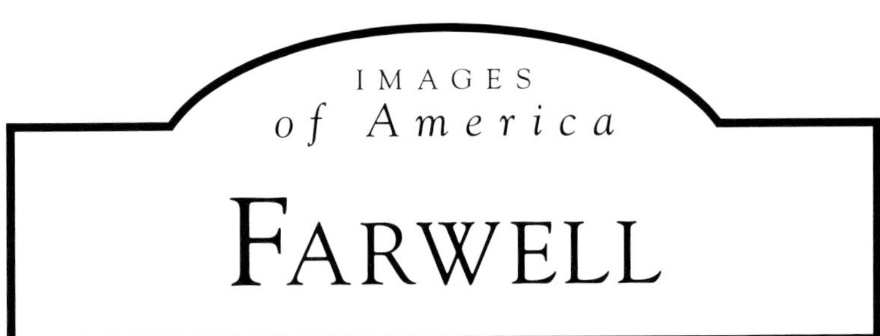

Angela Kellogg and Nick Loomis

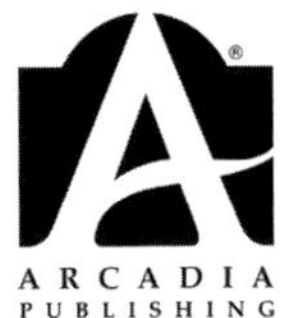

ISBN 978-1-4671-1706-7

Published by Arcadia Publishing
Charleston, South Carolina

Printed in the United States of America

Library of Congress Control Number: 2016930605

For all general information, please contact Arcadia Publishing:
Telephone 843-853-2070
Fax 843-853-0044
E-mail sales@arcadiapublishing.com
For customer service and orders:
Toll-Free 1-888-313-2665

Visit us on the Internet at www.arcadiapublishing.com

For Dad, Barry A. Henry Sr., and his hometown.

Contents

Acknowledgments

Many thanks to those who were supportive of this book and contributed photographs, family history, and information: Jared Clouse, James Graham, Patrick Graham, Janet Hagg, James Hannum, Toni Hayes, Barry Henry Sr., Joe Manley, Sarah Moore, Gary Saxton, and Scott Welty.

Special thanks to Clare County Historical Society members Andy Coulson, Martin Johnson, Robert Knapp, Jon Ringleberg, and Sam Sellers, who are always willing to research, preserve, promote, and have fun with history. This book was possible because of their encouragement and willingness to help research, find, and scan material and provide valuable input.

Thank you to Cody Beemer for permission to put in print for the first time photographs of the Lake George & Muskegon River Railroad and sharing his extensive knowledge about railroads, logging, and Clare County history.

Thank you to Connie Calkins, Cindy Hoefling, Dannielle Rogers, Miranda Reyes, and Cheryl Wagner, staff at the Harrison District Library, for patience and support as this book took shape. A special thank-you to Sheila Bissonnette and Mary-Jane Ogg for encouragement and guidance.

The community of Farwell owes a great debt to the Farwell Area Historical Museum for its excellent preservation of local history. Many thanks to Alice Wilson for her support of this book and her many contributions to preserving Farwell history.

The work of Forrest Meek continues to be the foundation that all Clare County historians reference, and his collection is an invaluable resource.

Images in this volume appear courtesy of the Harrison District Library (HDL), the Forrest Meek Collection (Meek), and the Clare County Historical Society (CCHS). All unattributed images are from the collection of the Farwell Area Historical Museum.

INTRODUCTION

Farwell was once the largest and most important community in Clare County. As the first county seat, it was the beginning of county government and a hub of lumbering and business activity. Although it was founded by wealthy and prominent businessmen, its success is owed to the families who first settled there. Educated and wealthy, the Hall, Hitchcock, Littlefield, and Woodruff families sought to bring culture and order to Farwell, unlike most other early Michigan lumber towns. The families were related through the marriages of Edmund Hall's sisters Mary (Littlefield), Abigail (Woodruff), and Martha (Hitchcock.) A testament to the women's influence on Farwell was the Ladies' Library Association. They also brought to Farwell books, nice furniture, and the expectation of a civilized village.

The Farwell City Company was formed by Gurdon Corning, Lorenzo Curtis, Edmund Hall, James Hay, Thomas Merrill, James Pearson, Erza Rust, and Ammi Wright in 1870. These men were successful lumbermen and businessmen led by Edmund Hall, who had the contract to build the state road from Ionia to Houghton Lake. By 1875, Edmund Hall had bought out the other members of the Farwell City Company and later sold most of those holdings to his nephew Josiah Littlefield.

Farwell was off to a prosperous beginning, and many businesses came to Farwell to serve the lumber camps, settlers, and new residents. This was interrupted in July 1877 when the courthouse burned in a suspicious fire. Fortunately, most county records survived the fire. The cause of the fire was never determined, but it sparked controversy and debate that continues today.

A temporary courthouse was put in use, and the squabble began over where to locate a new one. The county seat was sought after as it brought jobs, business, and prominence to wherever it was located. Clare and Farwell both lobbied for the county seat, but there were many other factors to take into consideration. The Michigan legislature had passed a law that county courthouses must be as centrally located as possible. Though it was still just wilderness, the town of Harrison, in the middle of the county, was being planned as the Flint & Pere Marquette Railroad was making its way north.

There are conflicting stories about influential lumbermen like Winfield Scott Gerrish paying his men in drink to go to the polls to vote for keeping the county seat in Farwell. His logging railroad was nearing the Budd Lake area as he continued to clear lumber and profits from his Lake George & Muskegon River Railroad. This story was likely newspaper fodder to rally the farmers against lumbering and business interests by claiming men like Gerrish could influence their men to vote any way they wished.

The *Farwell Register* editor James (nicknamed "Jeems") Holden and *Clare County Press* editor Alvardo Goodenow fanned the fires of contention in their papers, turning Farwell and Clare against each other. The mudslinging grew personal, and much more was made of it than the real issue at hand—where to locate the courthouse.

Eventually, the vote was accepted that the courthouse would be located in the future town of Harrison. In a final act of antagonism, the supervisors did not fully fund the project and only built the courthouse and not the jail, with troublesome results for the new county seat. Farwell's planned courthouse square later became the site of a beautiful new home for the Hitchcock family, and Farwell went about its business as a prosperous new town. Many lawyers and businessmen followed business to the new county seat and set up shop in Harrison while still keeping their main interests in Farwell.

Throughout the 1880s and 1890s, Farwell was a successful and growing community. Officially incorporated as a village in 1879, farming was prospering south of Farwell in Gilmore Township, business was growing downtown, and lumber operations were at full speed in every direction. Hotels, shops, churches, and other businesses were flourishing even without the county seat. In addition to the Flint & Pere Marquette Railroad, the Toledo & Ann Arbor Railroad reached Farwell in 1887.

After the large lumber operations moved on, small lumber work continued for many years. Attention was turned to the land for farming, and tourism started very early on the many beautiful lakes around Farwell. Excursion trains were taken as early as the 1890s to Crooked Lake. Train service made it easy to travel to the Farwell area, and later the automobile made tourism a success by bringing city dwellers up north to enjoy hunting, fishing, boating, and other outdoor sports year-round.

One

Farwell

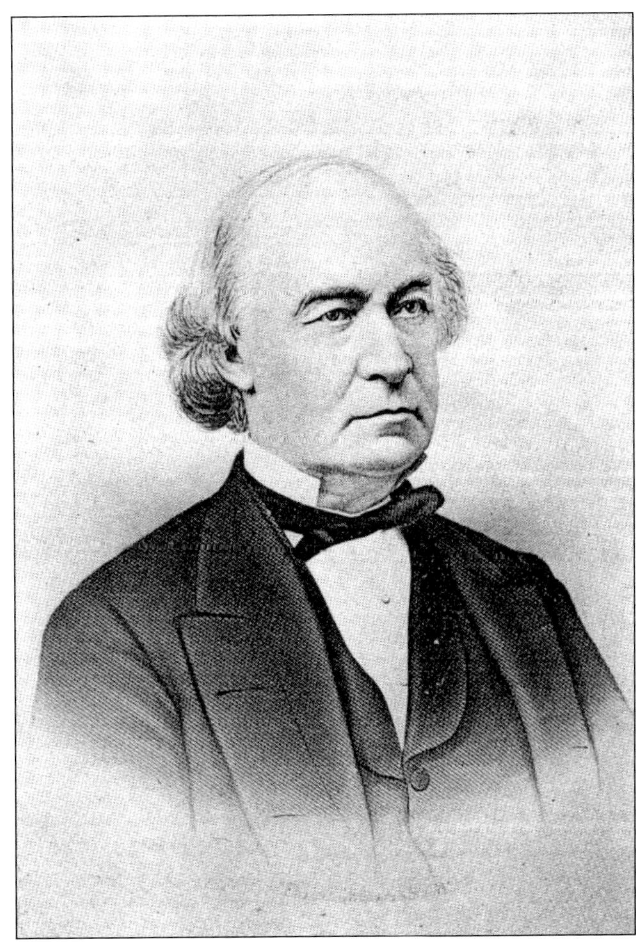

Farwell was named for Samuel Farwell of Utica, New York, vice president and principal shareholder in the Flint & Pere Marquette Railroad. He was an influential man with a long, successful career in canal building, construction, and the railroad. It is not known if Samuel Farwell ever visited the new city that was named after him. He died in 1875 at age 80 and is buried in Utica.

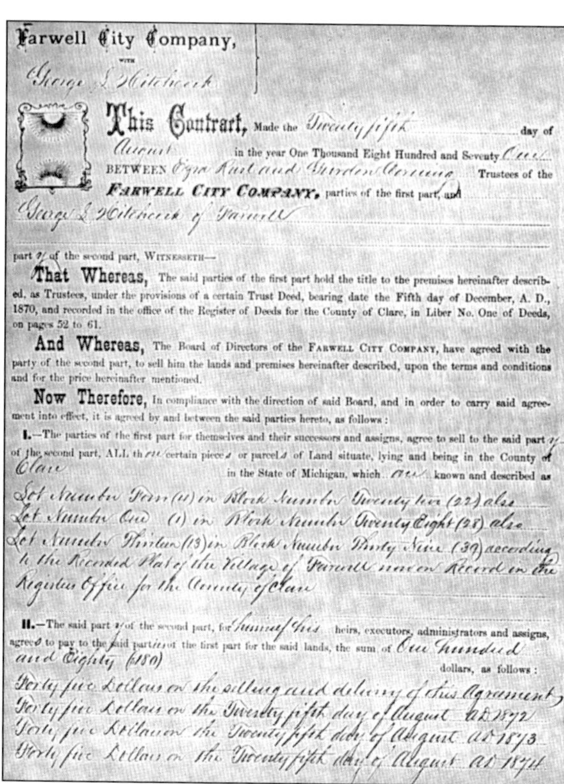

Farwell City Company,

WITH

George L. Hitchcock

This Contract, Made the Twenty fifth day of August in the year One Thousand Eight Hundred and Seventy One BETWEEN Ezra Rust and Gurdon Corning Trustees of the FARWELL CITY COMPANY, parties of the first part, and George L. Hitchcock of Farwell

party of the second part, WITNESSETH—

That Whereas, The said parties of the first part hold the title to the premises hereinafter described, as Trustees, under the provisions of a certain Trust Deed, bearing date the Fifth day of December, A. D., 1870, and recorded in the office of the Register of Deeds for the County of Clare, in Liber No. One of Deeds, on pages 52 to 61.

And Whereas, The Board of Directors of the FARWELL CITY COMPANY, have agreed with the party of the second part, to sell him the lands and premises hereinafter described, upon the terms and conditions and for the price hereinafter mentioned.

Now Therefore, In compliance with the direction of said Board, and in order to carry said agreement into effect, it is agreed by and between the said parties hereto, as follows:

I.—The parties of the first part for themselves and their successors and assigns, agree to sell to the said party of the second part, ALL those certain pieces or parcels of Land situate, lying and being in the County of Clare in the State of Michigan, which are known and described as

Lot Number Four (4) in Block Number Twenty two (22) also Lot Number One (1) in Block Number Twenty Eight (28) also Lot Number Thirteen (13) in Block Number Thirty Nine (39) according to the Recorded Plat of the Village of Farwell now on Record in the Register Office for the County of Clare

II.—The said party of the second part, for himself his heirs, executors, administrators and assigns, agrees to pay to the said parties of the first part for the said lands, the sum of One Hundred and Eighty (180) dollars, as follows:

Forty five Dollars on the selling and delivery of this Agreement

Forty five Dollars on the Twenty fifth day of August AD 1872

Forty five Dollars on the Twenty fifth day of August AD 1873

Forty five Dollars on the Twenty fifth day of August AD 1874

Farwell City Company was formed as a joint stock company in 1870 by the efforts of prominent businessmen Gurdon Corning, Lorenzo Curtis, Edmund Hall, James Hay, Thomas Merrill, James Pearson, Erza Rust, and Ammi Wright. These businessmen, lumbermen, and mostly millionaires invested widely in many business ventures, of which Farwell was one. Several streets in Farwell are named for founding members of the company.

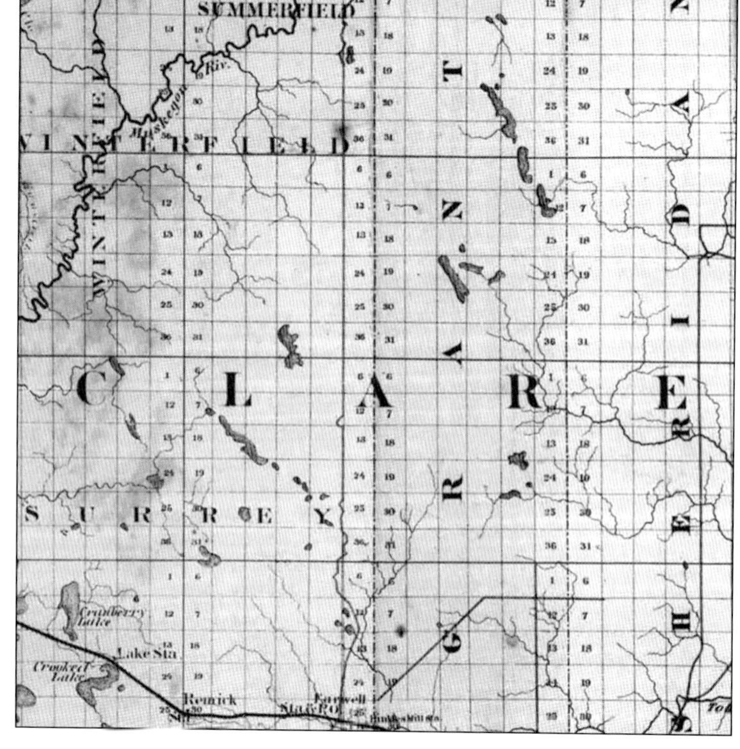

The location for Farwell coincided with the Flint & Pere Marquette Railroad route, and changes were made to the Ionia to Houghton Lake state road by Edmund Hall to travel through Farwell, making it an important locale in the early days of Clare County. It supplied lumber camps and provided a route for early settlers. The state road is just to the left of the center line of this 1875 Clare County map. (Meek.)

Farwell was designed to be a planned community and did not develop as shacks surrounding a sawmill or railroad siding like other lumber towns. A clause in every deed sold stated that buildings had to be at least one and one half story high with two coats of good oil paint. It also excluded the sale of liquor and the establishment of saloons until January 1876. It is not likely the village remained dry, as more lumber operations moved into the area by 1875.

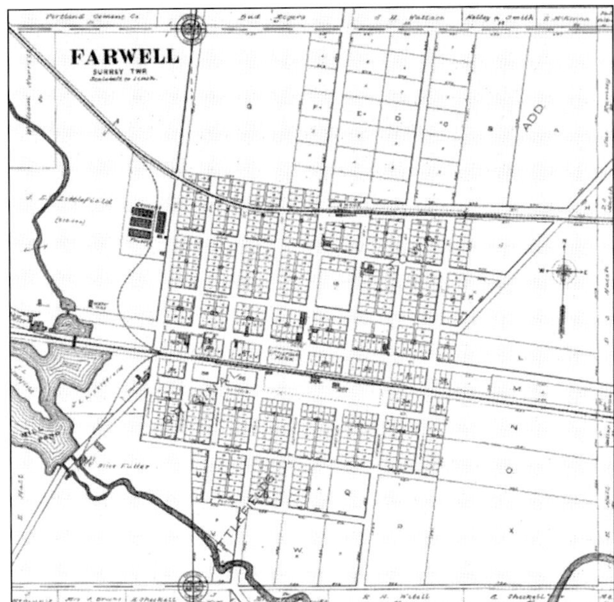

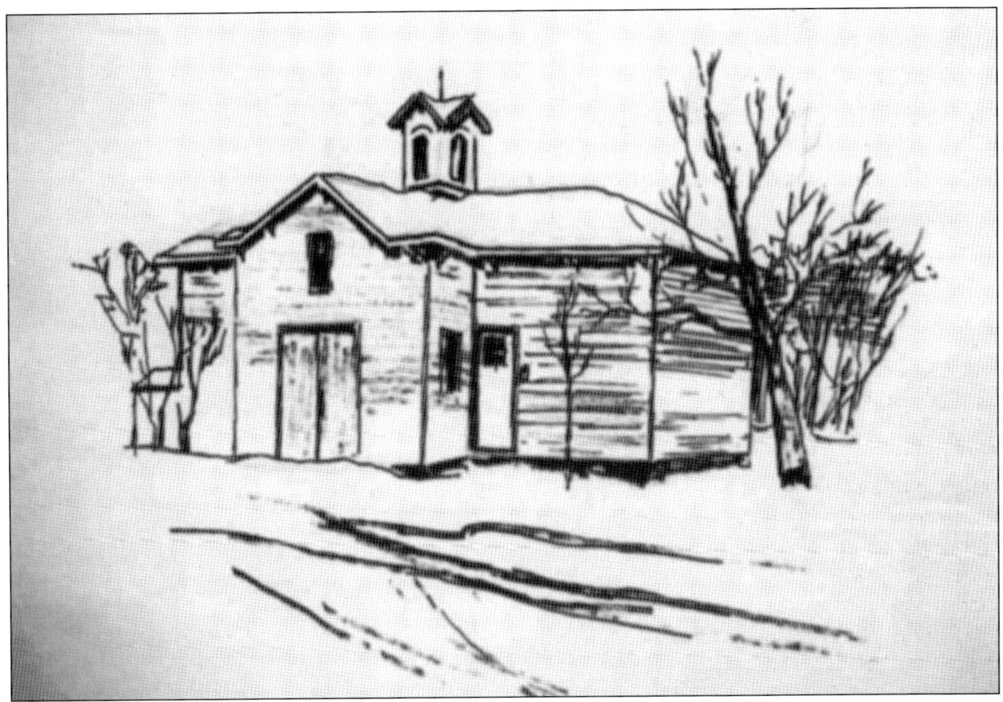

The county seat was officially begun in Farwell on May 11, 1871, and the courthouse built in 1872. It burned down in a suspicious fire in 1877, though arson could never be proven, despite a cash reward being offered. A temporary courthouse was in use at Farwell after the fire until a new one could be constructed at Harrison. This sketch of the first county courthouse first appeared in *Michigan Timber Battleground* by Forrest Meek. No photographs are known to exist of the courthouse, so this sketch may have been taken from a firsthand account describing the courthouse, a photograph in a newspaper, or a general artist's rendition of what a small rural courthouse would have looked like at the time. (Meek.)

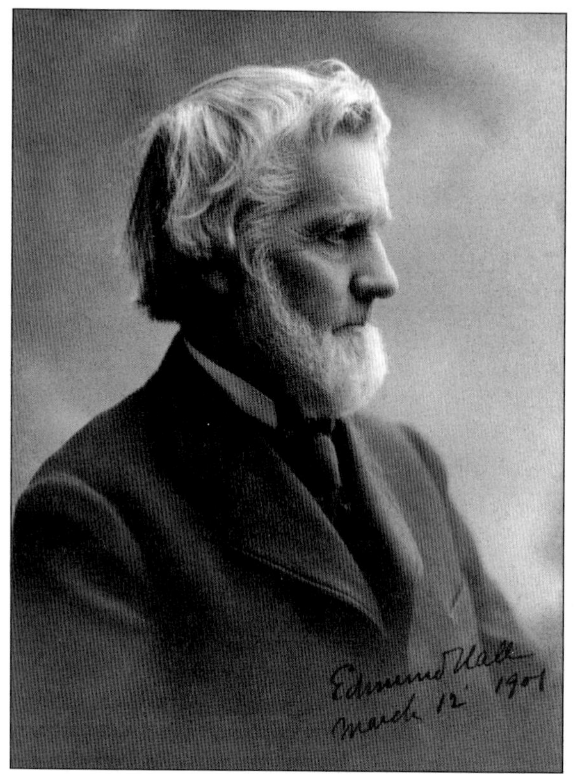

Edmund Hall was a lawyer from Wayne County. He came to Michigan at 14 years of age from New York and later went to Oberlin College in Ohio. He passed the bar in 1847, invested in land in Gibralter, and served on the Detroit School Board. He eventually gave up law to pursue business, and acquired contracts to build state roads in Isabella, Clare, and other counties, often taking his pay in land. He became a timber operator, making his fortune in lumbering. Though his permanent home was in Wayne County, Hall and his family were instrumental in developing Farwell.

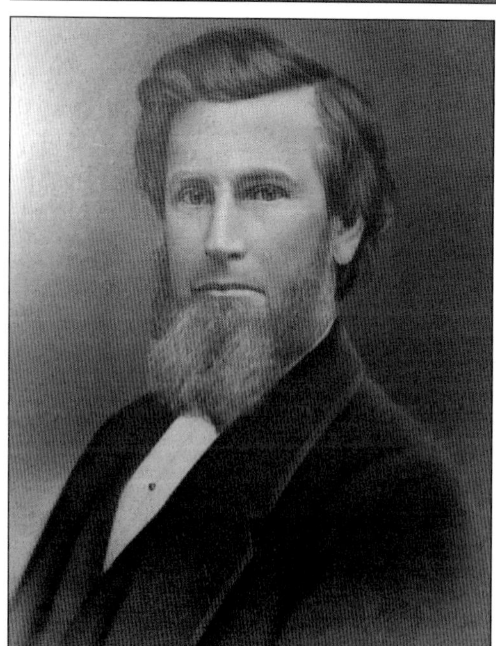

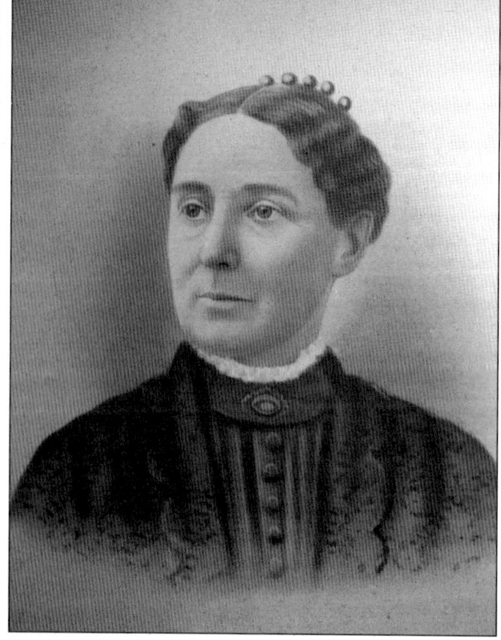

George Hitchcock was married to Edmund Hall's sister Martha Hall Hitchcock. Martha sought to influence the cultural atmosphere of the new village in the wilderness. George was the first treasurer of Clare County. The founding families that would dominate politics and the social scene in Farwell were well educated and adept.

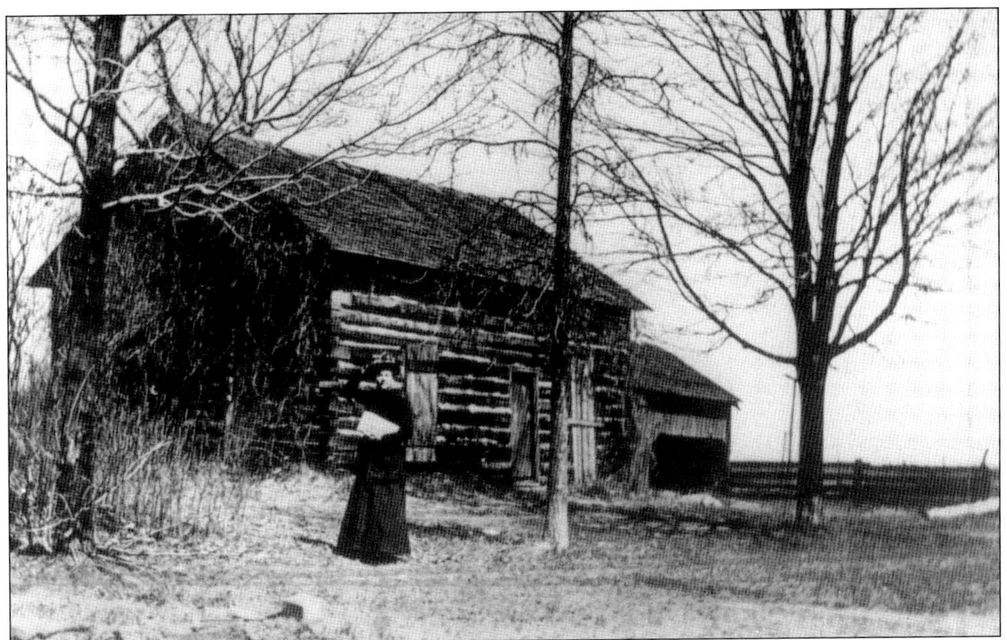

The Hitchcocks are noted as the first permanent residents of Farwell. This cabin was the first in Farwell, and it became the stopping place for everyone who passed through or came to Farwell. Their original home was later moved to Crooked Lake and used as a cabin by their daughter Alice, her husband, William Fuller, and their family. The cabin does not stand today. (Meek.)

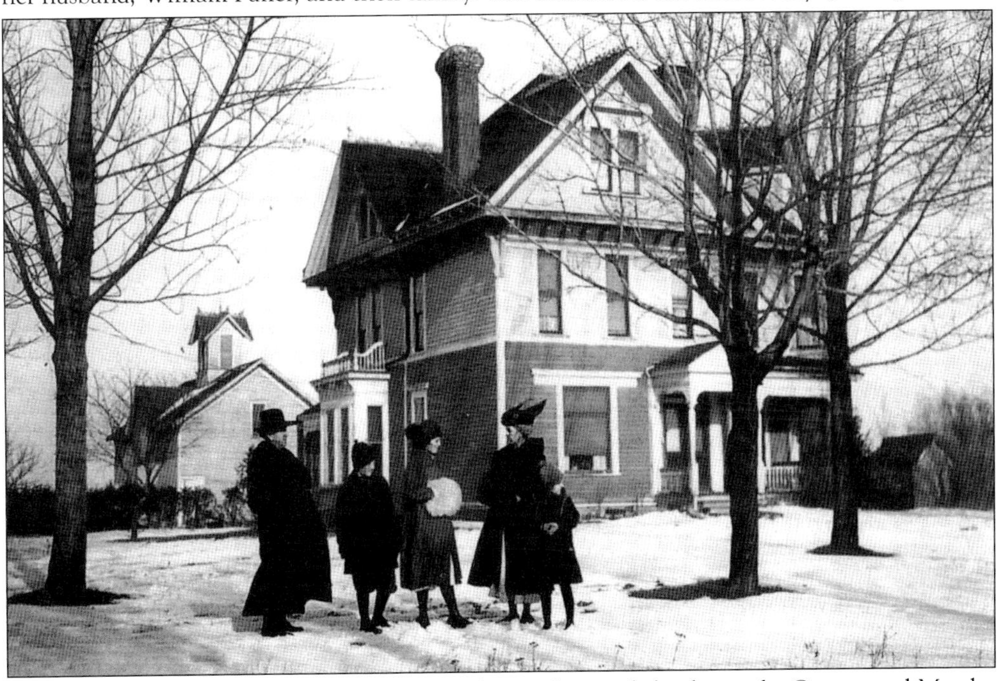

The prestigious Detroit architects Mason and Rice designed this home for George and Martha Hitchcock. They built it on the courthouse square lots after the county courthouse burned and was moved to Harrison. Their daughter Alice inherited the home, and her family is shown here in 1916. From left to right are William, George, Martha, Alice, and Marion Fuller.

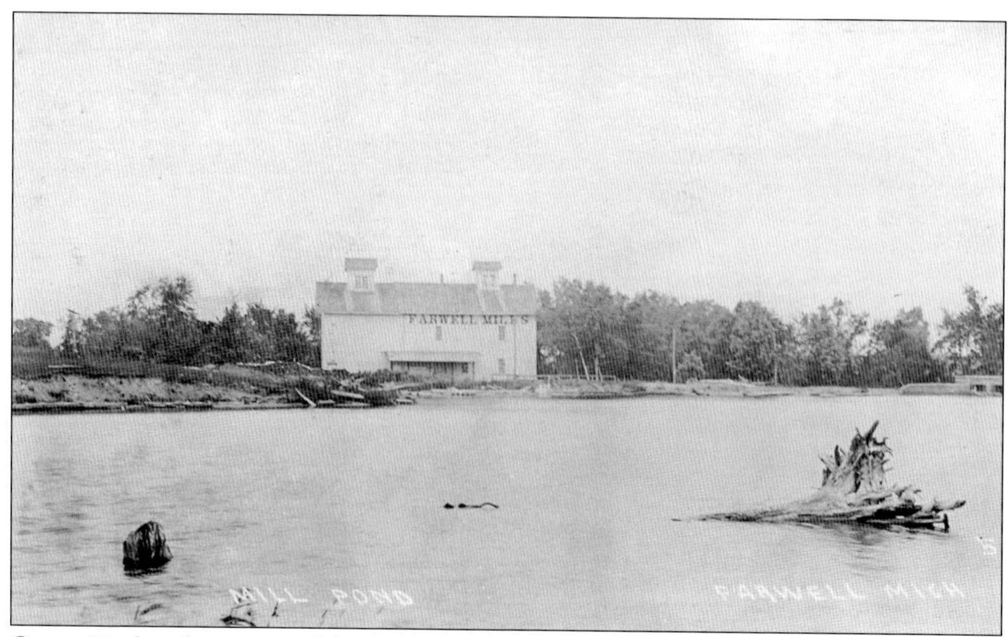

George Hitchcock constructed this gristmill and flour mill in the mid-1870s. It was sturdily built of local hemlock and pine and held together with wooden pegs. People from all over the area utilized the mill to grind their grain, and it helped transition the area to agriculture from lumbering. It was in operation for over 125 years.

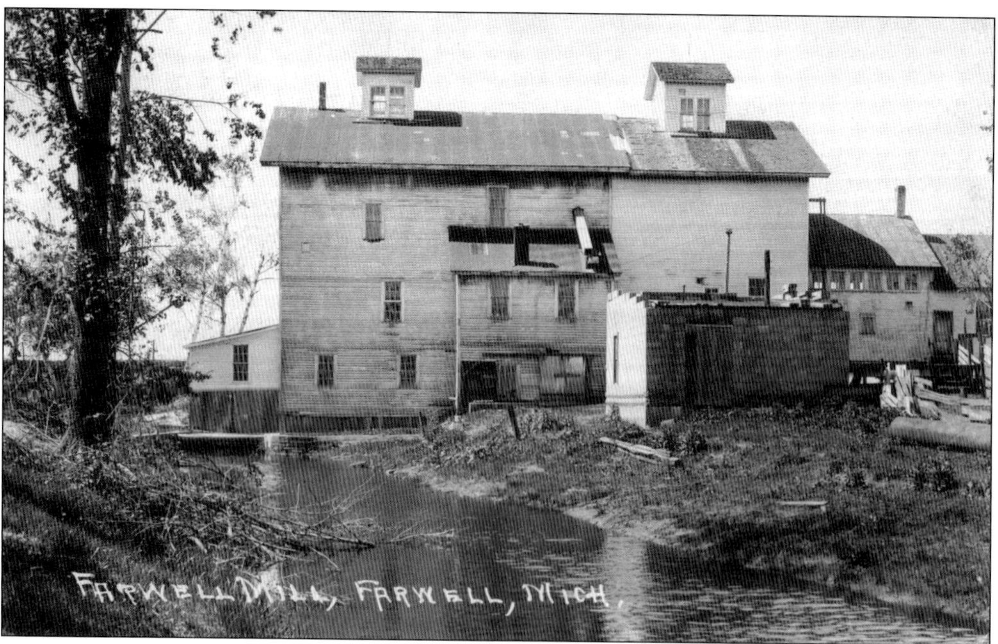

This postcard shows the back of the Farwell Mill in the 1920s. Duane and Laurie Warner purchased the mill in 2001 and began to make repairs on the turbines and refurbish the buildings. It was a landmark in Farwell until it was destroyed by fire on July 3, 2003. The cause of the fire was never determined. (HDL.)

Fred Siegle was born in Germany, where he apprenticed, receiving his master millers license. He immigrated to America in 1923. Siegle's dream of owning his own mill was fulfilled in Farwell when he purchased the Farwell Mill in 1927. Siegle operated the mill until he was 94 years old.

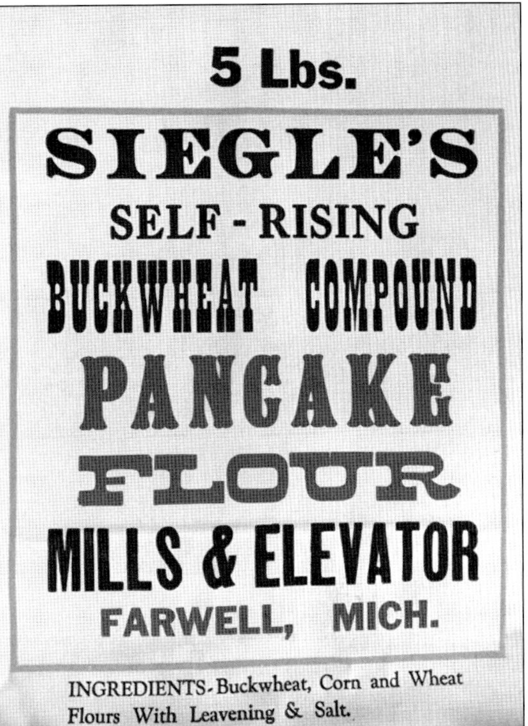

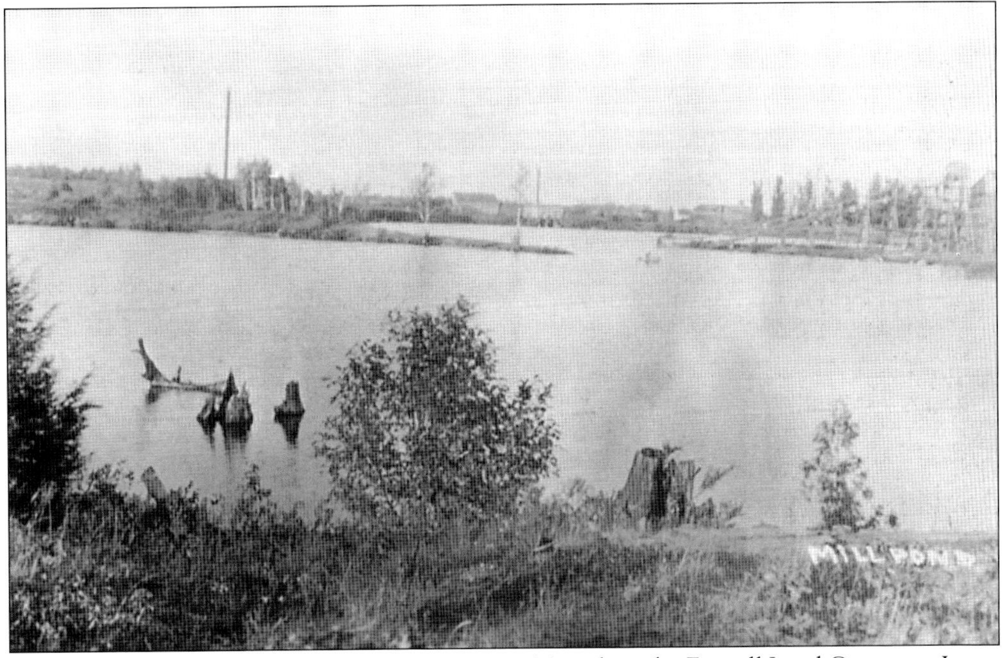

The dam was built on the millpond by the original founders, the Farwell Land Company. It was built for log drives and storing logs to be milled but later served as valuable waterpower with a concrete overflow and water wheels. Efforts in the 1990s to develop the millpond by selling subdivided lots and deepening the pond failed due to environmental and local opposition. The power station is pictured at center, and the mill and ice works are to the right.

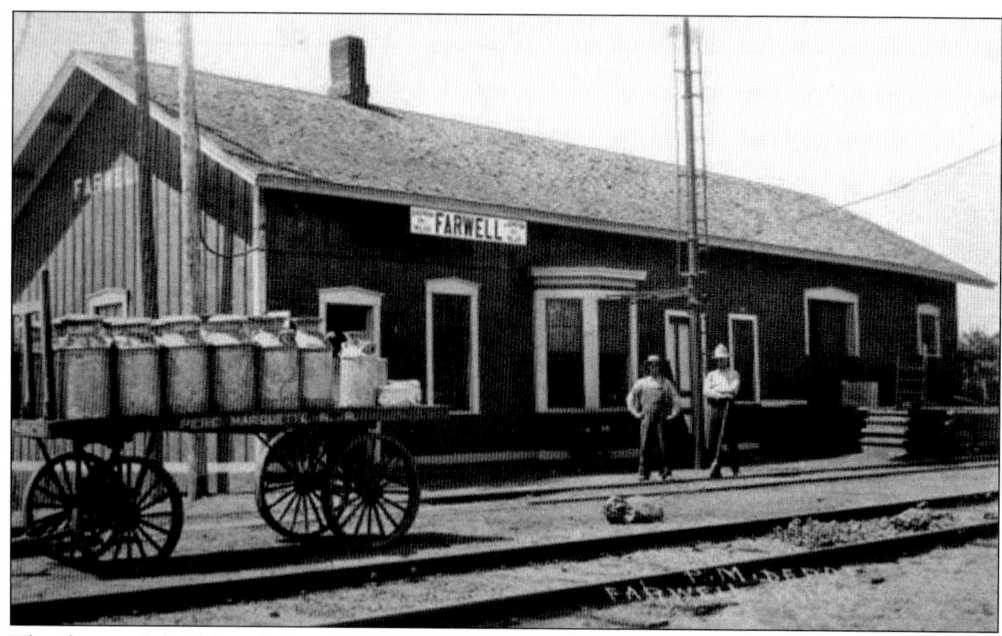

The depot of the Flint & Pere Marquette Railroad was built in 1871 one block south of Main Street. It was the focal point of activity as Farwell grew, serving as meeting place, post office, and general store. Freight was delivered by horse and cart to businesses and homes throughout town. The railroad tracks were removed in 1987 and later became a rails-to-trails bike and footpath.

D. R. WAIT,

DEALER IN FINE FAMILY

Groceries and Provisions,

TOBACCO, CIGARS, YANKEE NOTIONS, &c.

Manufacturer and Dealer in Pine and Hardwood Lumber of all kinds and Shingles.

Orders solicited and will receive prompt attention. Satisfaction guaranteed.

FARWELL, - - - - - MICHIGAN.

The Farwell Register,

JAMES S. HOLDEN, Publisher,

FARWELL, Clare Co. - - MICHIGAN.

ESTABLISHED IN 1872.

The REGISTER is the only Newspaper published in Clare County; has a large local and general circulation; especially devoted to Local News, the Lumber and General Interest of Northern Michigan. The REGISTER gives more information in regard to Lumber matters than any other paper in this portion of the State, Northwest of Saginaw. Manufacturers and dealers will find it to their interest to patronize its columns. The REGISTER is an 8 page, 6 column paper, published weekly at $2 per annum.

FARWELL HOUSE,

H. WOODRUFF, Proprietor,

FARWELL, - - - MICHIGAN.

This Large and Commodious House is centrally located in the business portion of the town. Large Sample Rooms on first floor for commercial travelers. Good accommodation. Large Barns in connection.

Farwell was securely on the map as a successful place to do business by 1877 as advertisements in the *Michigan State Gazetteer and Business Directory* by R.L. Polk & Co. suggest. James Stuart Holden was the owner of the *Farwell Register* and had a long career in the newspaper business. Born in Ireland in 1840, he came to Detroit as an infant with his parents. He apprenticed at the *Midland Sentinel* and worked for the *Detroit Tribune* before coming to Farwell in 1872. He was also the postmaster of Farwell from 1875 to 1879.

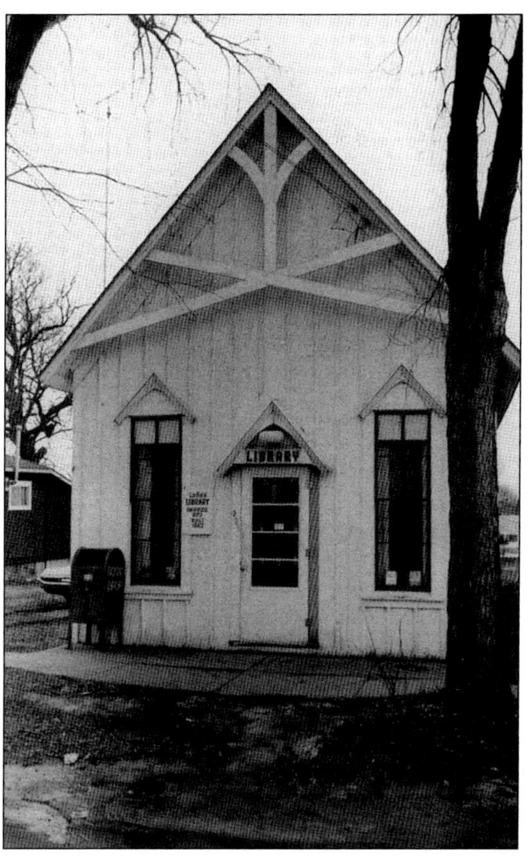

Abigail Woodruff and her sister Martha Hitchcock organized the Ladies' Library Association in 1872 to bring culture to Farwell. It was incorporated in 1879. The Farwell Land Company gave them the lot to erect a building. For a few years, the Methodist and Congregational Ladies Aid held 10¢ dinners here. During World War I, the activities included Red Cross work. In 1931, the township rented the building for a public library until the present library was constructed. After the new library was built, the Ladies' Library Association turned it over to the historical society. Today, the building houses the Farwell Area Historical Museum.

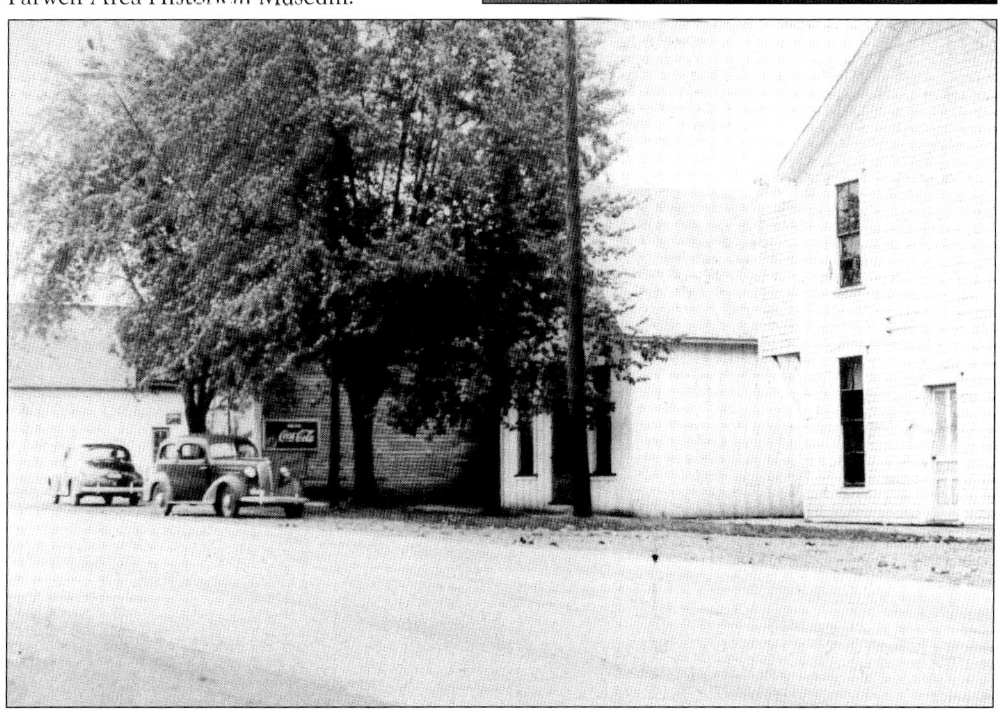

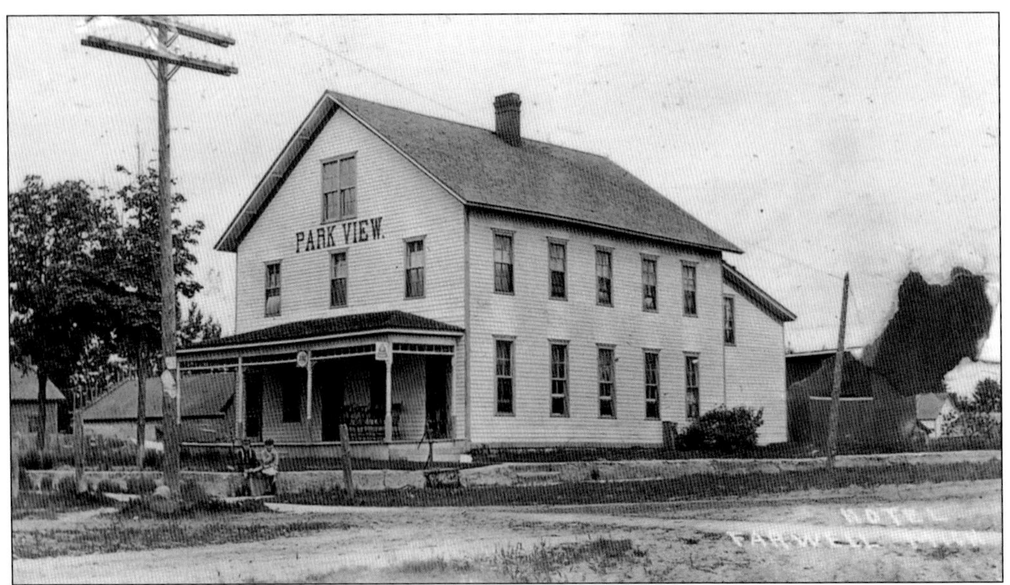

The Rust House was built in 1872 to accommodate the growing town and its need for boarding rooms. By customer demand, it was the first hotel to break the temperance agreement by serving alcohol in 1875. It was later called the New Farwell Hotel and partially burned in 1910. It was rebuilt with more modern amenities, and the third floor and front half were removed. After 1916, it was known as the Park View Hotel, and it was torn down in 1998.

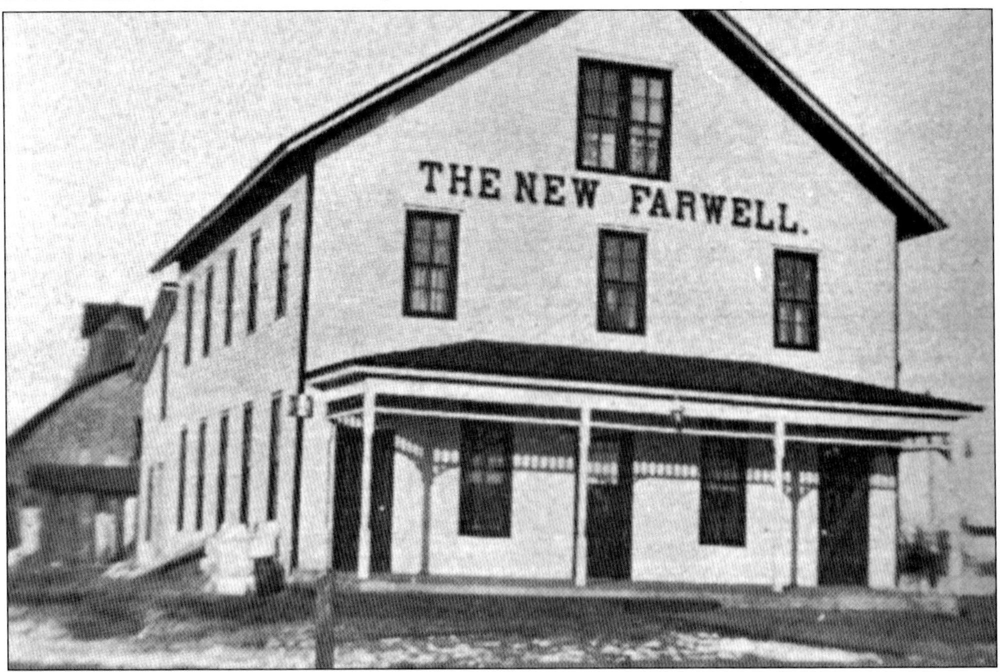

The New Farwell Hotel was probably named "new" so it was not confused with the Woodruff Hotel, commonly referred to as the Farwell House. The Woodruff was built in the early 1870s by Henry Woodruff to replace his original little boardinghouse that was too small to accommodate the growing number of shanty boys and businessmen coming to Farwell. This photograph is from the 1906 *Standard Atlas of Clare County*. (HDL.)

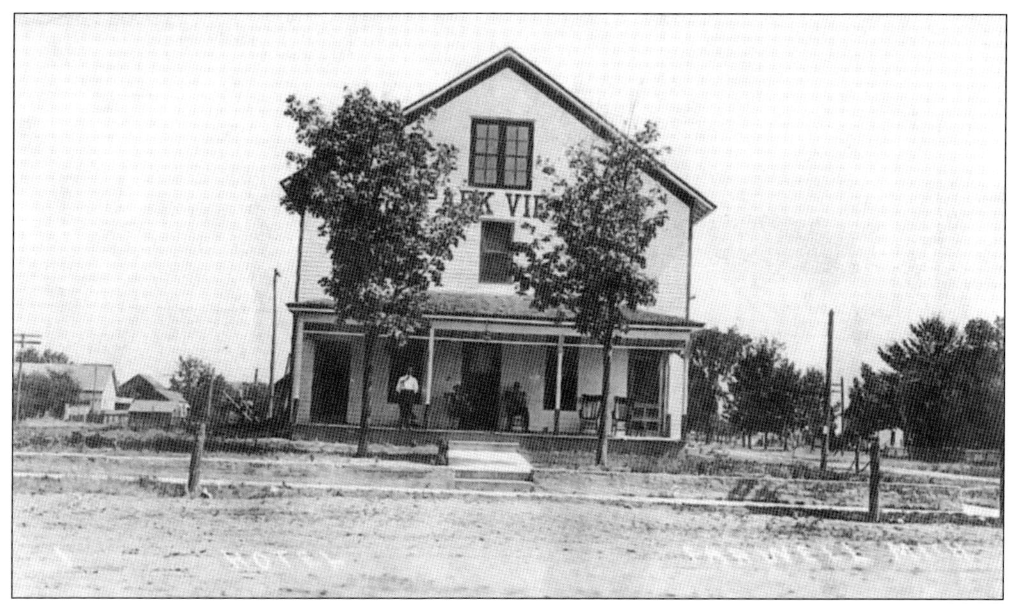

The Park View Hotel was located on the north side of Main Street across the street from Littlefield Park. Though Farwell did not have the reputation for shanty boy bawdiness that other Clare County towns had, the hotels of Farwell still saw their share of bad behavior.

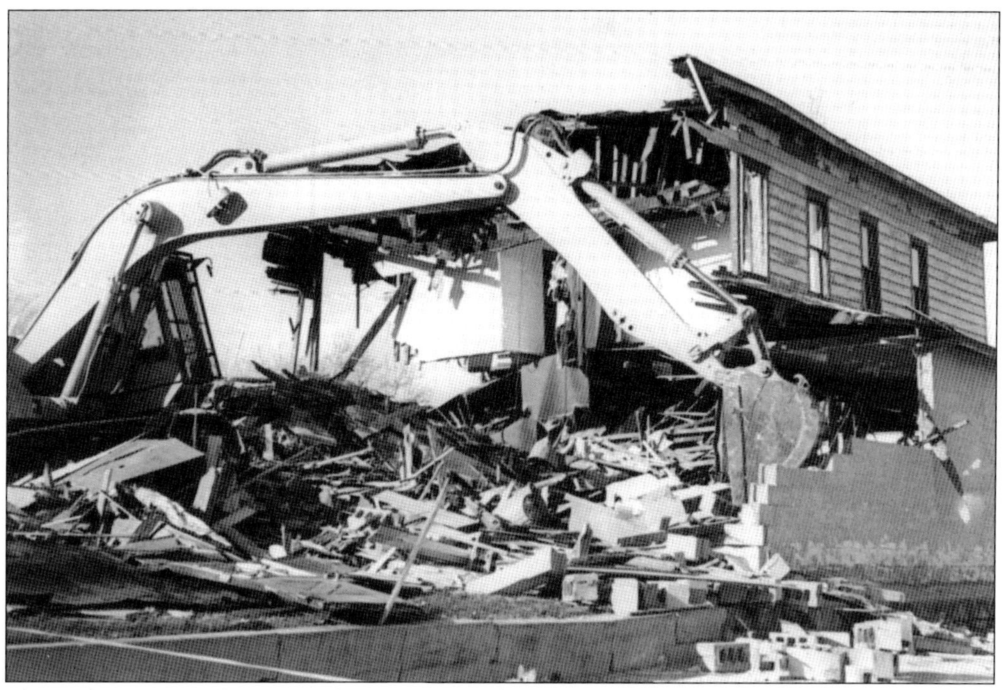

The Park View Hotel was torn down in November 1998. It was one of Farwell's oldest buildings when it was razed.

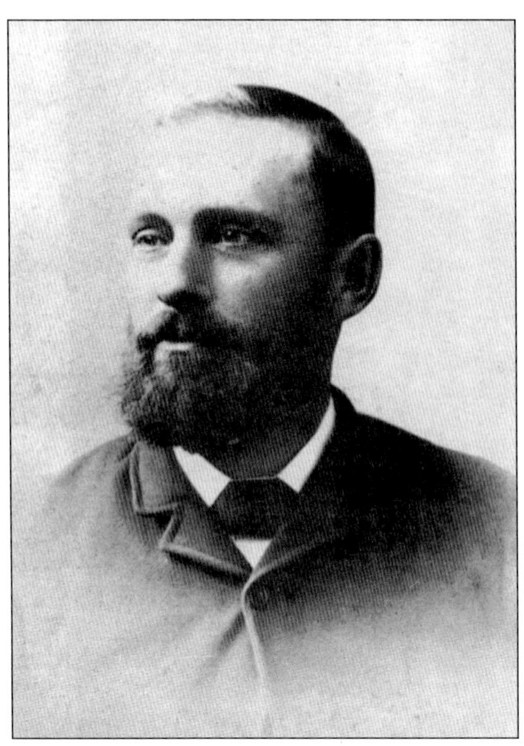

Of all the early residents, the person with the most lasting impact on Farwell was Josiah Littlefield. He graduated from the University of Michigan with a civil engineering degree in 1871. Littlefield was called to help survey a better route for the Ionia to Houghton Lake state road while still at the university by his uncle Edmund Hall. He returned after graduation to survey Farwell and make it his home for the rest of his life.

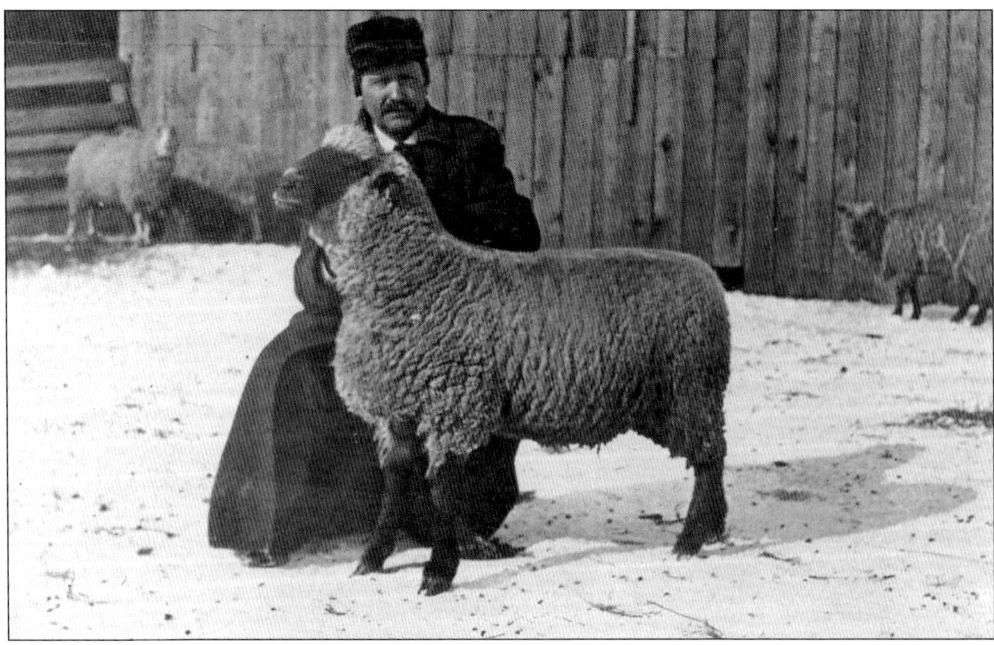

Throughout his life, Josiah Littlefield strove to better the lives of the citizens of Farwell through his business and community endeavors. His autobiography suggests he viewed himself as the benevolent fatherly figure of Farwell. Whether the citizens of Farwell embraced his self-appointed title is questionable. One can only imagine they felt the same mix of admiration, envy, and resentment most small-town folks feel about their more affluent neighbors. He is shown here with a prize Hampshire ram.

Josiah Littlefield was born in Flat Rock in Wayne County, Michigan, in 1845. He married Ellen Hart, and she died in childbirth in Farwell in 1875. Their daughter Ellen Hart Littlefield was primarily raised by her grandmother, Littlefield's mother, Mary Hall Littlefield. Littlefield is shown here with his second wife, Emma Layle, and their two children, Hazel Grace and Franklin Floyd.

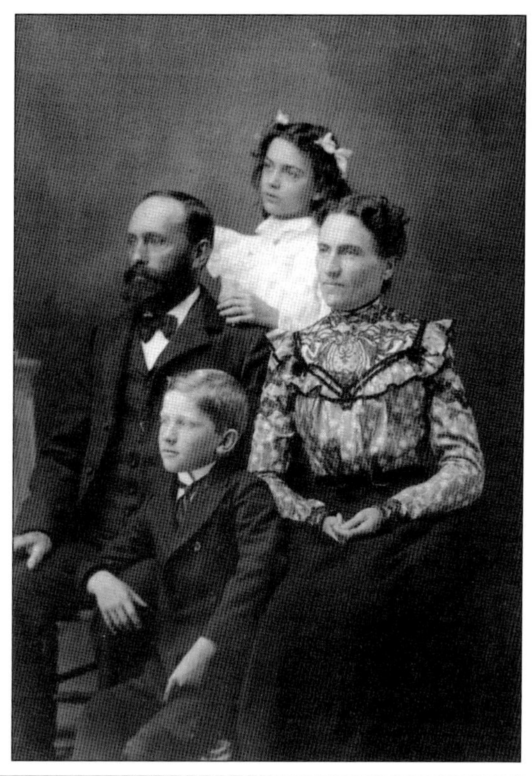

Josiah Littlefield (far left) is shown in a rare pose, looking directly at the camera with his lumbermen in 1897. Typically, when pictured with his men, he looked to the left, reminiscent of kings and emperors signifying their leadership. Several of the men in front are wearing crudely made leather aprons. Such aprons were worn by blacksmiths and saw operators.

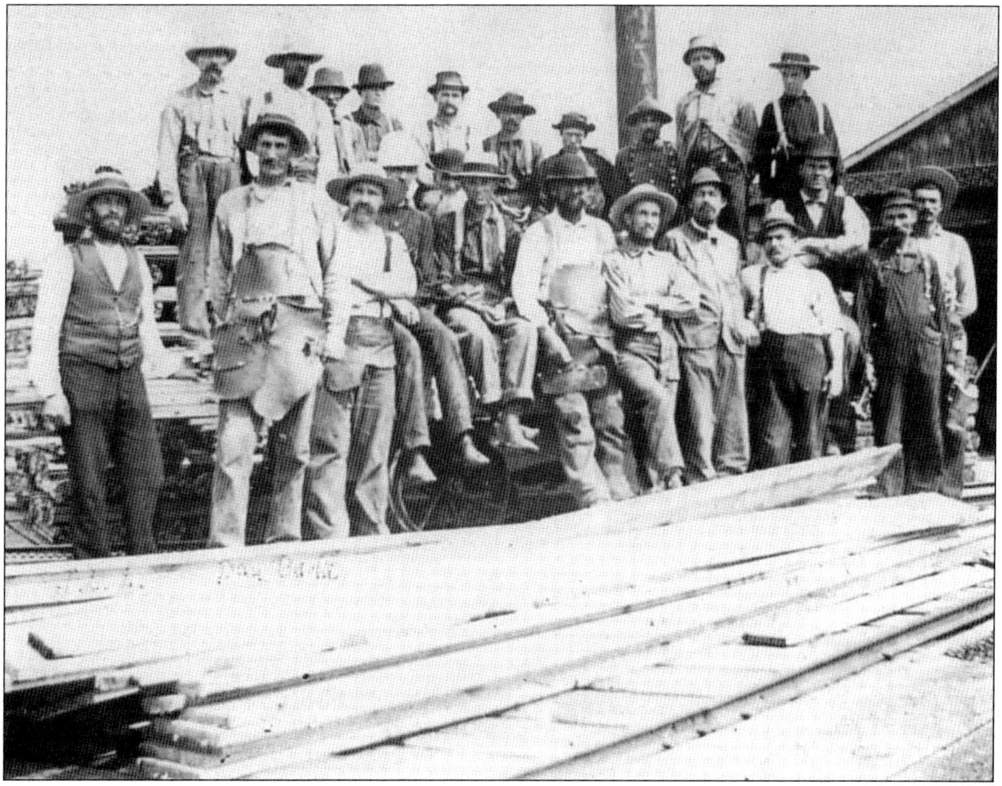

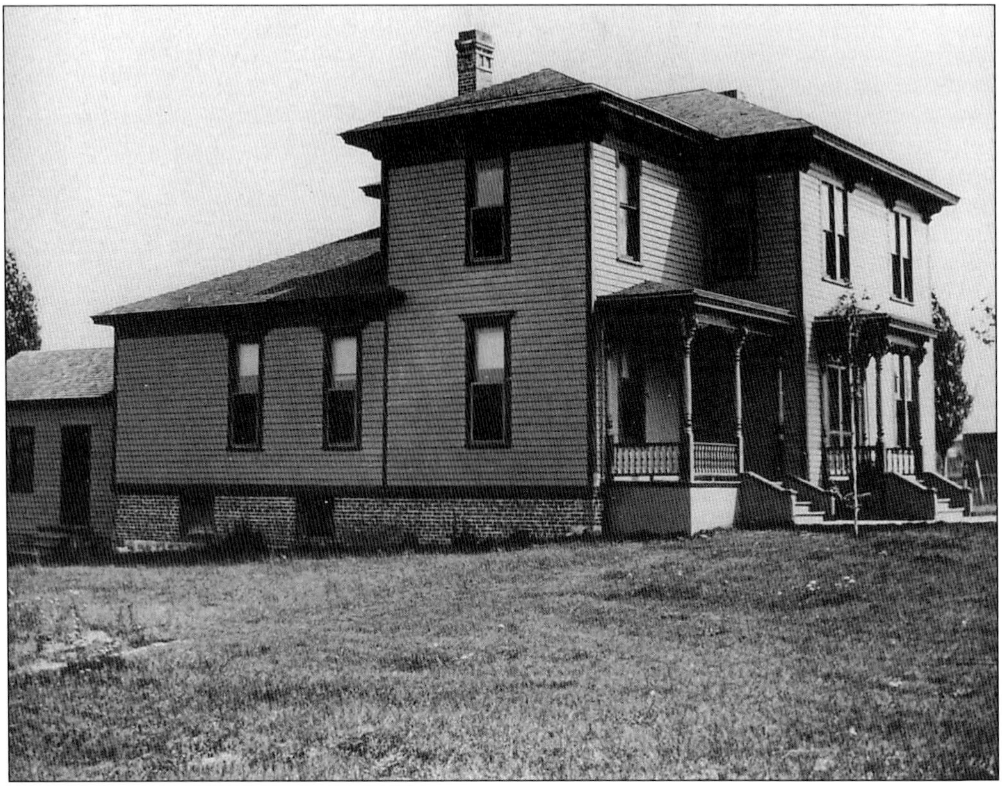

The Littlefields' home still stands today as the Campbell Stocking Family Funeral Home. Frank and Hazel Coker purchased the home in 1952 and moved their family and their business there. In 1962, a large chapel was added to the original home. In recent years, the interior and exterior were renovated by Paul Campbell and Stacy Stocking to retain its historical integrity as a Victorian-style home.

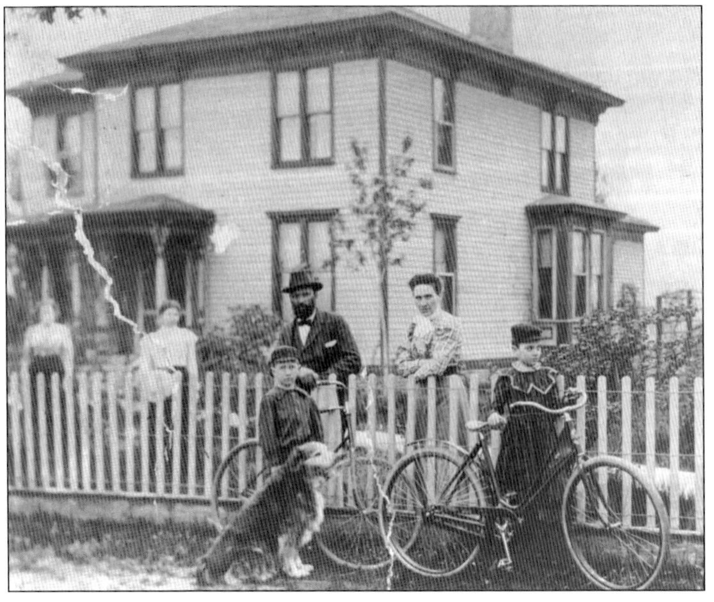

The corner of Main and Corning Streets was where the Littlefield home stood since it was completed in 1890. Construction started in 1889 by a local mason, a Mr. Thomas, and carpenter Dan Black. With access to his own planing mill, Littlefield finished rooms in different types of woods, from red oak to cherry and cedar, along with three fireplaces.

Farwell was a family affair for the Hall, Littlefield, Hitchcock, and Woodruff families. Pictured here from left to right are (first row) Franklin and Hazel Littlefield; (second row) Wesley Littlefield (J.L. Littlefield's brother), Mary (Hall) Littlefield (his mother), and J.L. Littlefield; (third row) Mary (Stoflet) Hall, Edmund Hall, Blanche (Maynard) Littlefield, and Emma Littlefield.

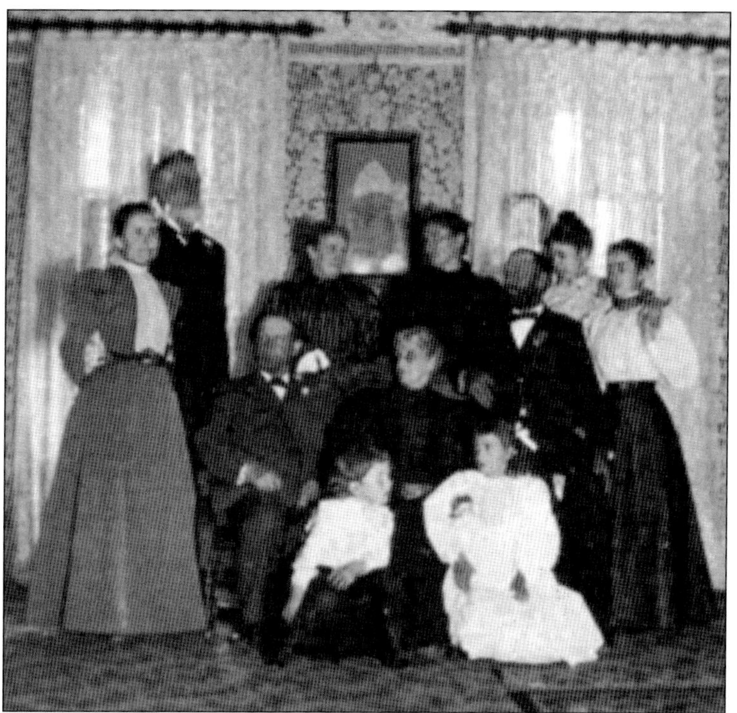

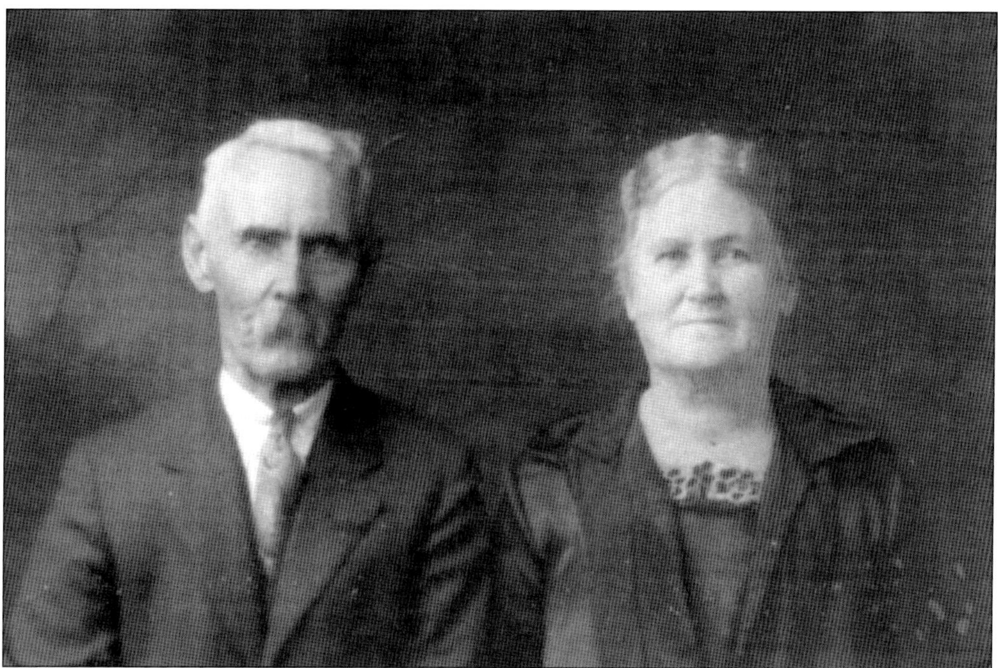

John "Jack" Barton and his wife, Sarah, worked for the Littlefield family for over 40 years. Jack worked as a lumber foreman and camp boss at Littlefield's Beechwood logging operation, and Sarah cooked and boarded men from the lumber camp. They were both born in Ontario but lived most of their lives in Farwell. At the time of both of their deaths in 1934, they were considered pioneer residents.

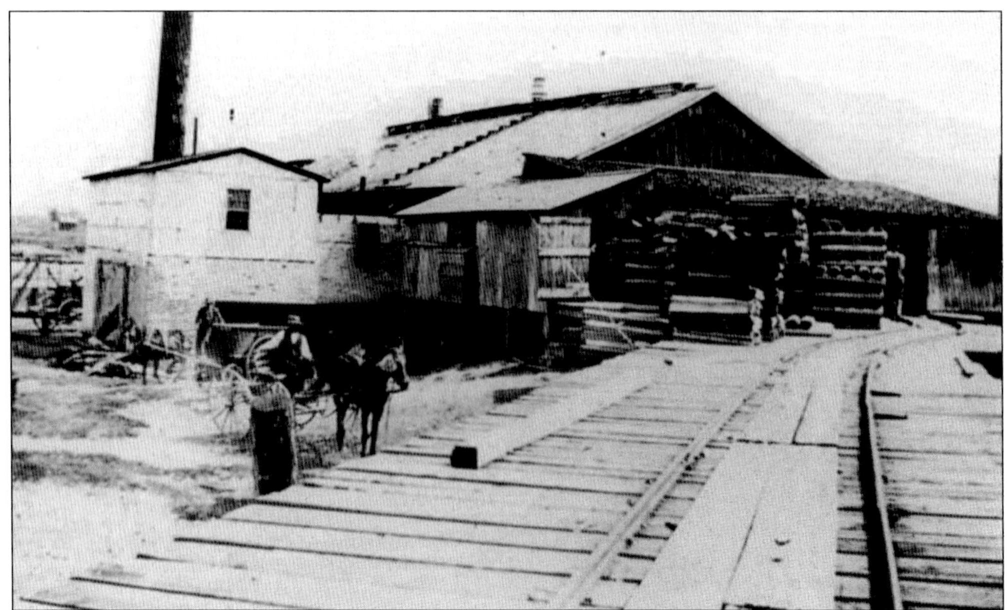

The Littlefield Planing Mill was part of the Littlefield family's farming, logging, and other business interests. The family had a large impact in the area, evidenced by place names such as Littlefield Road and the memories of many people who worked and depended on their business operations for their livelihood. The collected papers of Hazel Littlefield Smith reside at the Bentley Historical Library at the University of Michigan, where much of the Littlefield family and business life is preserved.

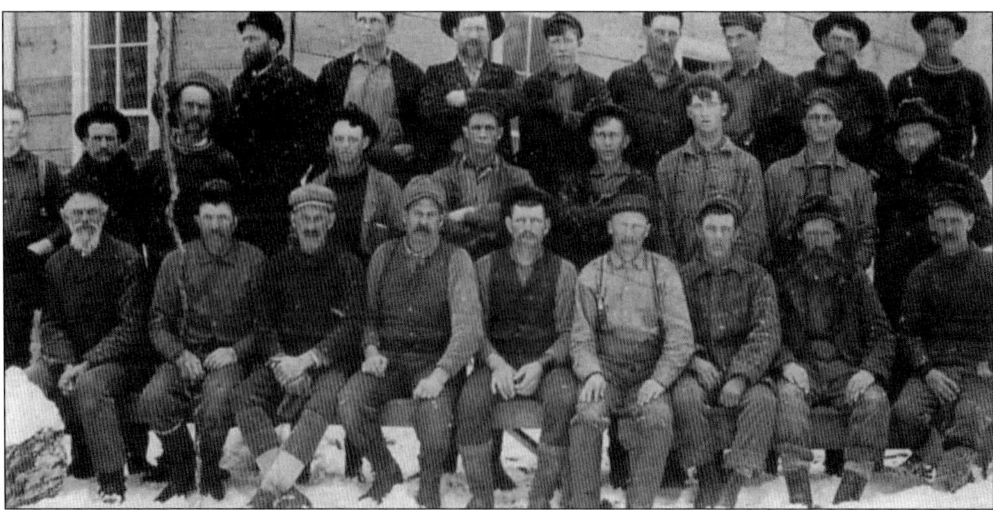

Littlefield is pictured with his men, top left, in his iconic picture-taking pose, turned to the left. He took very seriously his self-assigned role of creating varying industries, creating jobs, and keeping the town prospering.

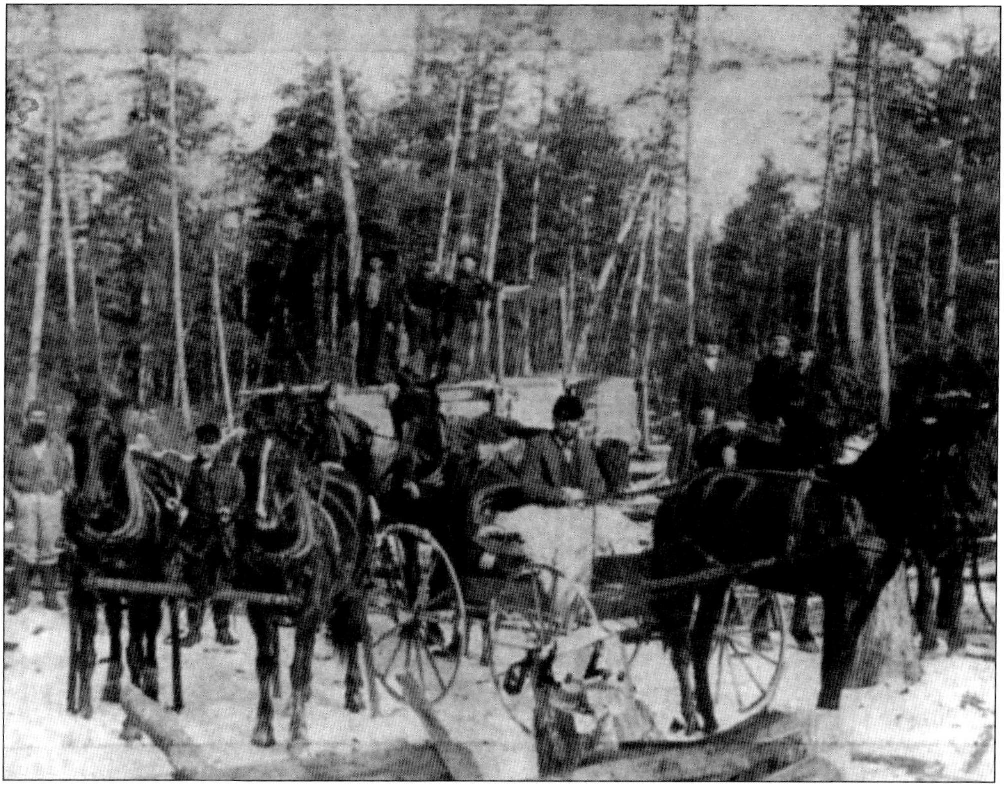

In addition to his mill, Josiah Littlefield's first logging efforts began in 1882 with the start of his own camp on property purchased from his uncle Edmund Hall. Josiah Littlefield is in the cart at center.

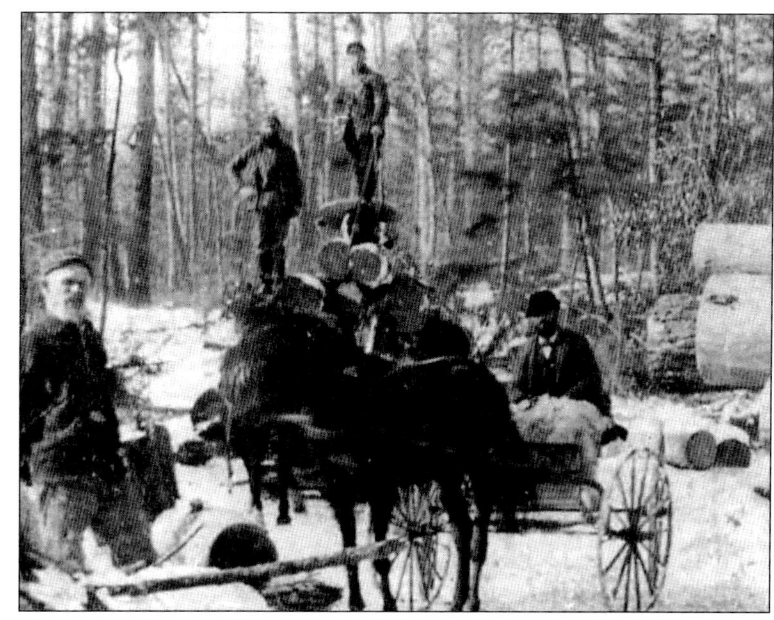

Littlefield poses in his cart in front of a load of logs. Note the sizeable logs stacked to his right. Intending on staying in Farwell, unlike many of the transient lumber operators, Littlefield had the idea from the beginning to eventually farm and reforest his land.

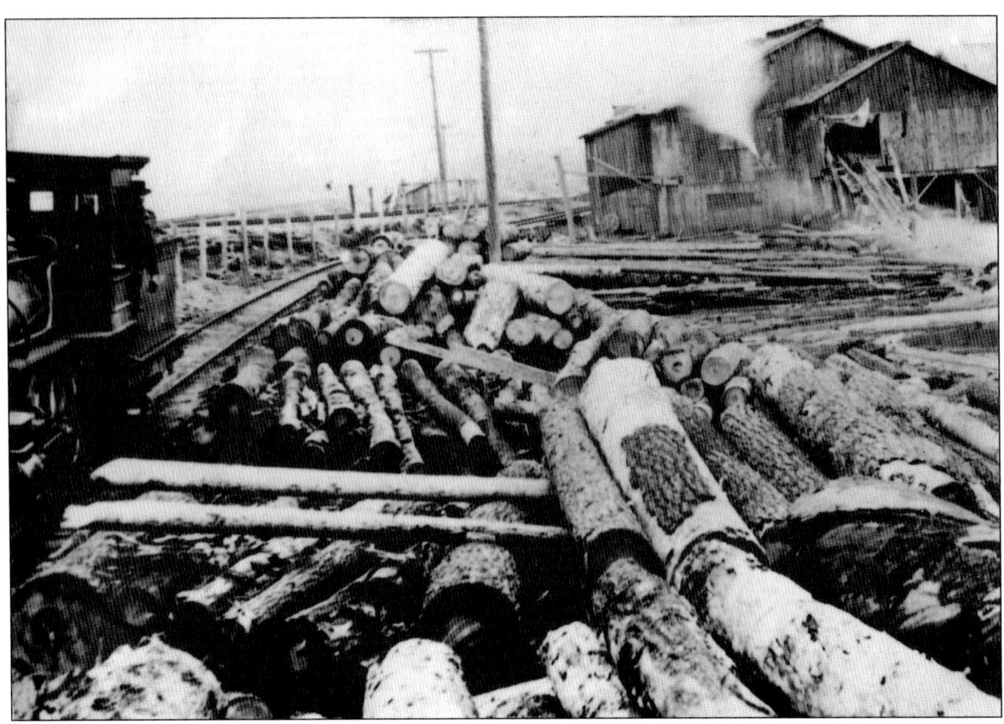

The planing mill, shown here in its heyday, ran until 1912. The machinery sat idle for a few years until World War I, when there was a high demand for metal and it was sold for scrap.

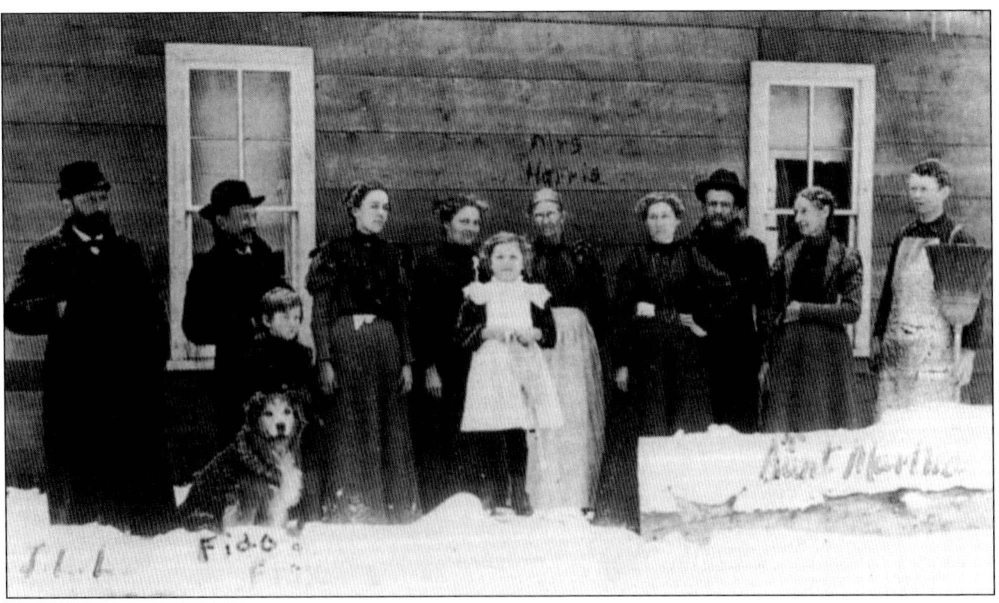

Josiah Littlefield (left) is shown with his family, most likely at Beechwood when it was operating as a lumber camp. Littlefield owned sections 7, 8, and 9 and half of sections 15, 16, 17, and 18 (over 3,000 acres) of Surrey Township, which he finished logging and stumping so he could raise crops and livestock and replant trees.

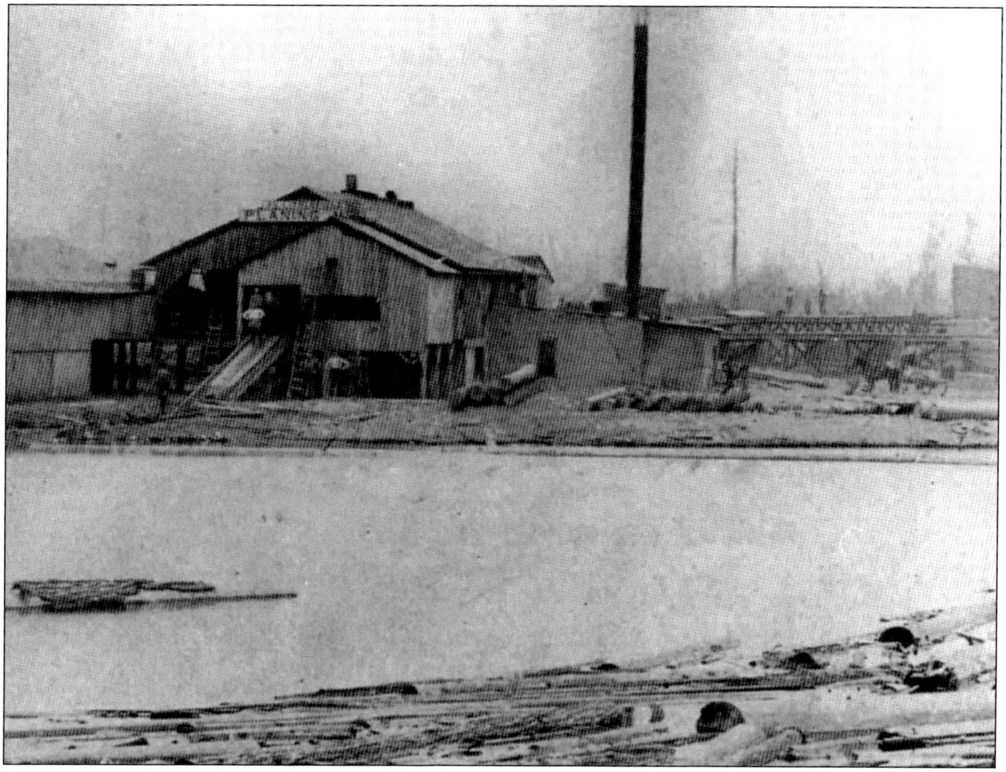

Josiah Littlefield built his planing mill in 1874 and changed and adapted it over the years. Shown here in 1888, it was the longest-running mill on the pond. It was first equipped with a planer and marcher molding machine and resaw. In 1881 it was expanded, and circular saw machinery was added. In the 1890s, a band saw was added.

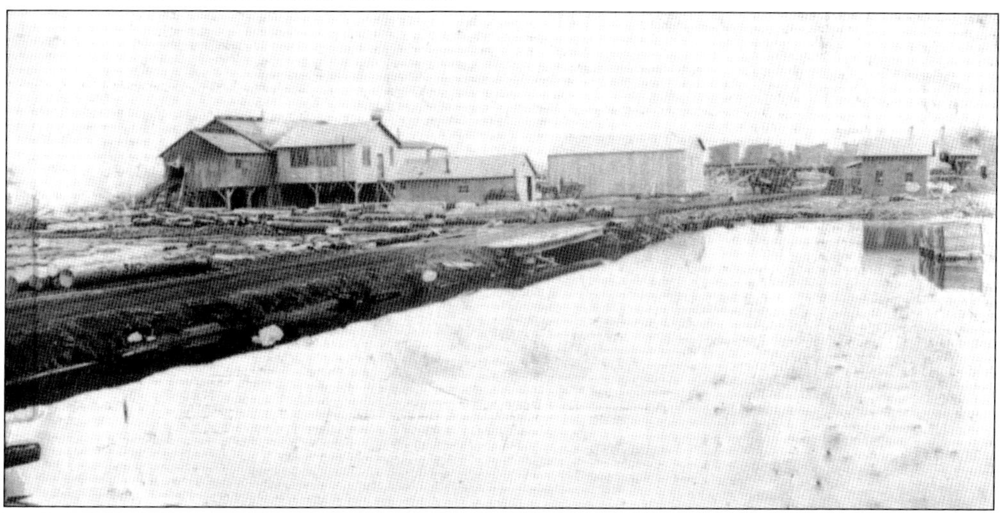

Littlefield's mill, shown here, was just one of the many mills that operated on the millpond. In 1871, the first sawmill was operated by George Hitchcock and Aaron Linton of Saginaw. A shingle mill was started by Thomas Hilson and Steward Linton about the same time. Baker and Company, Dave Branch, and J.W. Youngs were just a few of the many mill operators, large and small, around Farwell before 1900.

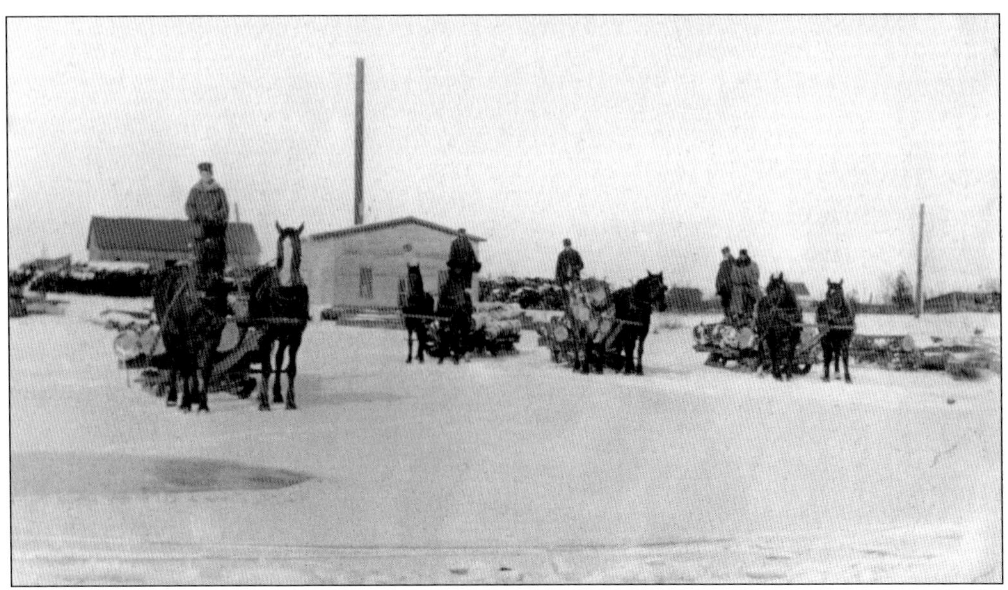

Teams hauling logs to Littlefield's mill pause for the photographer. Logs were hauled on sleighs over iced logging roads so the horses could easily haul large loads. The powerhouse and mill outbuildings are in the background.

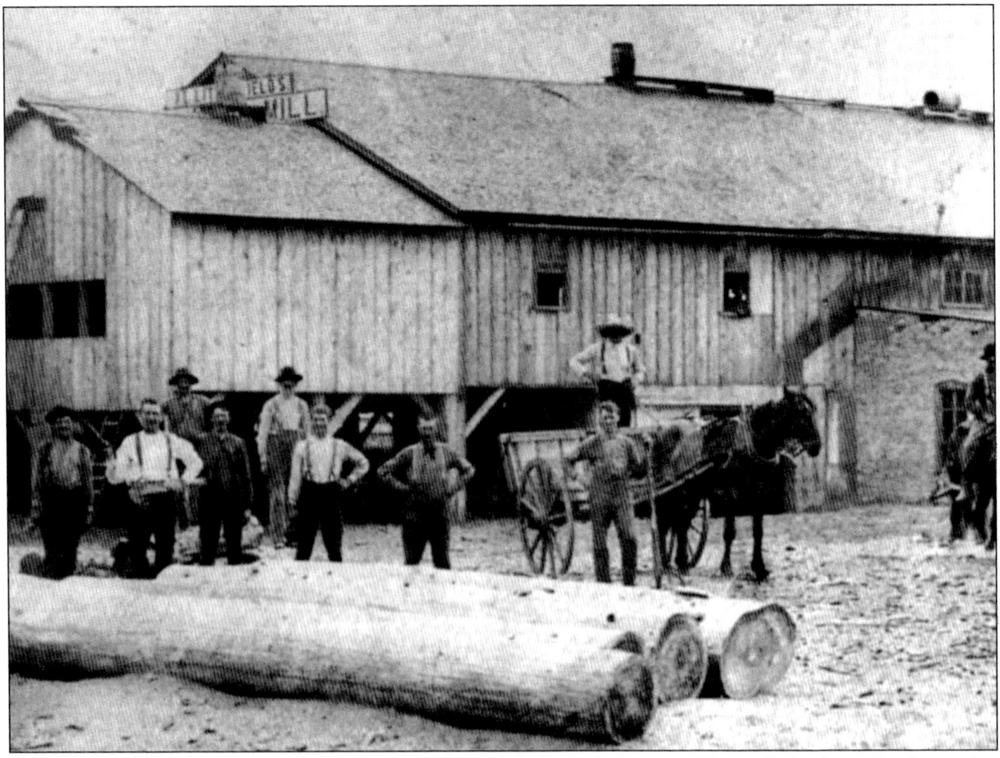

Note the sign on the roofline reading "J.L. Littlefield's Planing Mill," and the barrels along the roof for fire protection. Sparks from trains and other machinery were common hazards at the mill. Littlefield's mill survived several small fires, which were always put out before they could cause any catastrophic loss.

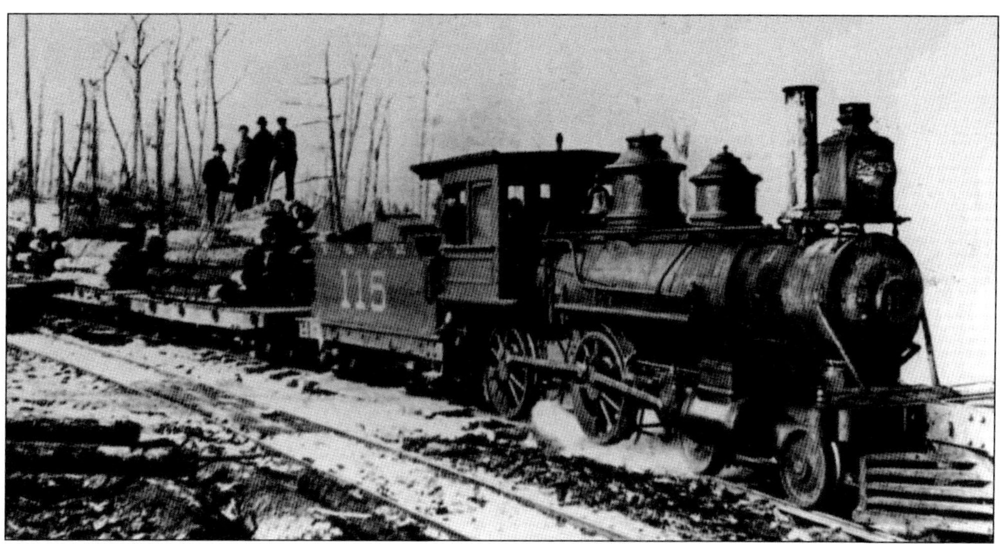

The logging train of Josiah Littlefield, No. 115, carried timber from his land in southern Missaukee County to his mill in Farwell. This portion of railroad grade near Farwell became part of the route for Highway 115. M-115 begins in Clare and ends in Frankfort. It was first designated in the 1920s, with the Clare County portions added in the 1930s.

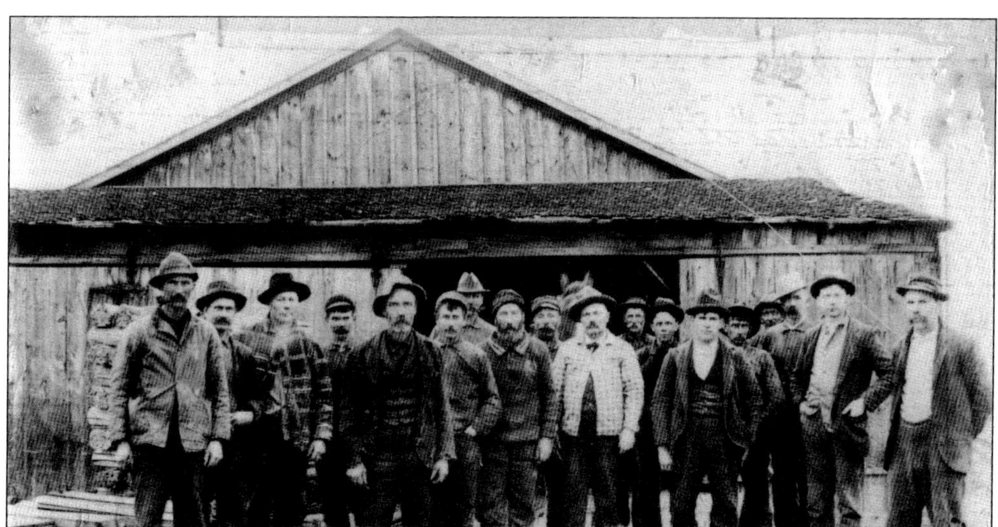

Littlefield kept his own accounts and paid his workers directly. He sometimes would give a man only part of his wages if he felt him irresponsible and would deliver the rest to his wife for the assurance of the care of his family. Many lumber operations paid their men in scrip, which was usually only good at the company store. Saloons would often cash the scrip for less than it was issued for, and many shanty boys had little to show for their week of work. Mill workers are shown here.

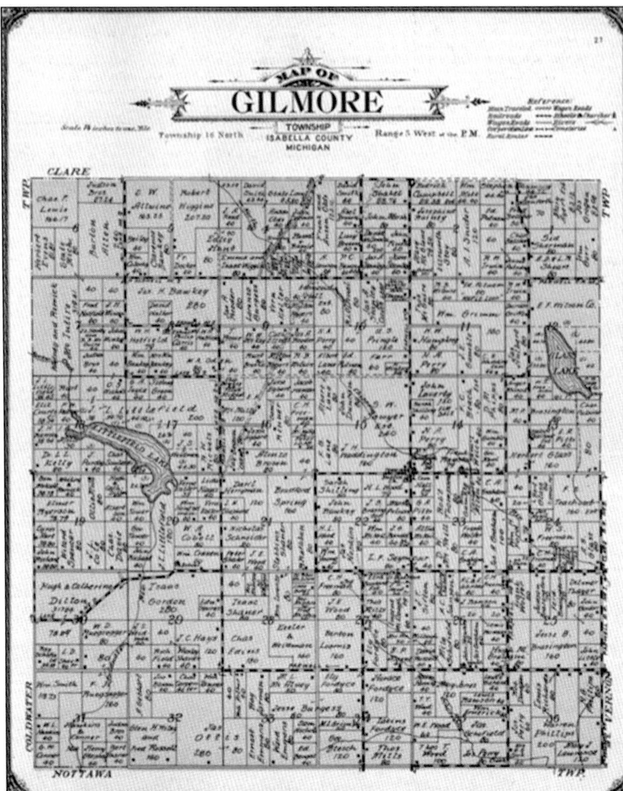

Gilmore Township was organized in 1870. Farwell was the closest town for many Gilmore Township residents, and the two communities were closely connected. Schoolchildren from Gilmore attended school in Farwell. Jesse Wood was the first postmaster in 1891, and the post office operated there until 1906. The center of Gilmore for many years was the general store of Jesse's son James.

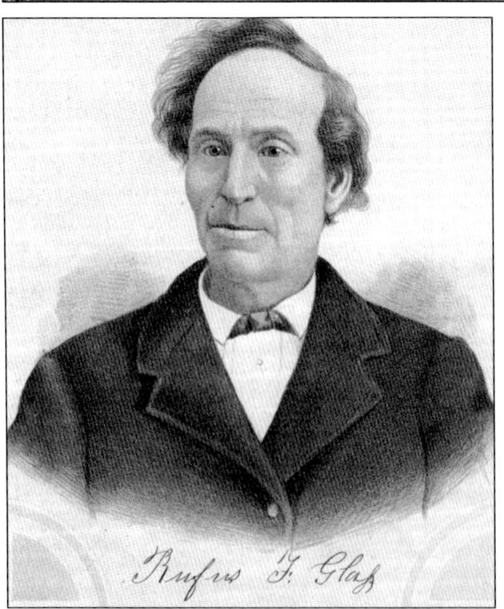

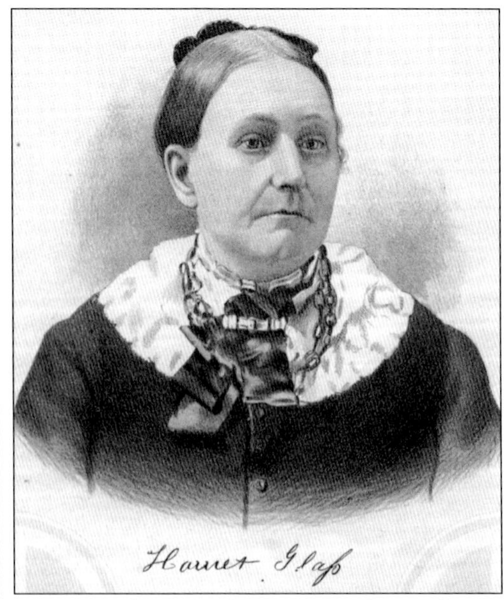

Rufus and Harriet (Gould) Glass were among the first settlers of Gilmore Township and were a prominent pioneer family. He named the township after Civil War general Quincy Adams Gilmore. Glass was a farmer and a carpenter. He served as the first justice of the peace and the first supervisor and held those positions for many years. The school near their home was known as the Glass School.

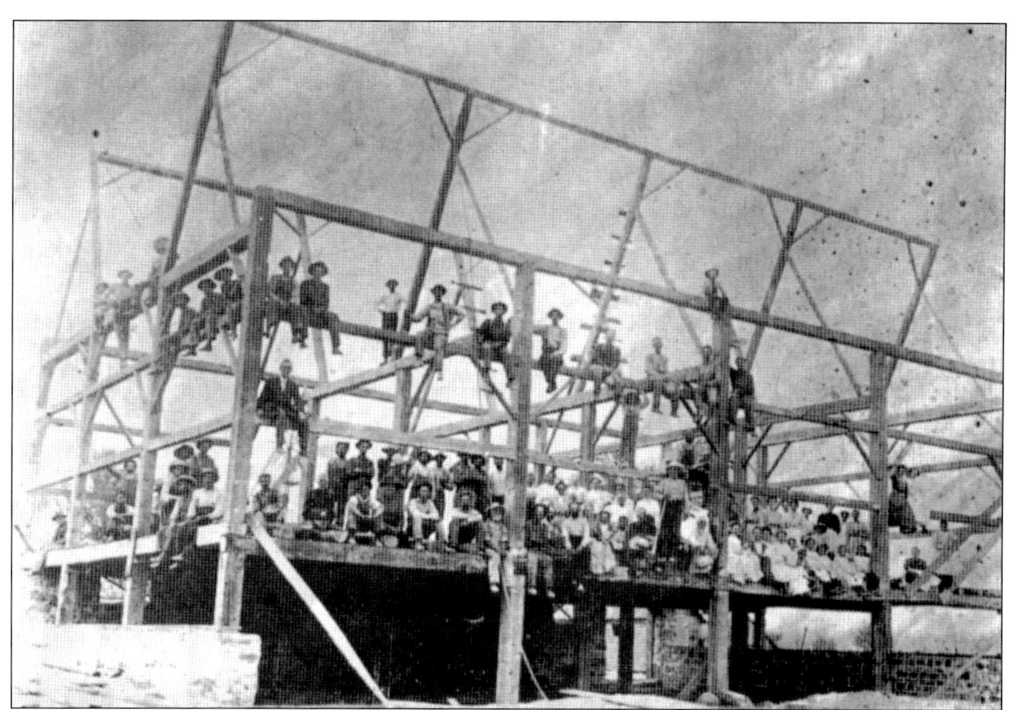

After the lumber was logged off, agriculture was very successful in Gilmore Township and brought many farmers to the area. By the turn of the 20th century, Gilmore had 112 farms. A barn raising brought the community together and bonded families together.

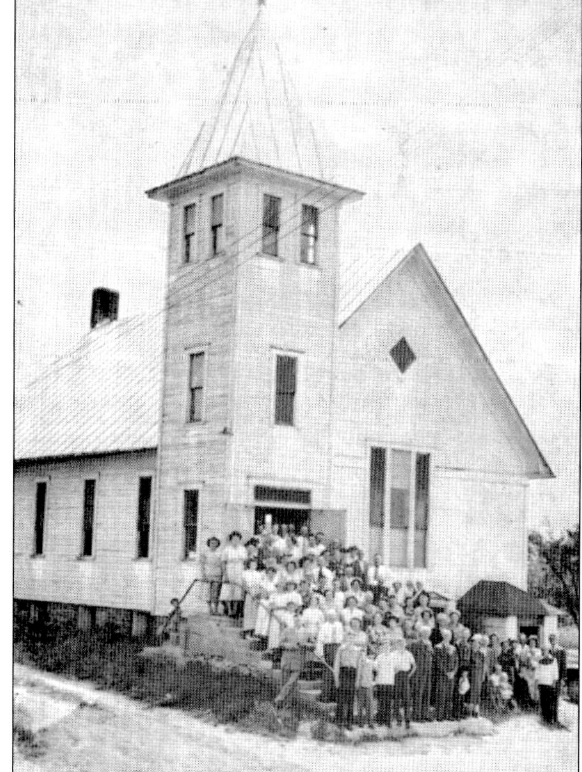

The Gilmore Church of Christ, just six miles south of Farwell, started as a Sunday school in the Schofield schoolhouse. The church was formally organized in 1882, and the church shown here was built in 1901. Still recognizable, it stands today with some changes made over the years.

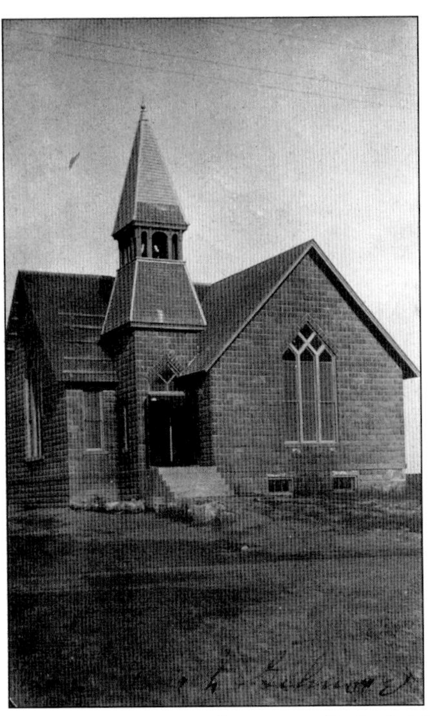

The Gilmore Methodist Church was built around 1915, but by the late 1920s, it had fallen into disuse. It was donated to the Indian school (officially called the Mount Pleasant Indian Industrial Boarding School) and carefully removed. It was reconstructed about four blocks from the school and used for church meetings, as well as community center.

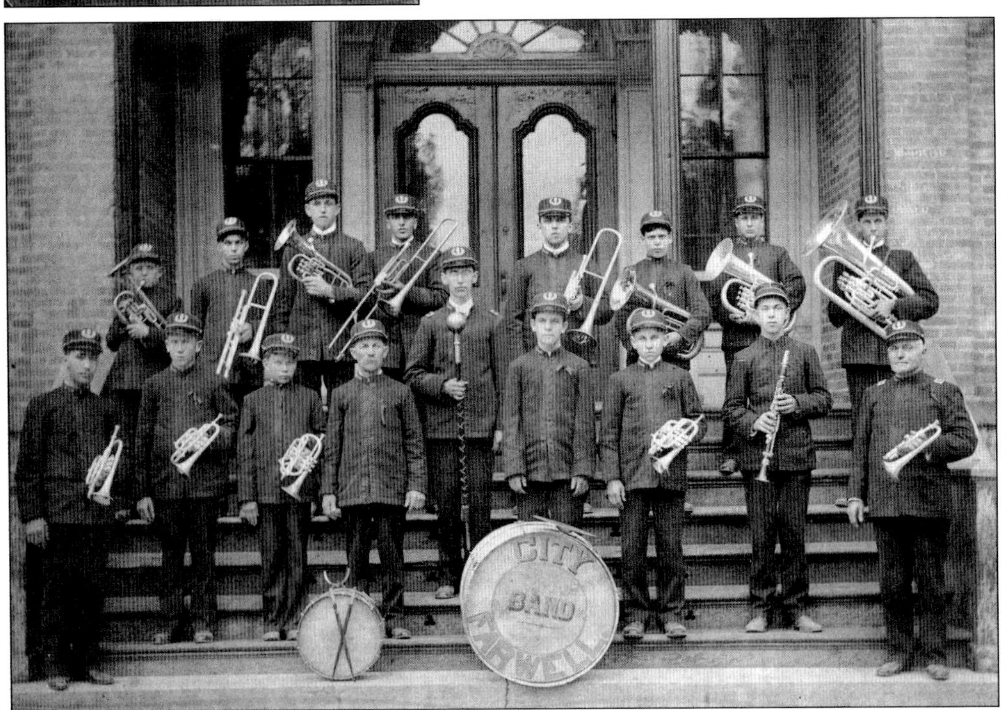

The Farwell City Band was founded by C.F. Lyon in 1886 and taken over in 1887 by Eugene "Dutch" Eager, who led it for over 38 years. Pictured here are, from left to right, (first row) Albert Weisman, Fred McQuire, George Hayward, Dan Rowe, Ronald Barton, Styrie Perkins, Persis Saxton, Charles Belding, and Eugene Eager; (second row) Linus Gardner, Ossie Rowe, Carl Updegraph, Tom Hilson, William Burston, Wilmot Carpenter, Bernard Weisman, and John Armstrong.

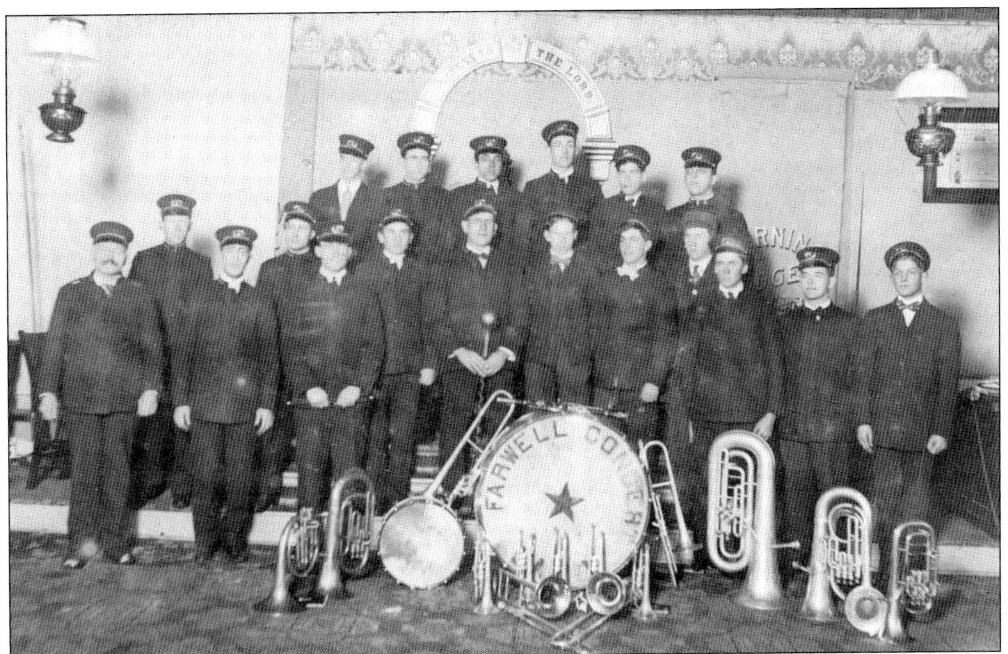

A band was a fixture and a point of pride in every early American town. Farwell had several bands over the years under many different names, such as the Farwell Cornet Band, Farwell Band of Hope, and Farwell Concert Band (pictured). In 1874, the Farwell Band of Hope was part of the Methodist-Episcopal Church.

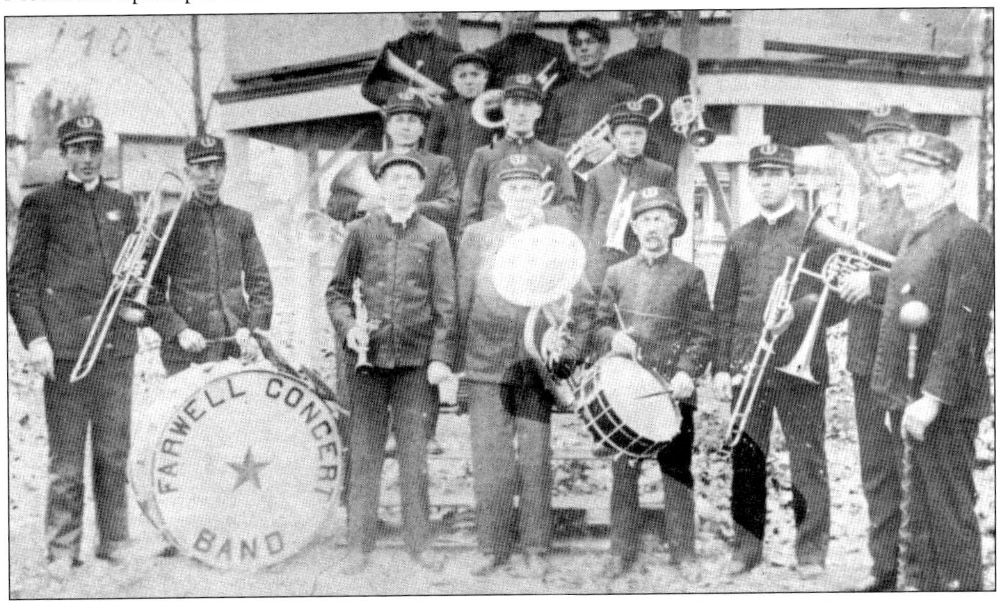

The band played at most community events and parades and would travel to other communities to make a good showing for their hometown. The Farwell band in 1906 consisted of, from left to right, (first row) Tom Hilson, Ron Barton, Charlie Belding, John Armstrong, Dan Rowe, William Burston, Carl Updegraff, and Nate Trumble; (second row) Bernie Weisman, Albert Weisman, and George Heyward; (third row) Linus Gardener, Wilmot Carpenter, Fred McGuire, Oass Tow, and Percy Saxton. (Meek.)

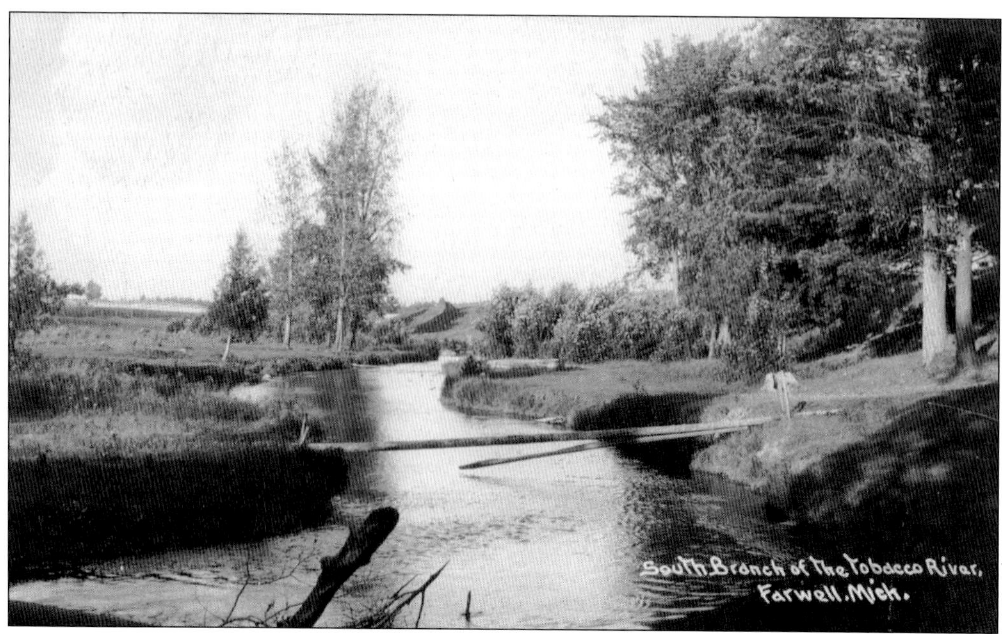

The south branch of the Tobacco River flows from Deadman Lake through Farwell and southern Clare County on its way to join rivers flowing to Saginaw Bay. The Native Americans called the river Samaquaebing or Assemoqua. Many log drives were held on the river during the lumber era, and it was dammed in several places to create larger areas to float logs. (Courtesy of the Moore family.)

. JANUARY 2, 1901.

GREEN WILL BE TAKEN TO MICHIGAN FOR TRIAL

Steadfastly Refuses to Repeat His Confession of the Murder of Feeney.

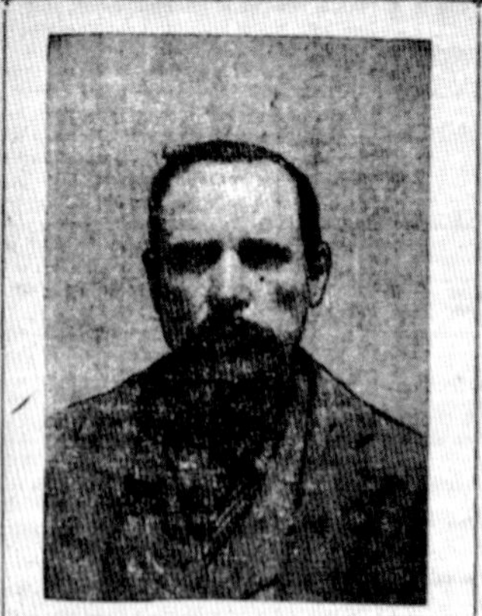

H. GREEN, WHO CONFESSED TO SACRAMENTO'S POLICE THAT HE KILLED A MICHIGAN MAN TWENTY-FIVE YEARS AGO.

SACRAMENTO, Jan. 1—H. Green, who walked into the police station on Christmas night and confessed to the murder of "Bill" Feeney in a Michigan lumber camp in the seventies, still declines to repeat his confession under oath, or to aid the officers in fastening the crime upon him. It is expected that a Michigan officer will soon come from the East to take him back to the scene of the crime.

District Attorney Baker has received from W. D. Elliott, formerly of Claire County, Michigan, but now a resident of Seattle, Wash., a letter detailing the circumstances of the Feeney murder. According to Mr. Elliott, Feeney, who was a sawyer in a lumber mill at Chippewa, had gone to Mount Pleasant with his wife on a visit and from there to a point south of Claire station. On their return home they took the stage from Claire to Mount Pleasant, and then took a northbound train for Chippewa. Feeney imbibed considerable whisky at Claire station, and after getting on the train, grew so boisterous that he had to be put off the train, his wife continuing on her journey to Chippewa, their home.

Feeney was not a drinking man, and save for this breach had never been intoxicated. He always carried sums of money, and this fact was well known to many who knew him. He was put off the train at Farwell station, and there went into a store and angered by the conductor's actions, in a boisterous way remarked that if there were any persons there who wanted to ride to Chippewa with him to come along, that he had lots of money to pay the fares, and then displayed his money. He then left the store, and never was seen alive afterward.

This was, according to Mr. Elliott, in the latter part of December, 1875.

About the last of May, 1876, an old hunter and trapper named Daggart, who was fishing in a small lake near Farwell, discovered Feeney's body in the lake, where it had been buried under the ice. Feeney's skull had been crushed, his throat cut, and his body had been loaded by weights tied around it. These had evidently become detached, and the body came to the surface after the ice broke up.

Feeney not returning to his home and work at Chippewa, the mill owners sent men to hunt for him, but no trace of him could be found, and nothing was known until his body was found by the old trapper.

Feeney's brother, who was a resident of New York, offered a large reward for the apprehension of the murderers, but the crime was never fastened upon anyone.

Mr. Elliott concludes his letter by saying that at that time he was a telegraph operator at Farwell, Michigan, three miles from where this murder took place.

Deadman Lake, west of Farwell, was so named because either Bill or Owen Feeney's body was found dead in the lake in 1876 after he turned up missing in 1875. Henry Green confessed but was never returned to Clare County to stand trial as he would not repeat his confession once pressed and the county would not extradite him. Green had previously spent six years in the Michigan State Prison at Jackson for burglary.

The Toledo, Ann Arbor & North Michigan Railroad reached Farwell in 1887. In addition to heavy freight traffic, four passenger trains and the mail ran twice a day between Toledo and Frankfurt. The tracks are still in service today and owned by the Chesapeake & Ohio Railroad. This map is dated 1888.

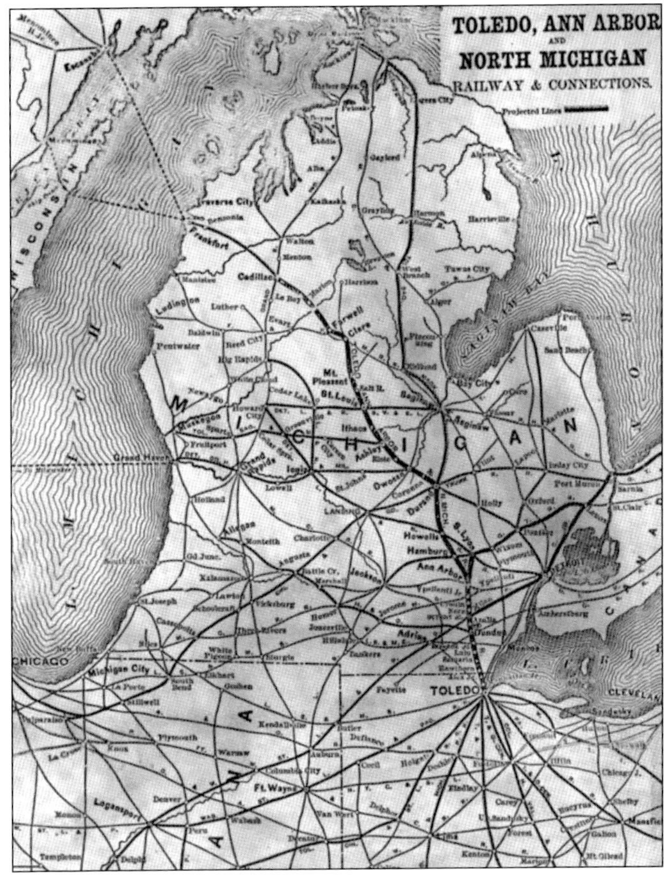

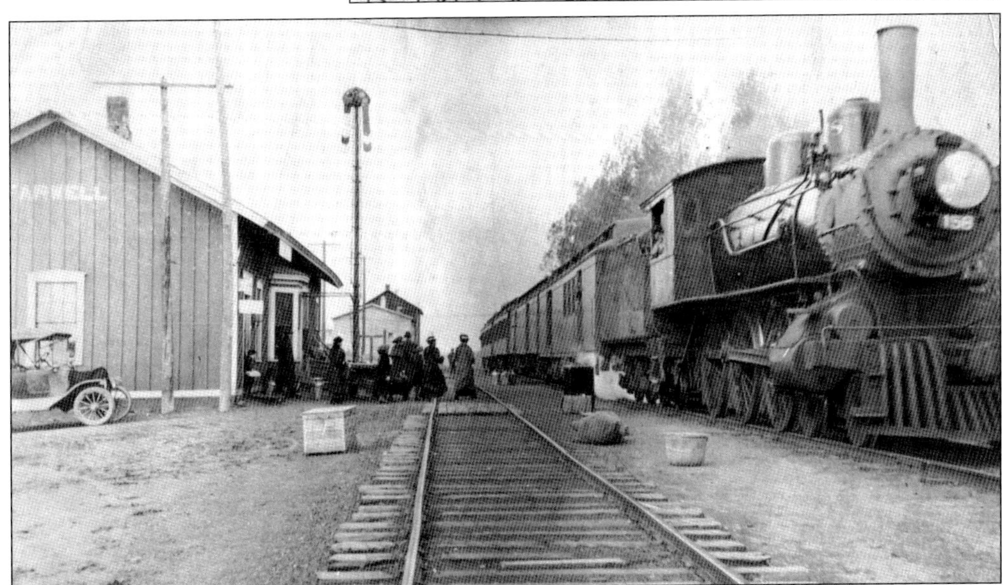

Passengers are boarding a train with their luggage at the Flint & Pere Marquette Railroad depot in Farwell. Four passenger trains ran daily between Saginaw and Ludington. The last passenger train ran in the mid-1940s.

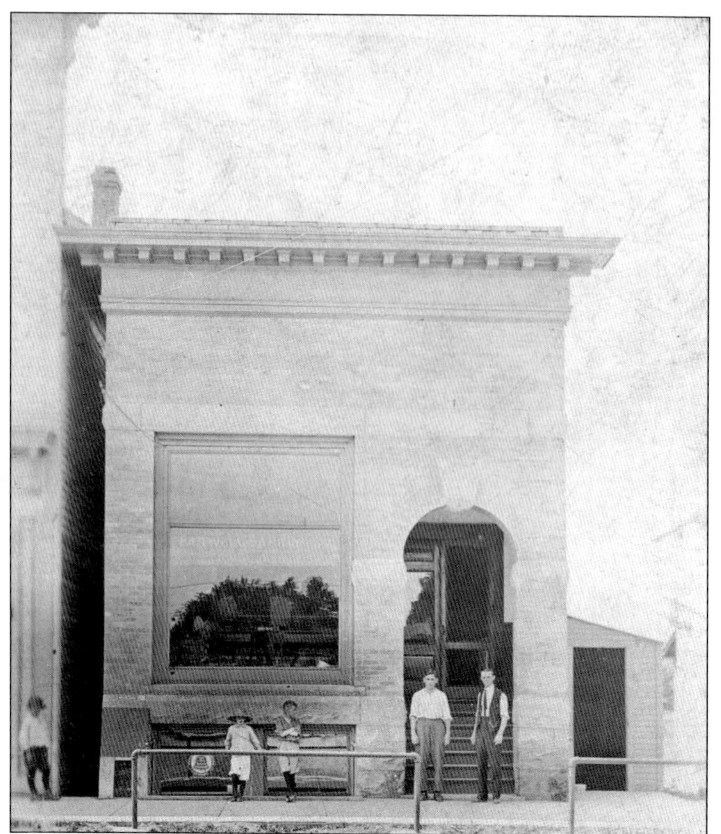

Louis Weisman was born in Germany in 1863 and came to Farwell in 1887 and opened a dry goods and general store. He started the Farwell Banking Company and ran it successfully until he sold it in 1910. He moved to Detroit and founded Weisman & Sons Company, a jewelry business, and married Lena Wolsey, and they had six children, most of whom were born in Farwell.

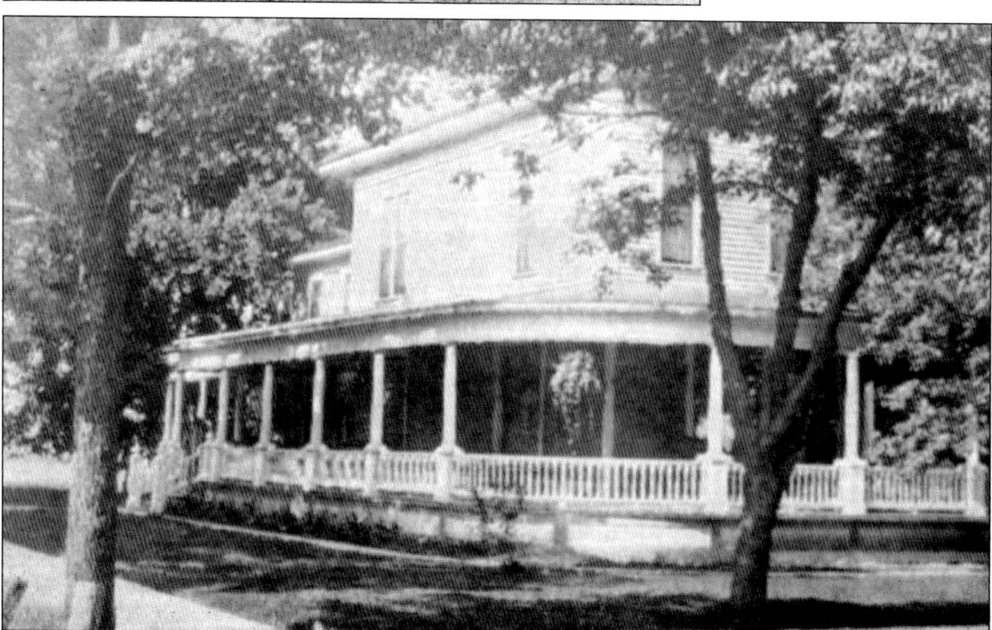

Louis Wiesman ran a dry goods store and lived with his family in Farwell for many years. He was active in the local government of the village and the school board, and was a Mason. Their beautiful home was on the corner of Webber and Michigan Streets.

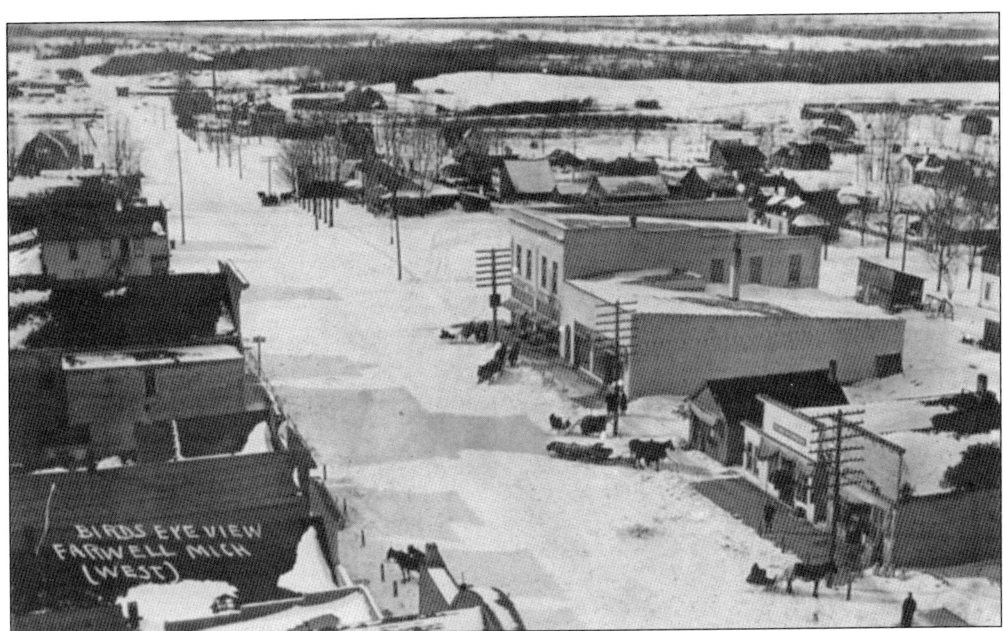

This aerial view most likely taken from the water tower sometime in the 1890s looks west. Residents have parked their sleighs and sleds while downtown doing their daily business.

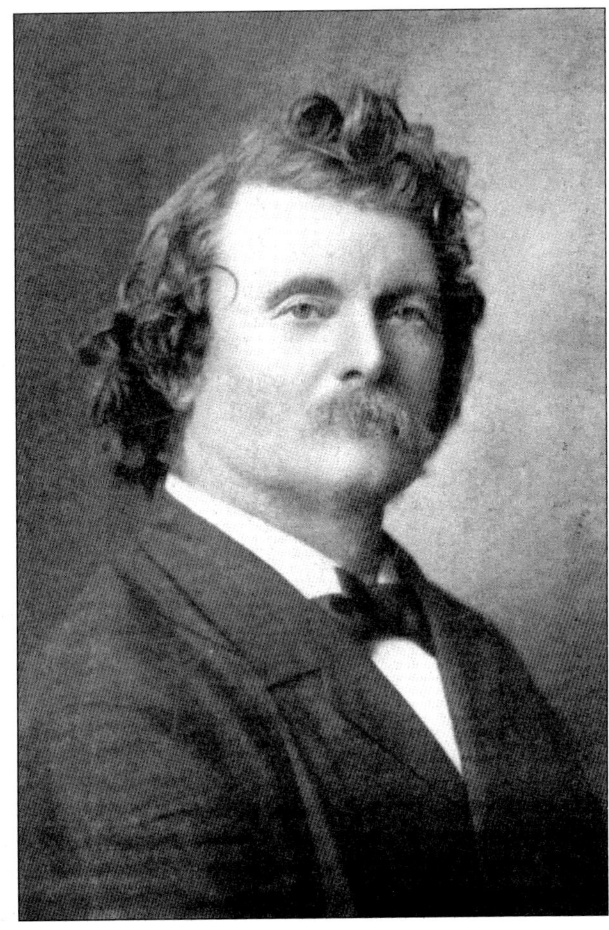

Newspaperman J.S. Holden married Fannie Burch, and they had eight children, many of whom also went into the newspaper business. The *Ogemaw County Herald*, the *Clare News*, and *Midland Sun* were also his publications before he moved to Oklahoma, still Indian territory, in 1890. He died there in 1920. Newspaper accounts suggest an affair of adultery was Holden's motive for moving out West. In Farwell, his editorial commentary on local events, particularly the temperance issue and the courthouse controversy, stirred up both sides, and his debates with Clare newspaper editors and politicians were numerous. Even after Holden left Farwell, he continued to comment about Clare County politics from his papers in neighboring counties.

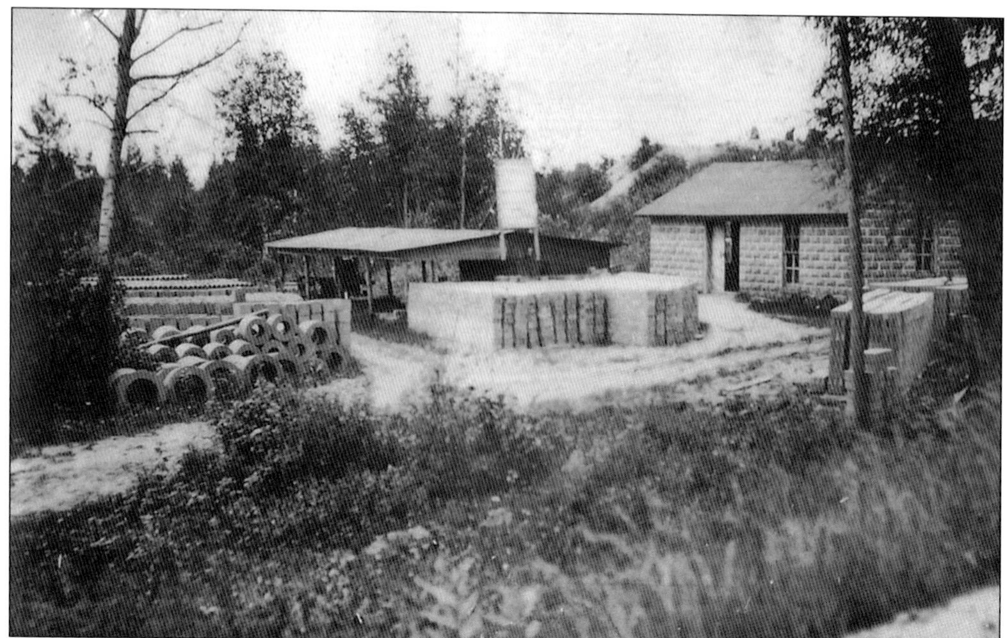

The brick plant of Sam Henry known as the Henry Cement Company was just south of the millpond on the west side of Vandecar Road. A brick or cement plant was an important part of building a successful town, making it possible to replace the hastily constructed wooden buildings of the lumber era with more permanent block or brick.

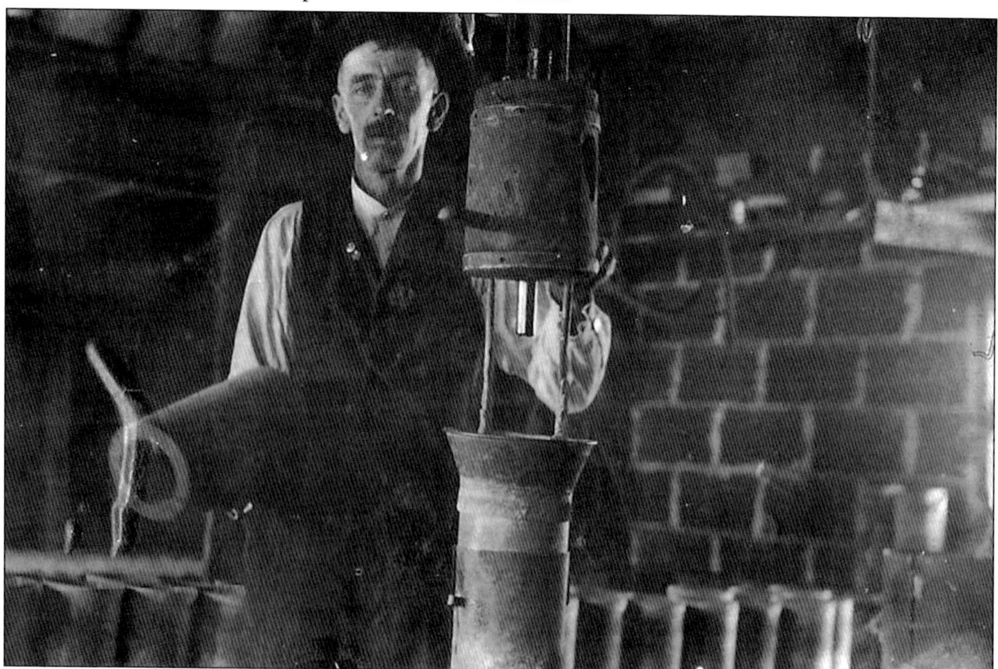

Sam Henry was born in 1860 in Pennsylvania and came to Farwell about 1886 with his mother and younger brother John. He married Alice Stine Cronk in Farwell in 1892. In addition to his own business, he worked for the Flint & Pere Marquette Railroad for 20 years and was the sexton of the cemetery for many years.

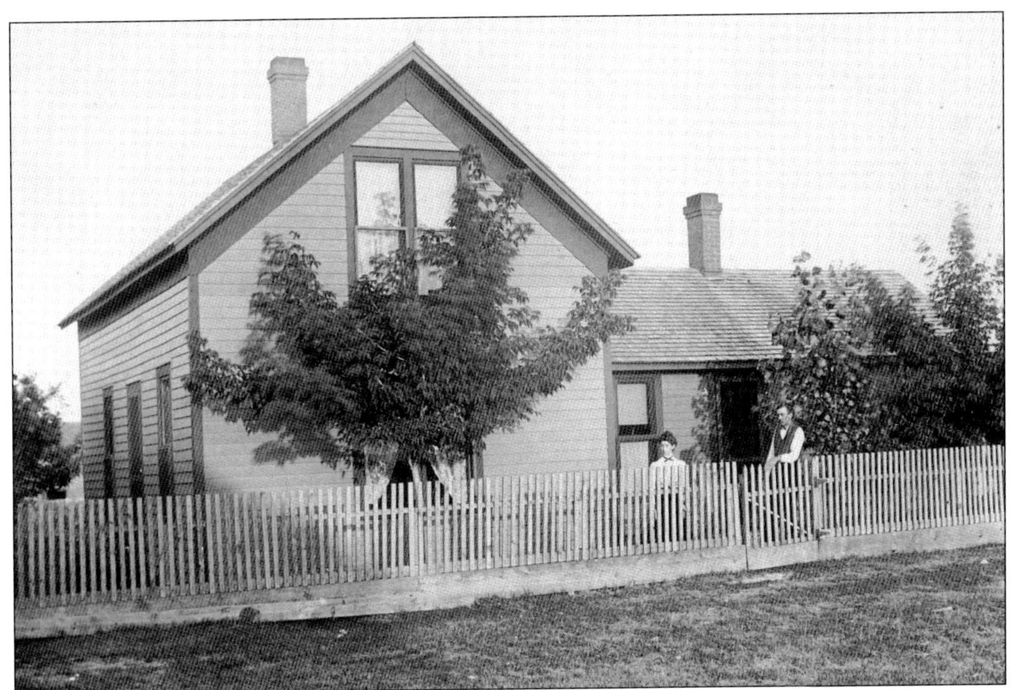

The home of Sam and Alice Henry was located at 237 South Wright Street. They had no children, and Sam passed away in 1940 after he was hit by a motorcycle on Main Street. Alice passed away in 1947, and they are both buried at the Surrey Township Cemetery.

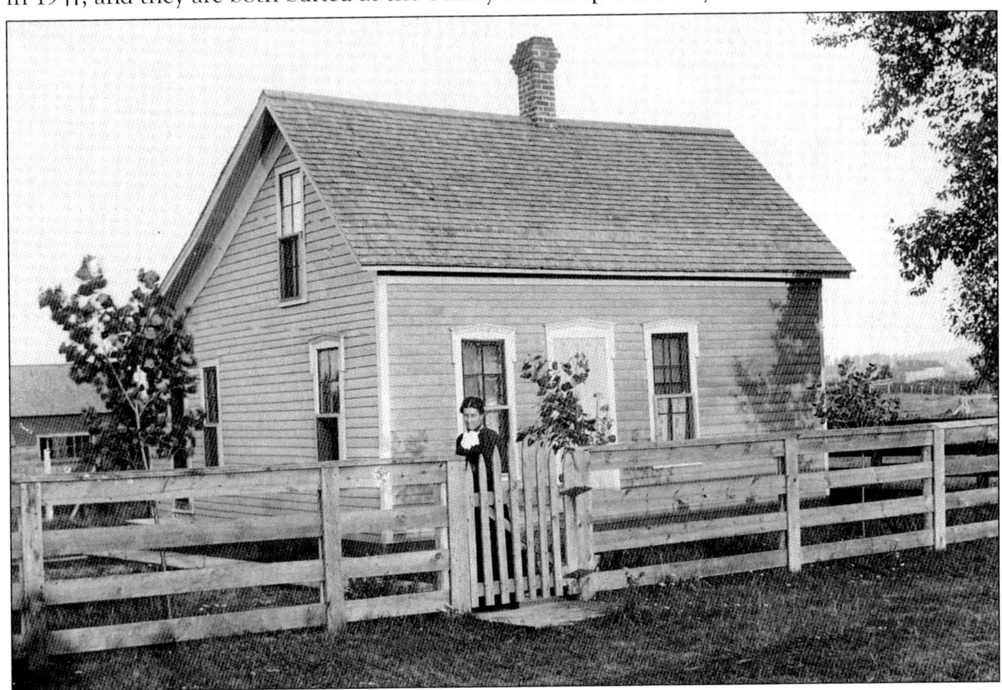

The home of John and Susan Cronk was later owned by Cecil and Ina Davison. The Cronks were married in 1879 in Farwell. Susan Cronk's only child, Alice, step-daughter to John Cronk, was married to Sam Henry.

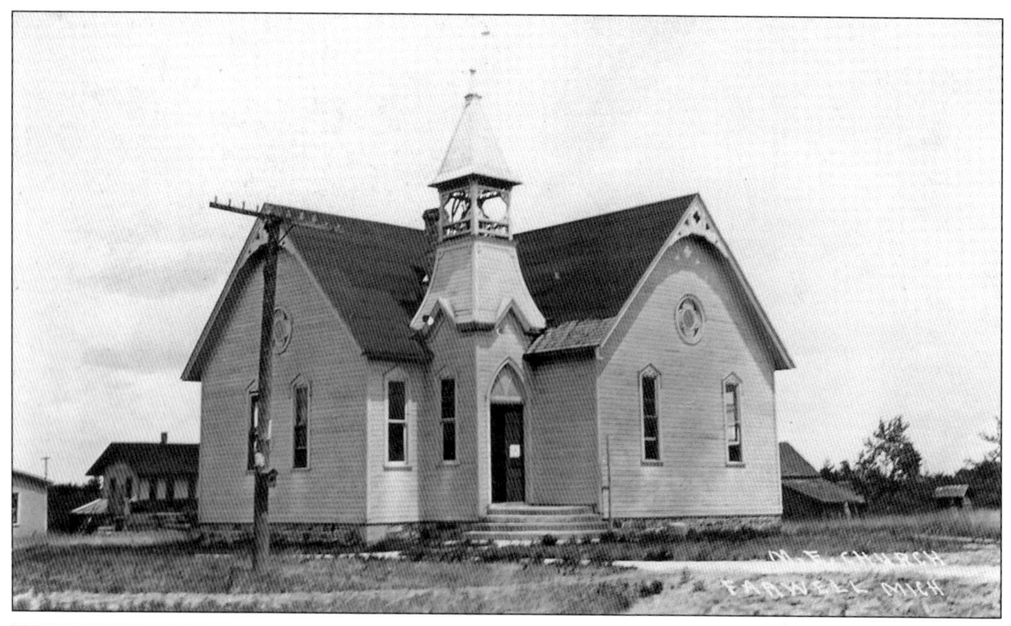

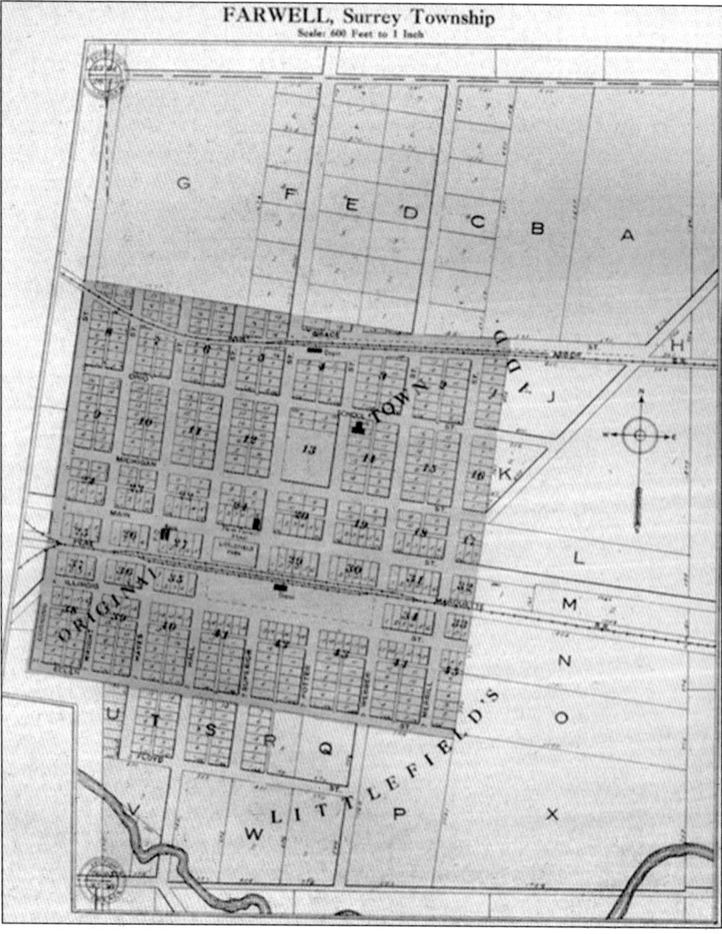

The cornerstone of the Methodist church was laid on June 20, 1884, on the corner of Superior and Ohio Streets. Josiah Littlefield donated the land and lumber. The original building is still in use today with many changes made over the years. The Ann Arbor railroad depot is to the left of the church.

This map of Farwell from 1916 shows the Littlefield Addition. Lot 13 is larger than the others and was the original location of the county seat known as courthouse square. The Hitchcock house was later built on the site after the courthouse burned.

The section lines for the townships were surveyed in the 1850s. Once claimed by other counties, Clare County had its first organizational meeting in 1871. Surrey Township was one of three townships to be established first in the county, along with Grant and Sheridan, replacing the originally planned Three Lakes Township. Surrey Township is shown here in the 1916 plat map. (HDL.)

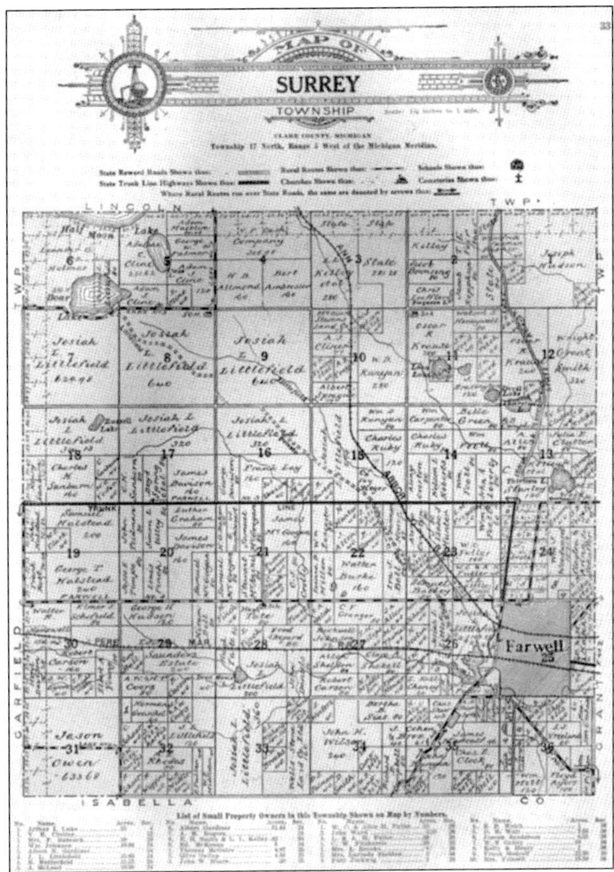

The job of clearing roads after the lumber era and stumping areas for settlement and farming was no easy feat. Josiah Littlefield stands on a road in Surrey Township in 1905 with his son-in-law Dennis Smith.

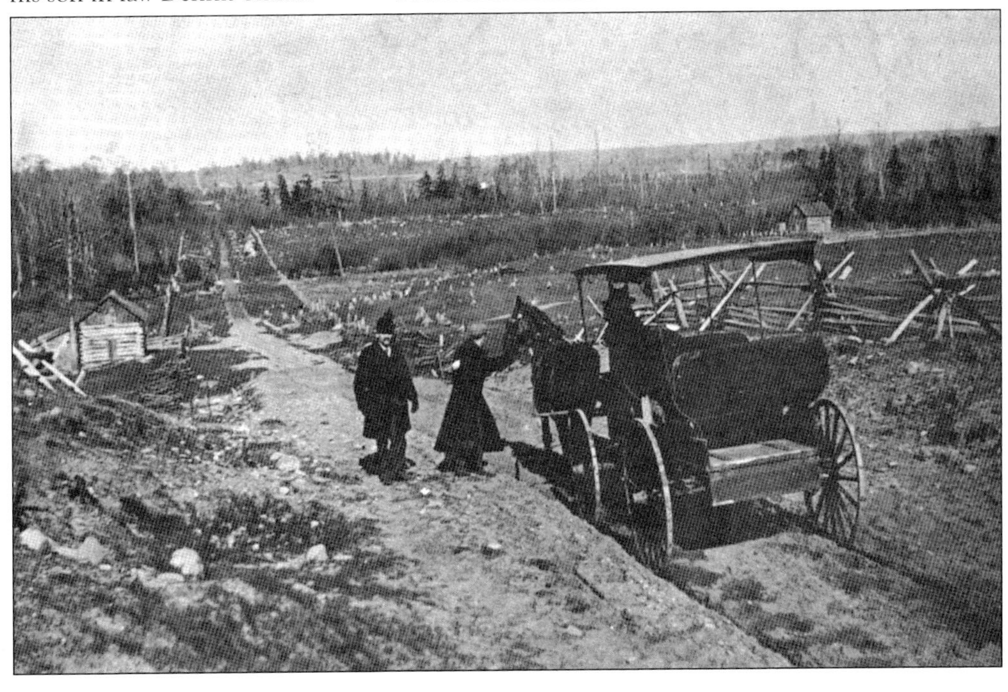

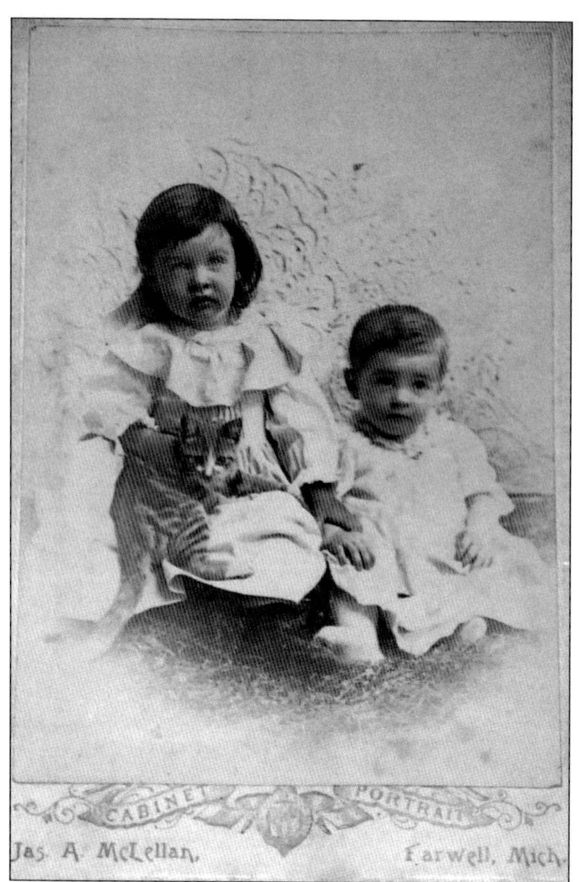

This cabinet card photograph of unidentified children was taken by Farwell photographer James McLellan. McLellan was in Farwell as early as 1880 as a grocer. His photography studio was open from 1892 to 1895. Other early area photographers included Richard Himes (1902–1903), John Scoffer (1910), and tinsmith turned photographer Nathaniel Watkins (1904–1911). (HDL.)

This bird's-eye view of Farwell shows a train on the Ann Arbor Railroad line puffing along at upper left, the Hitchcock house and barn (center), the school (upper right), and the Park View Hotel (bottom right). Note the new sidewalks on Main Street.

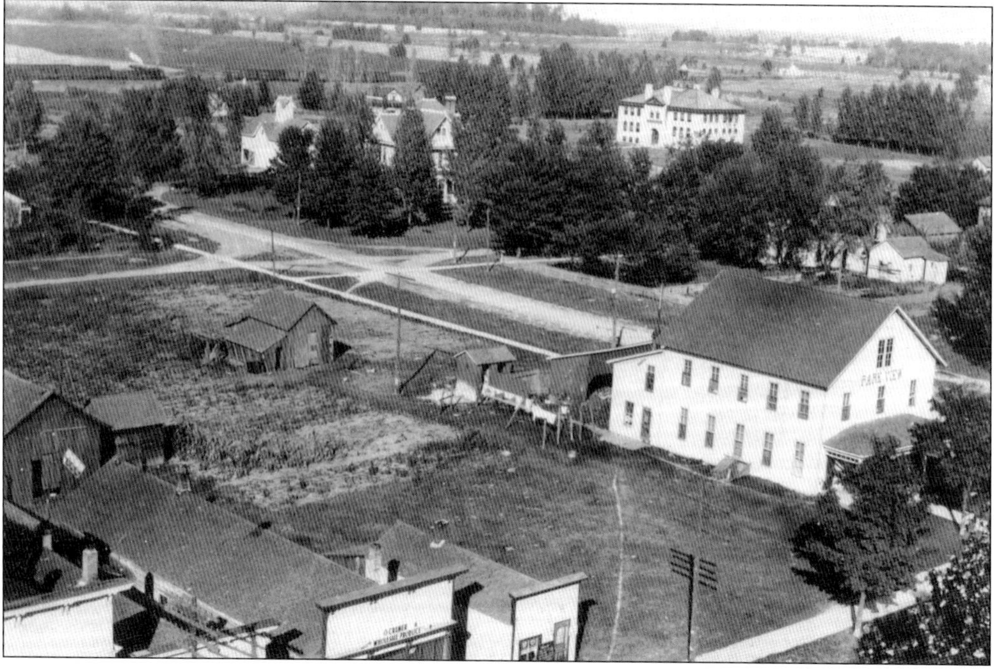

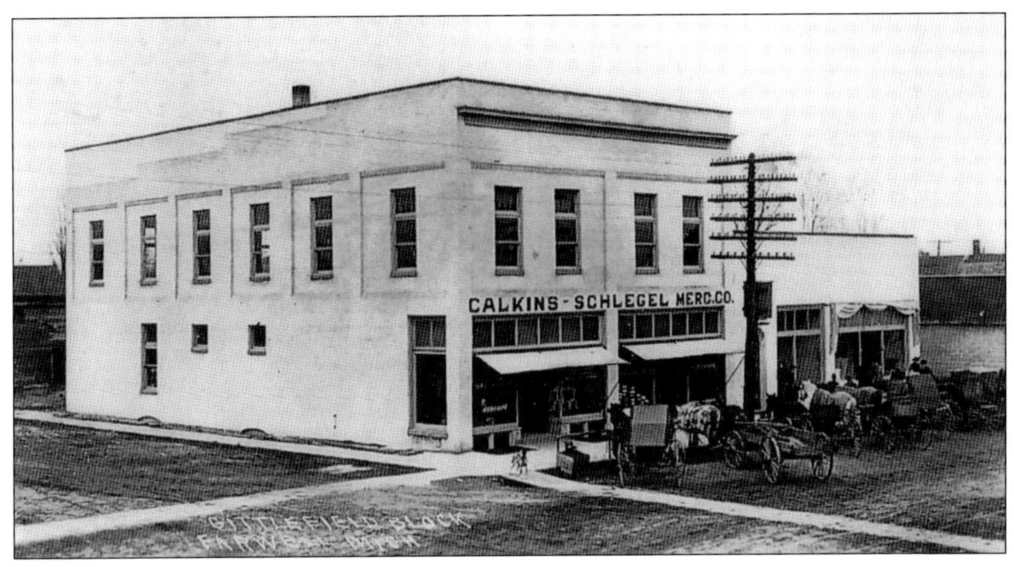

The Littlefield building, or Littlefield block as it was known, suffered several fires. The Calkins Schelgel Merchantile Company was in the lower level of the Littlefield building, and the opera house was above. The space was used for meetings, concerts, and other community gatherings. It was constructed in 1908 after a fire took the previous building, but in 1915, it was lost in a fire that was suspected as arson (below). Incidentally, the business of Charles Calkins and his nephew Irwin Schlegel moved to Farwell with their salvaged stock after a fire at their Lansing business. Their partnership later dissolved due to bankruptcy, a chattel mortgage, and disputes over stock and creditors.

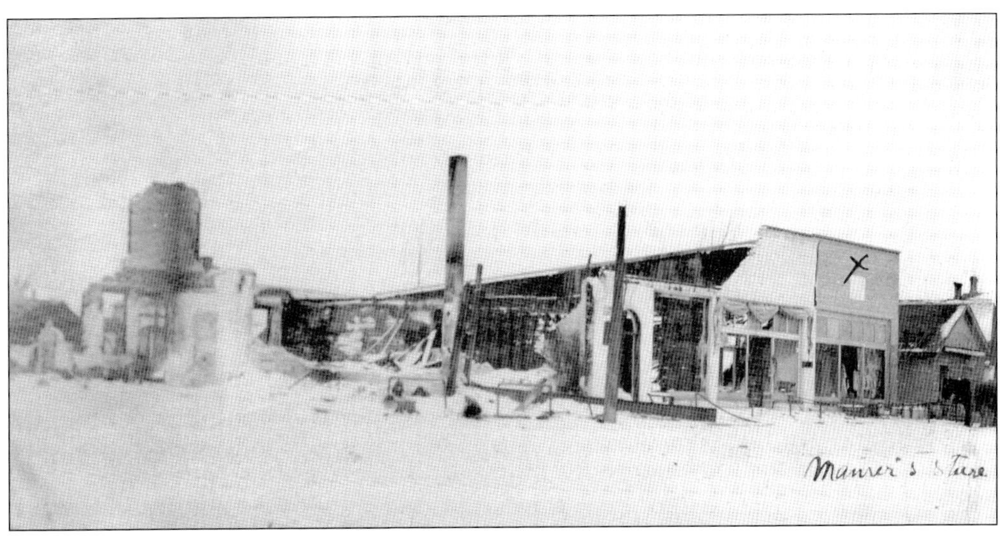

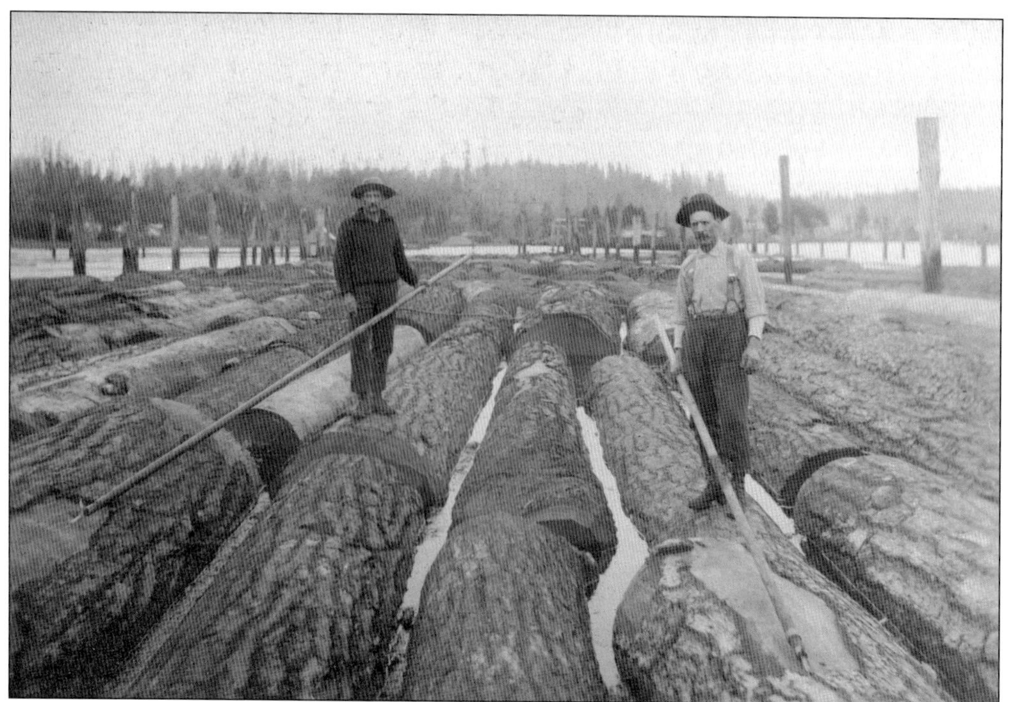

The millpond and other bodies of water have always been an important part of life in Farwell. Water was necessary for storing and moving logs to their destinations.

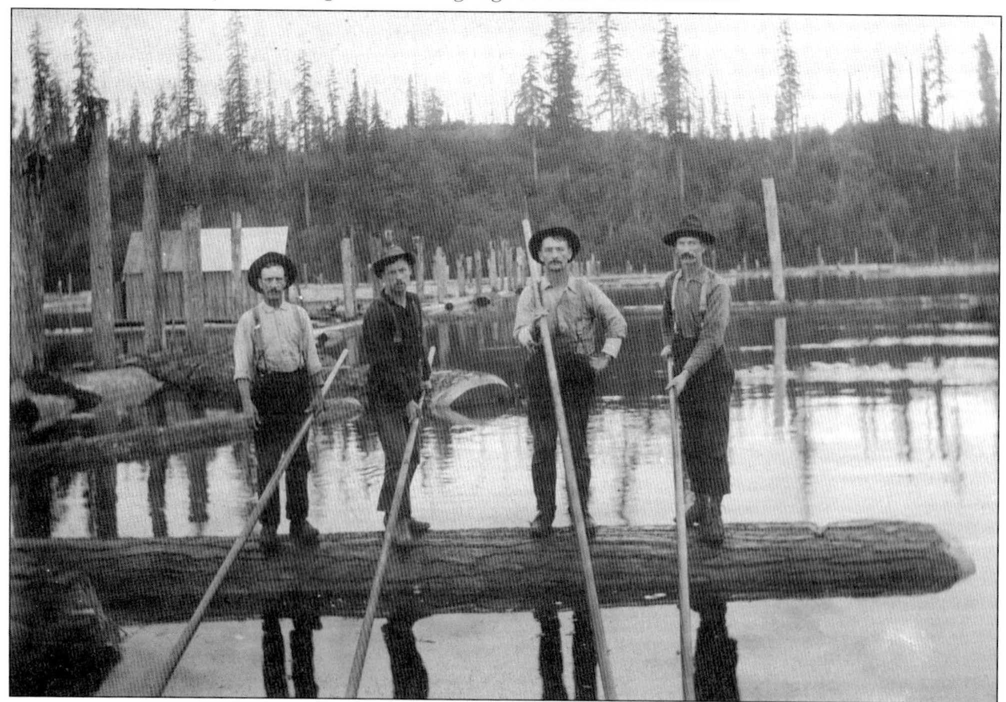

Logging has always been a dangerous profession. Men were regularly killed in and around the camps and mills. Men were killed while fighting, falling asleep, or drunk on railroad tracks, by rolling or falling logs, and other accidents.

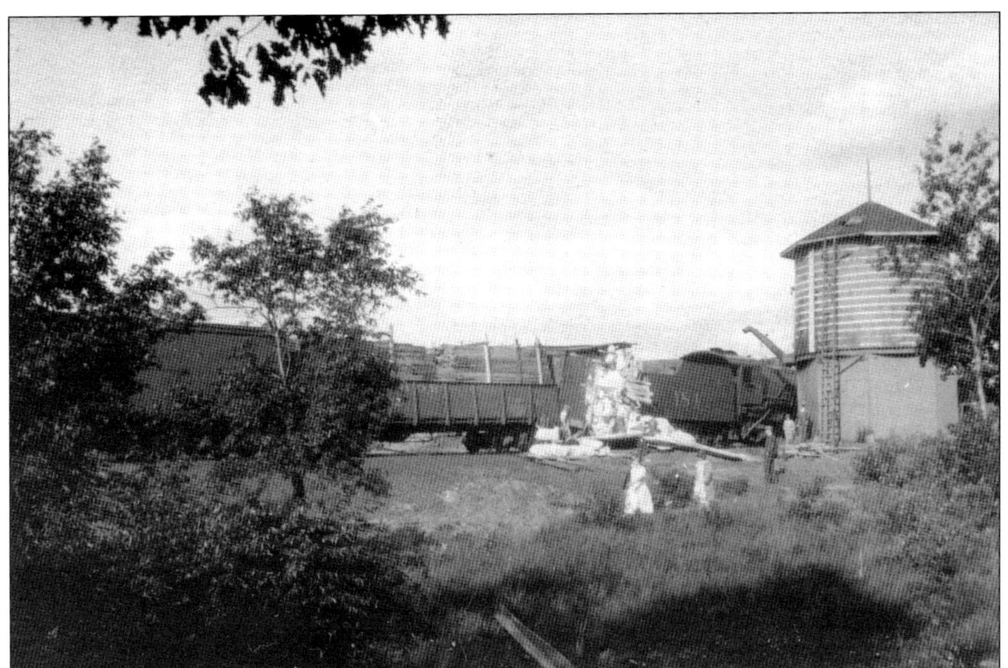

On July 29, 1925, a passenger train and a freight train had a head-on collision near the location of the water tower in Lake George. While stopped to take on water, the freight train was hit by the passenger train. Martin Enfield, the road master of the railway, was killed instantly, and there were other minor injuries. The lack of a block-signal and the failure of the operator at Farwell to deliver a copy of the meet order caused the accident. Local lore says the force of the collision only left one building standing in Lake George. Although it did not level the town, it was a serious accident still talked about today. (Both, courtesy of the Welty family.)

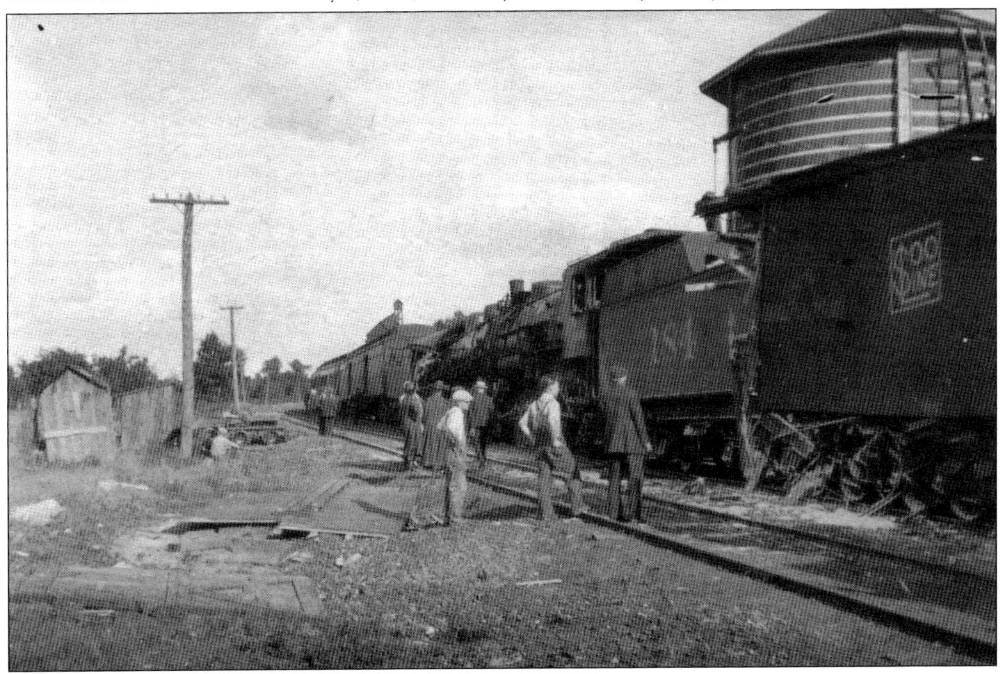

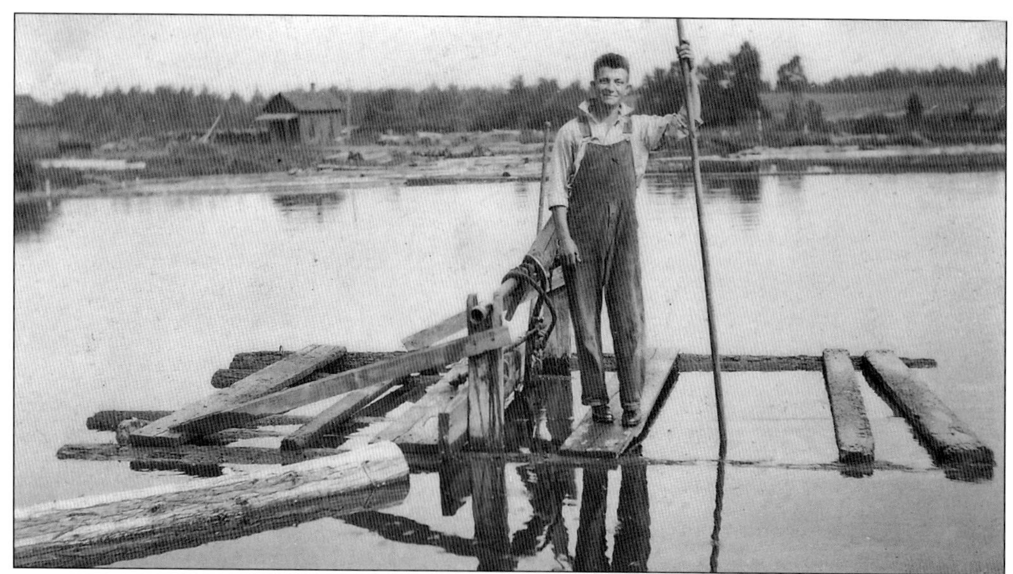

Lou Gee is shown pulling "deadheads" out of the Farwell millpond. Deadheads are logs that have been submerged and sunk in water. Deadheads were a common occurrence for many years in northern Michigan after the logging heyday was over. The 26-acre millpond is still popular for fishermen and children with a pole and some time on their hands.

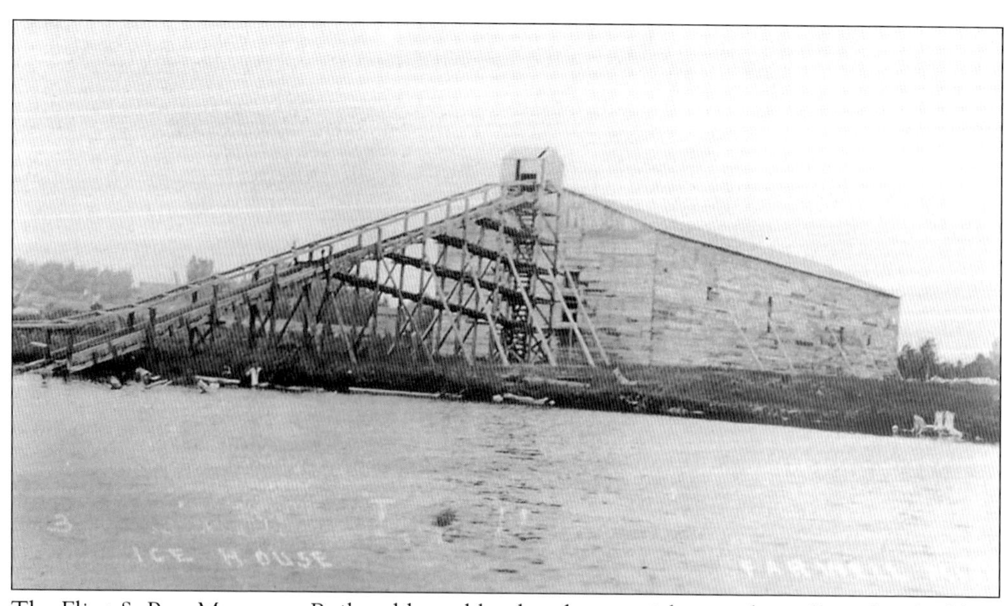

The Flint & Pere Marquette Railroad leased land and water rights on the millpond to build an ice works in 1923. Ice was cut and put into storage by electric elevators for local use. It was also shipped via the railway. The ice works burned to the ground in 1941, but by that time, better systems for making and storing ice had been invented.

An ill-timed business venture in the early 1900s in Farwell was the Portland Cement Company. This stock certificate belonged to Josiah Littlefield's wife, Emma, and shows that she owned 50 shares. The total capitalization was $350,000, or 35,000 shares at $10 each. (Meek.)

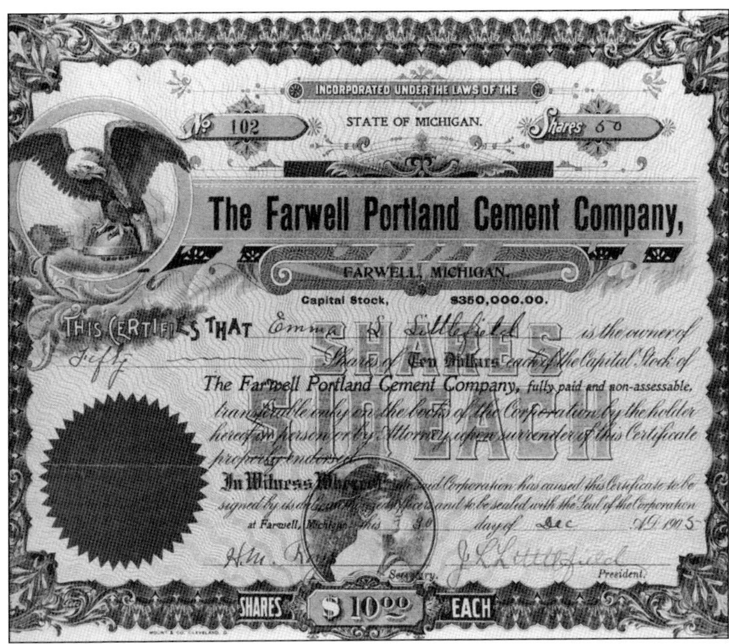

INCORPORATED UNDER THE LAWS OF THE

STATE OF MICHIGAN.

No 102

Shares 50

The Farwell Portland Cement Company,

FARWELL, MICHIGAN.

Capital Stock, $350,000.00.

This Certifies that Emma Littlefield is the owner of Fifty Shares of Ten Dollars each of the Capital Stock of The Farwell Portland Cement Company, fully paid and non-assessable, transferable only on the books of the Corporation by the holder hereof in person or by Attorney, upon surrender of this Certificate properly endorsed.

In Witness Whereof the said Corporation has caused this Certificate to be signed by its duly authorized officers and to be sealed with the Seal of the Corporation at Farwell, Michigan this 30 day of Dec A.D. 1905

Secretary. President.

SHARES $10.00 EACH

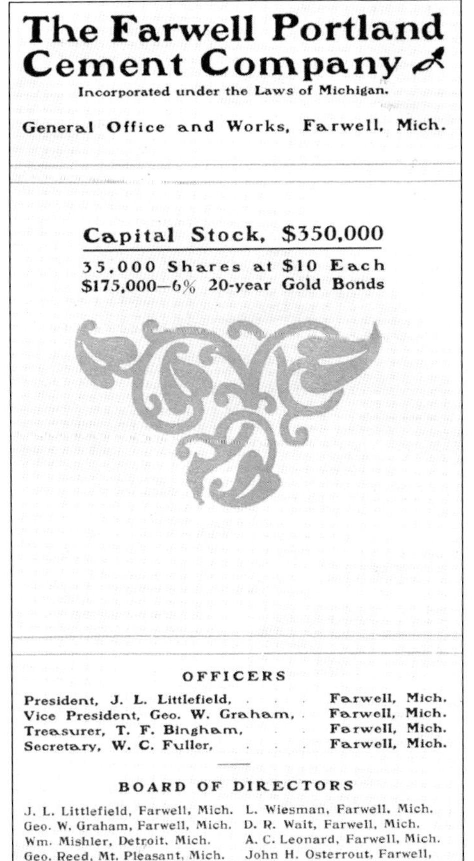

The Farwell Portland Cement Company

Incorporated under the Laws of Michigan.

General Office and Works, Farwell, Mich.

Capital Stock, $350,000

35,000 Shares at $10 Each

$175,000—6% 20-year Gold Bonds

OFFICERS

President, J. L. Littlefield, Farwell, Mich.
Vice President, Geo. W. Graham, Farwell, Mich.
Treasurer, T. F. Bingham, Farwell, Mich.
Secretary, W. C. Fuller, Farwell, Mich.

BOARD OF DIRECTORS

J. L. Littlefield, Farwell, Mich.
Geo. W. Graham, Farwell, Mich.
Wm. Mishler, Detroit, Mich.
Geo. Reed, Mt. Pleasant, Mich.
L. Wiesman, Farwell, Mich.
D. R. Wait, Farwell, Mich.
A. C. Leonard, Farwell, Mich.
John H. Osterrout, Farwell, Mich.
Fred. M. Shepard, Farwell, Mich.

Josiah Littlefield was president of the Portland Cement Company, and George W. Graham, T.F. Bingham, and William Fuller served as the board of directors and primary investors. The company was meant to create jobs and income after the decline of the lumber industry. The discovery of a new process for creating lime cement greatly reduced the price and availability of the product, and the factory was a failure. (Meek.)

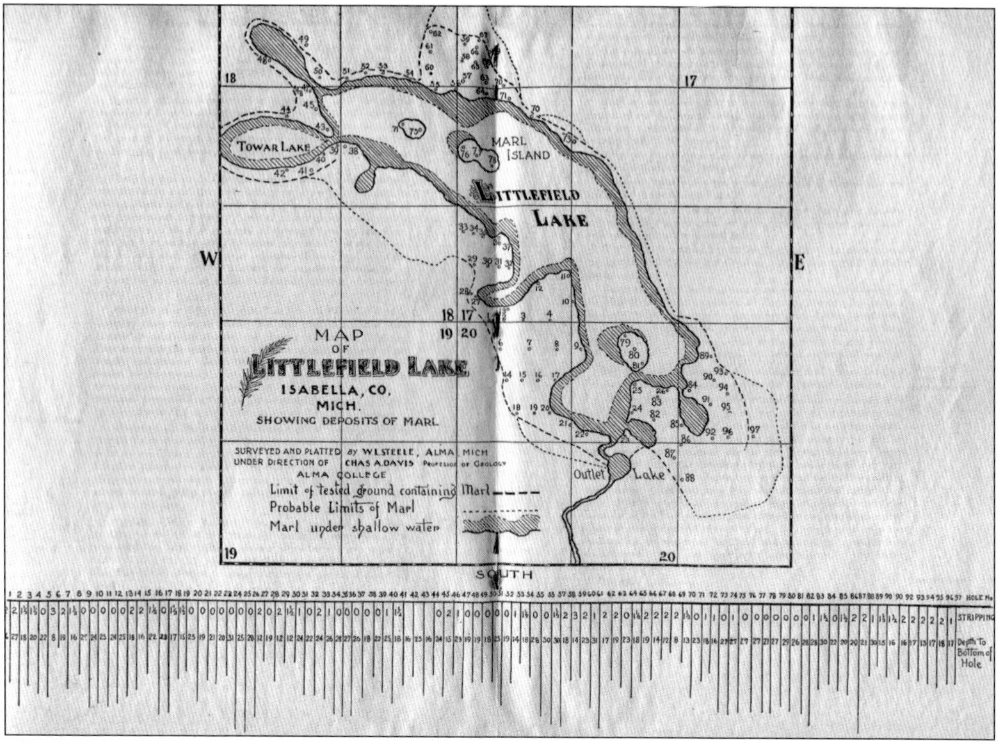

The failed Portland Cement Company intended to manufacture cement from marl deposits from Littlefield Lake in Gilmore Township. Josiah Littlefield owned most of the property surrounding the 183-acre lake at the time.

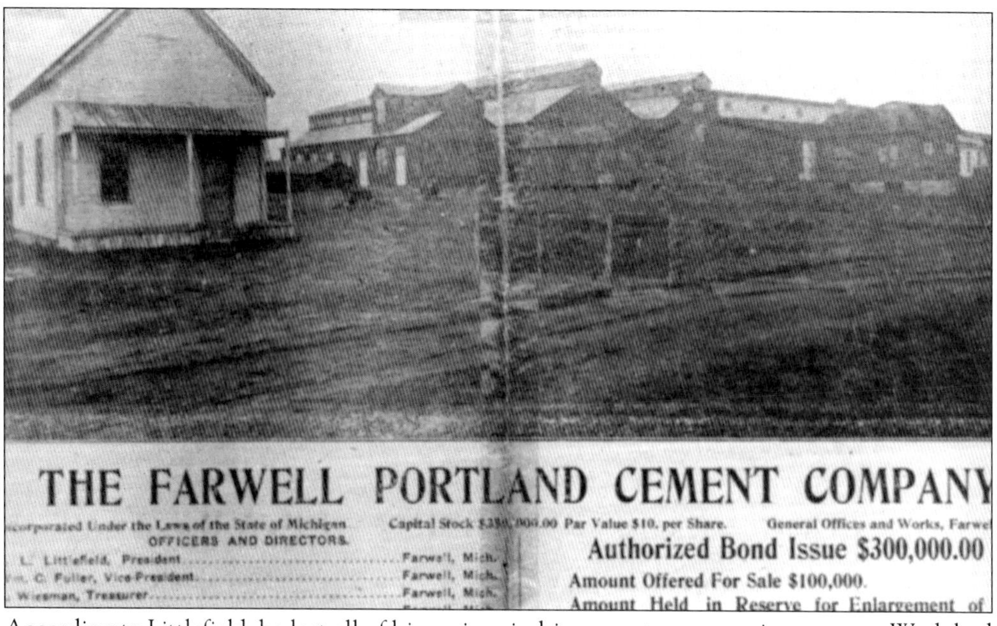

According to Littlefield, he lost all of his savings in his cement company investment. Work had begun on a railroad to the lake and most of the buildings were completed and ready to begin business before it was realized that the venture would not be successful.

George Graham was born in Ontario, Canada, and made his way to Clare County in the early 1870s. In Farwell he ran a stave mill and laid plank roads, and in 1885 was elected sheriff of the county at only 25 years of age. Along with a prosecutor named Burritt, he is credited with taming the lawlessness of Harrison and, in particular, cleaning up saloon and brothel owners like James Carr, who took advantage of the lack of law enforcement at the new county seat throughout the early 1880s. Graham is shown at right as a young man and below with his family in 1890. His son Arthur Stewart Graham (below, at center), born in 1885, was most likely the child playing on the floor at the jail/sheriff's residence when a prisoner made his escape and ran through the sheriff's home. Graham later followed his children and other family members out West in true American manifest destiny style. Though he died in Washington state in 1940, he was returned to Farwell and is buried at Surrey Township Cemetery. (Both, courtesy of Patrick Graham.)

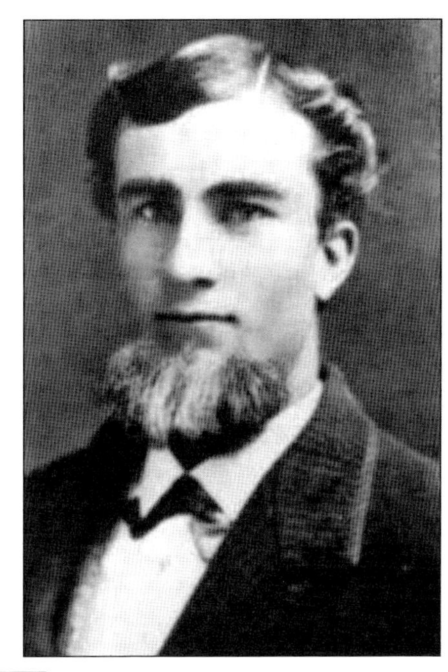

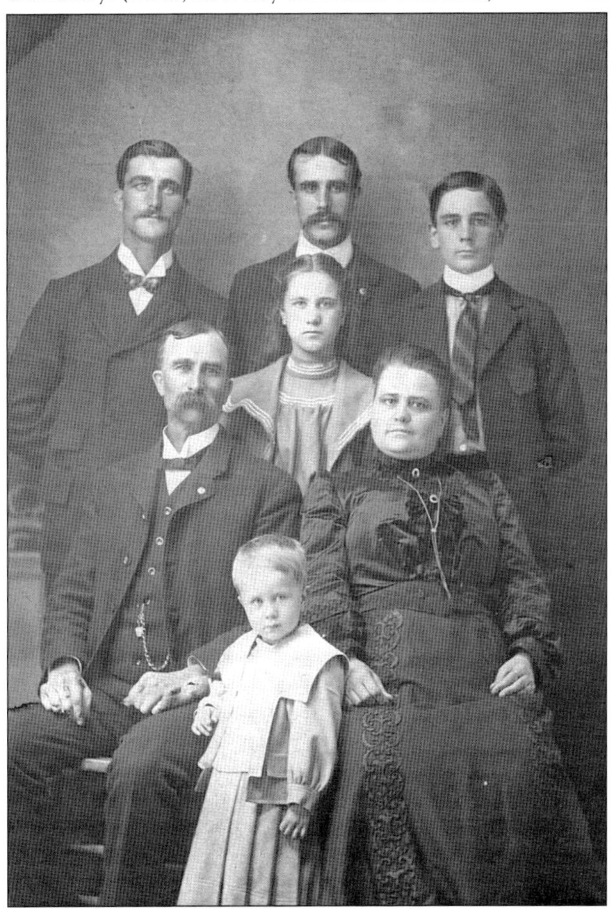

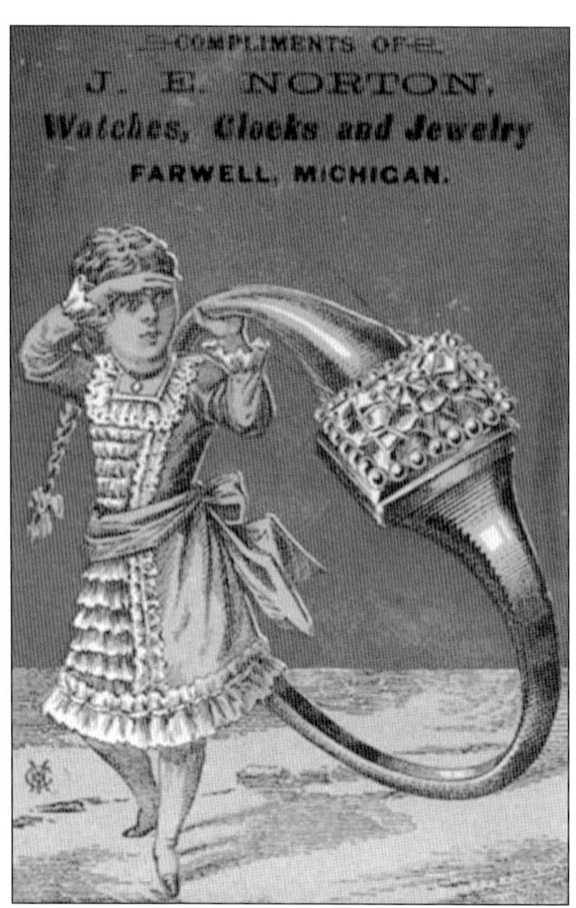

This 1890s trade card advertises one of the many businesses that came to Farwell—J.E. Norton, jeweler.

It is unclear what the gentleman on the far right is speaking of or what he could be selling, but the crowd in Farwell is dressed in their finery for the occasion. This postcard is aptly titled "When Farwell Celebrates," as the Labor Day festivities still draw huge crowds and bring native Farwell residents home to visit.

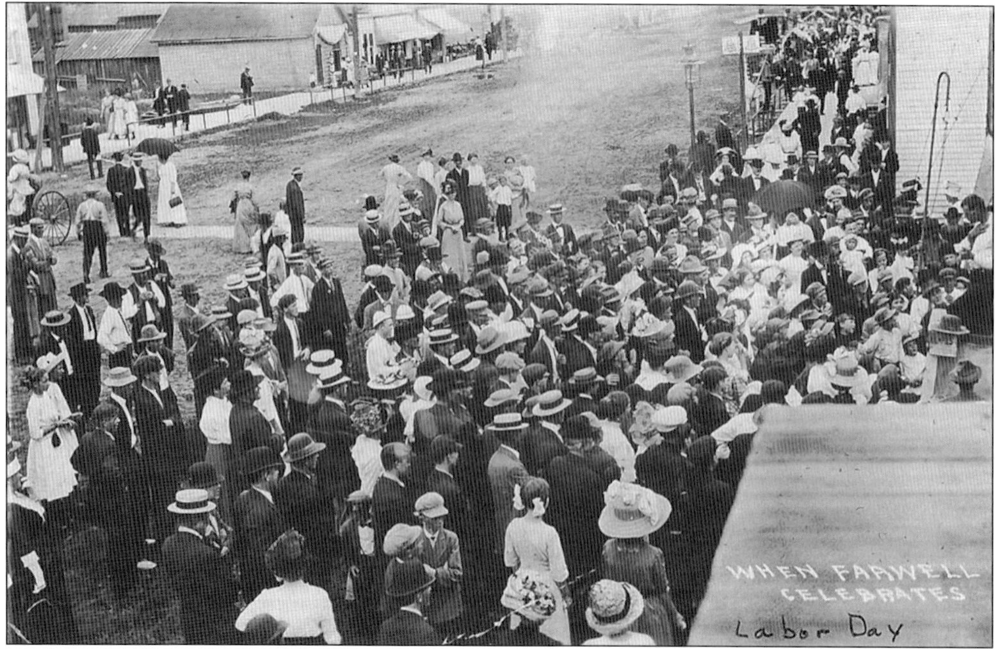

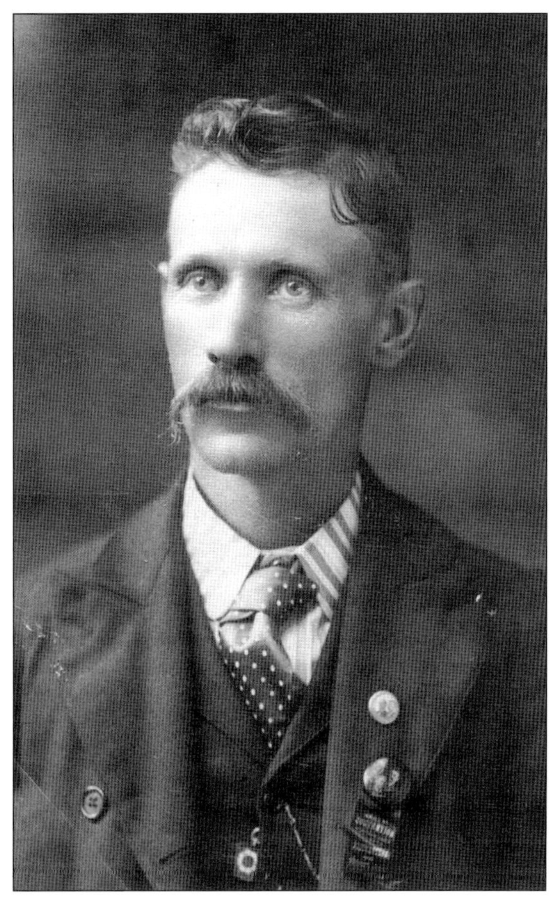

John J. Saxton came to Farwell in 1882 and worked as a store clerk. He moved with the store to Meredith, where he went into business for himself as a barber. He returned to Farwell in 1897 and was appointed postmaster. His first wife, Alice Foster, passed away in childbirth in 1900. In 1907, he also became an undertaker. Both of his children, Ethel and Percy, assisted their father when home as deputy postmasters. He was remarried to Adella Barrett Hammond. Saxton died in 1918 and is buried in the Surrey Township Cemetery. His brother William Saxton ran a stagecoach business on the Isabella–Tobacco River state road. (Both, courtesy of Gary Saxton.)

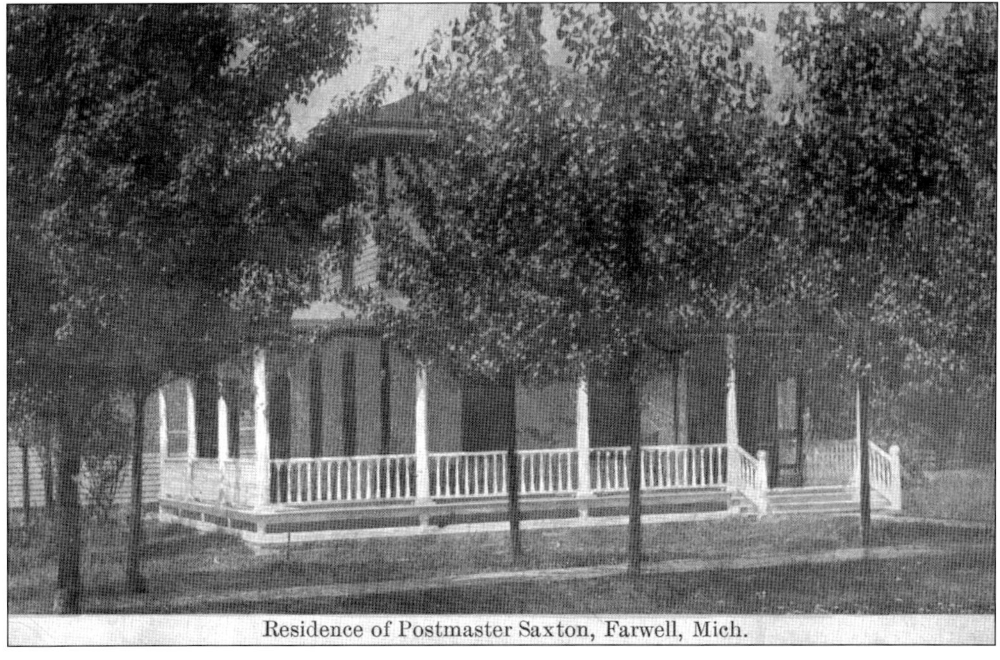

Residence of Postmaster Saxton, Farwell, Mich.

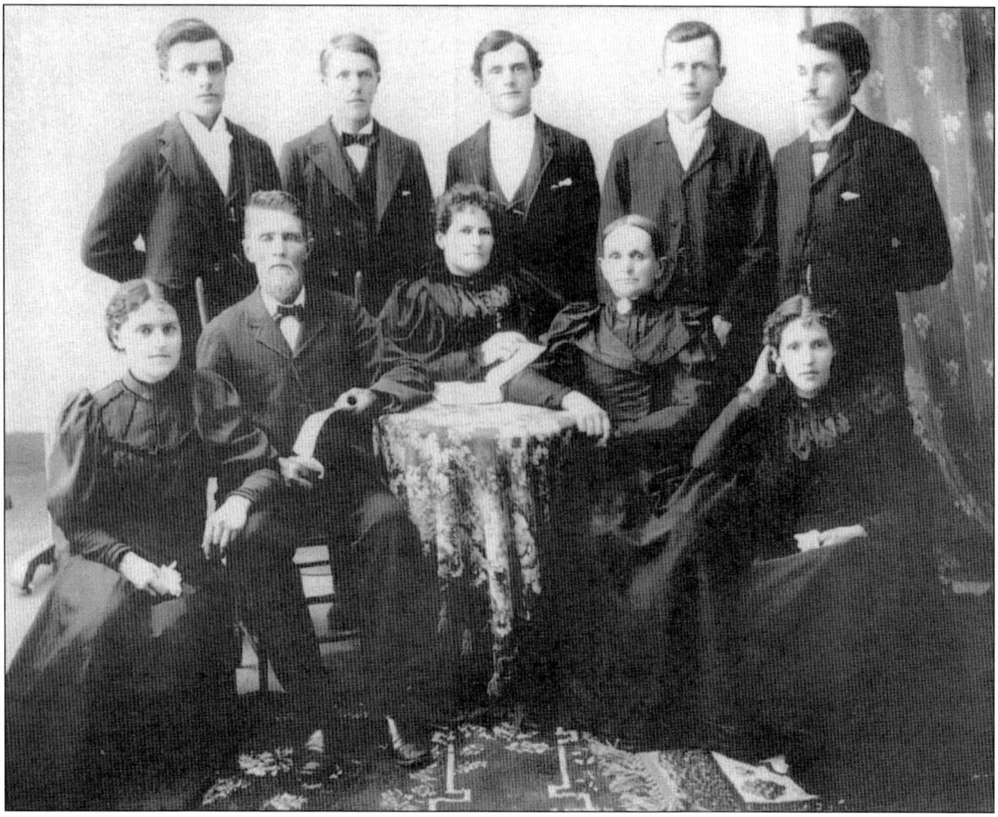

The Loomis family settled in and around the Farwell area. Benton Loomis was a respected member for the community for many years. He wed Goldie Fordyce, and they went on to have four children, one of whom, Kenneth, settled in Farwell. Benton Loomis spent the remainder of his years working at the Merrill-Palmer Motherhood School in Detroit, visiting his hometown often. The Loomis family is pictured here in 1905. From left to right are (first row) Kathryn, Hibbard, Dora, Mary (Tewksbury), and Clara; (second row) Benton, Chester, Frank, Sam, and Fred.

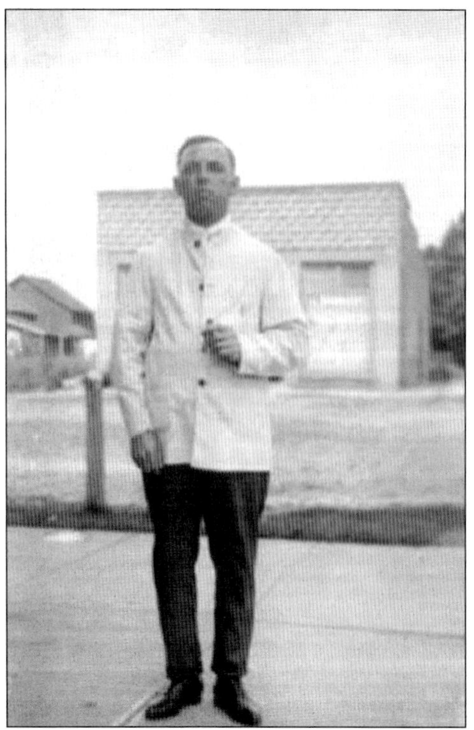

William Burston is pictured in front of his pharmacy, which he bought from H.M. Roys in 1906. Burston trained in Cadillac as a pharmacist. He became active in politics, in addition to being clerk of the Village of Farwell and clerk of Surrey Township. He eventually became president of the village.

As agriculture began to replace lumbering, Josiah Littlefield tried experimental farming with such crops as rye, alfalfa, and sugar beets. He also kept cattle and raised Aberdeen Angus and Herefords.

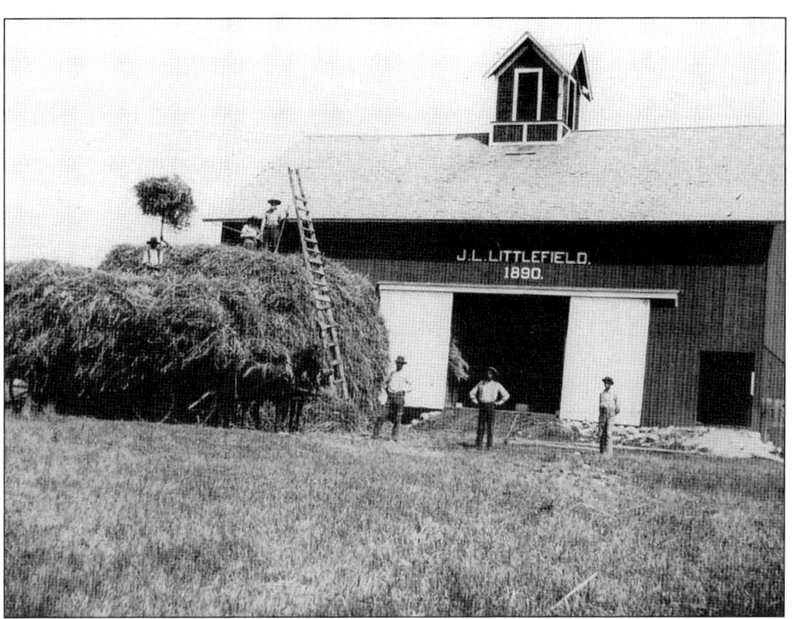

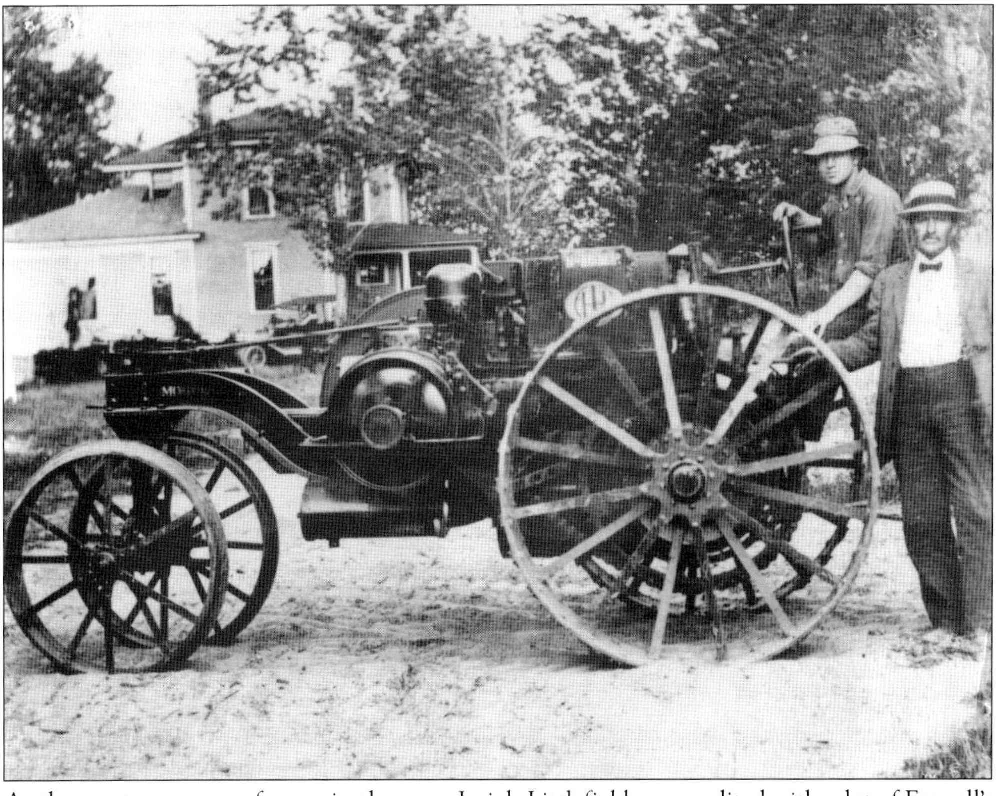

As the most prosperous farmer in the area, Josiah Littlefield was credited with a lot of Farwell's firsts. The first tractor is shown here with Franklin Littlefield in the driver's seat. His father stands beside him, and their home is in the background.

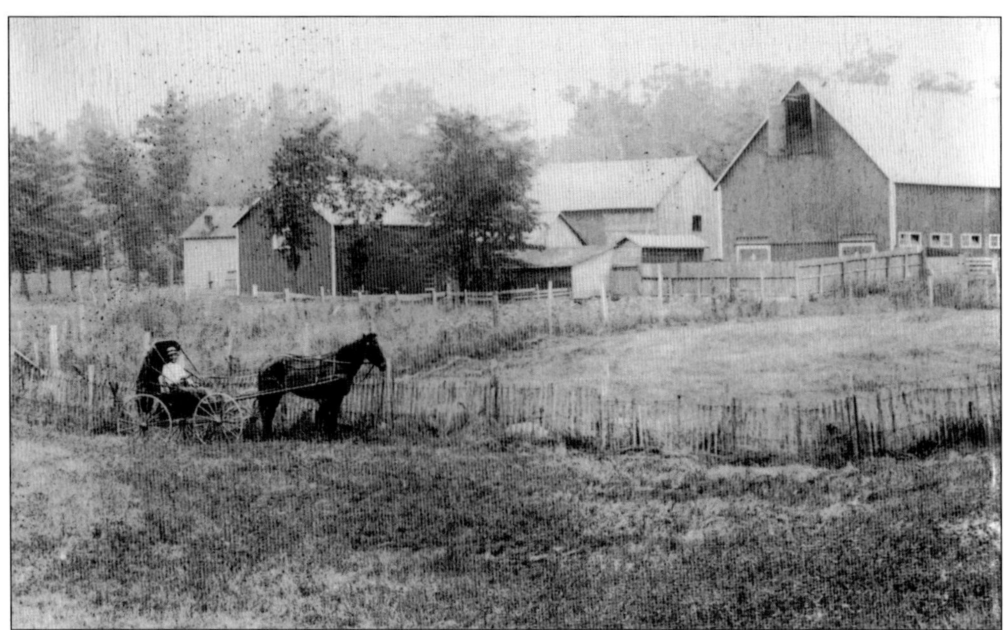

Josiah Littlefield is in his rig at his farming operation, known as Beechwood Farm. Littlefield began a Farmer's Institute in the county so farmers could meet and discuss problems and farming techniques. (Meek.)

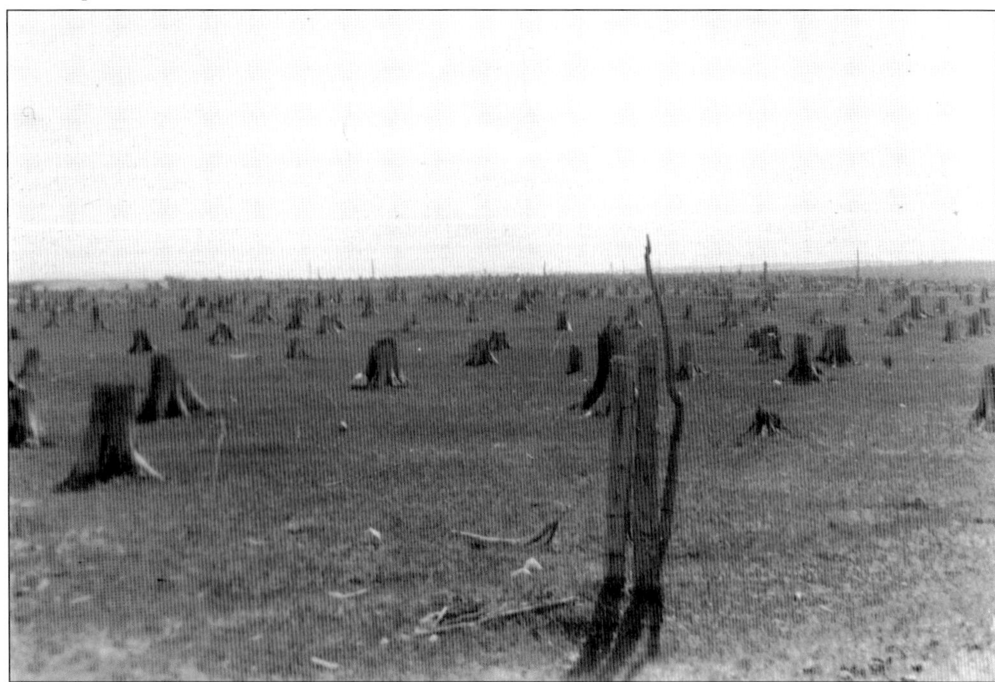

The stumps shown here on the Welty farm just north of Lake George were a problem faced by farmers who purchased land after it was logged off. Erosion, fires, and sandy soil were other challenges they faced. Farwell avoided many of the big fires that raged across Michigan as a result of logging in the 1890s. In 1884, fire completely surrounded the town, but the wind was favorable and the fire was contained in nearby swamps. (Courtesy of the Welty family.)

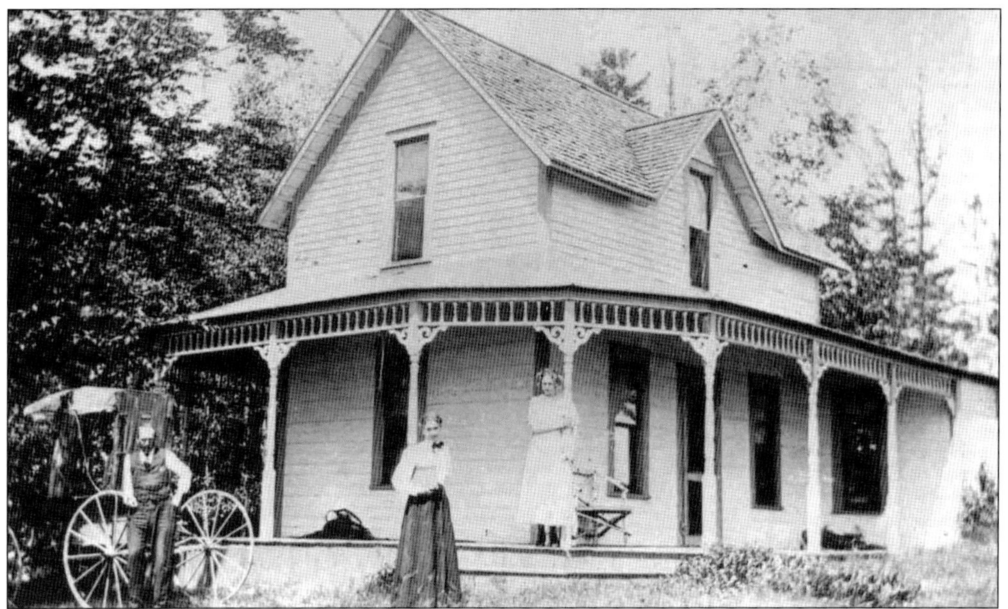

Lochabar Cottage, on the shores of Bear Lake, was built by Josiah Littlefield. The name comes from *loch* meaning "lake" in Scottish and *bar* meaning "bear" in German. The name honors the Littlefields' Scotch and German heritage. Lochabar was part of Josiah Littlefield's dream of a parklike setting inspired by his visit to Biltmore Estate in North Carolina. He purchased more land in Surrey Township after his visit to Biltmore for farming, grooming the land for groves of trees, roads, and scenic drives for pleasurable outings.

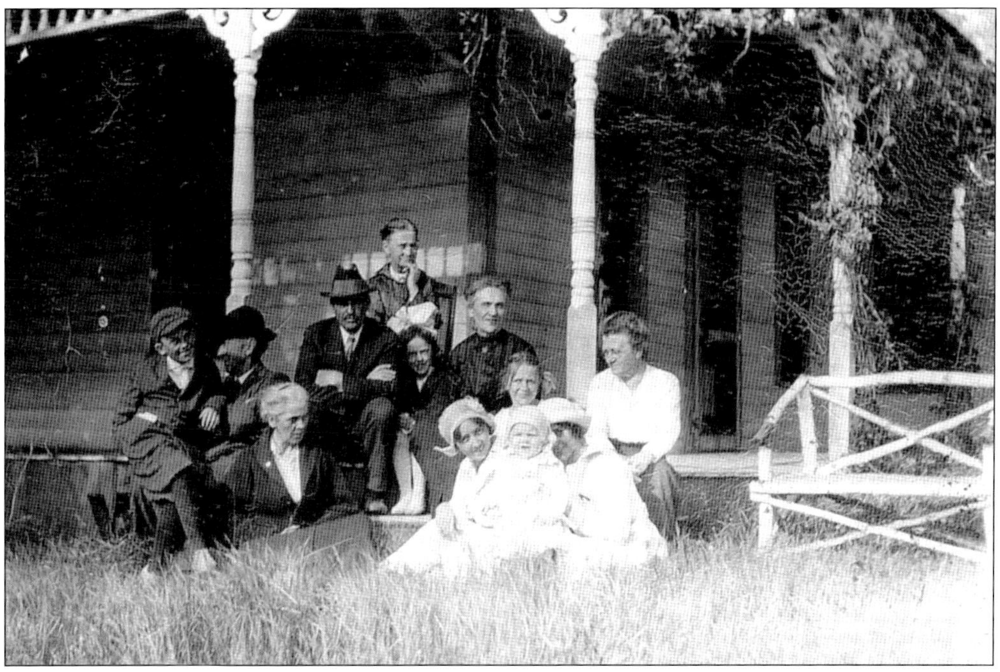

The Littlefield family sits with their extended family on the porch at the Lochabar retreat. Josiah and Emma Littlefield are pictured at center with a child between them. The cottage was built in 1896.

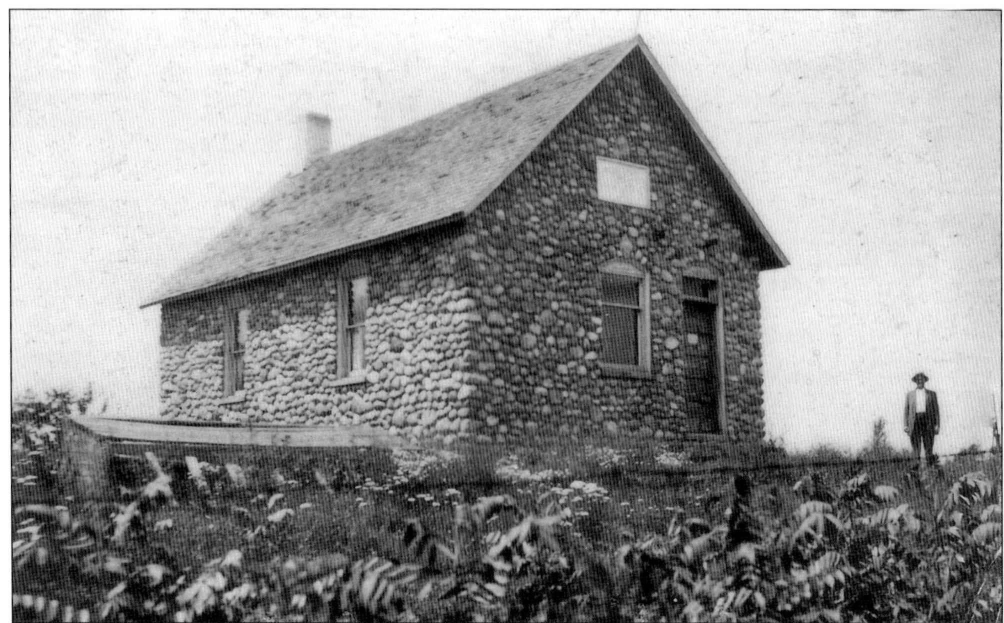

Lochabar School was built at Littlefield's own expense for the children in the area of Bear Lake. Members of the community that grew around Bear Lake identified their location as Lochabar and even formed a Lochabar neighborhood club with regular meetings. It also had its own social column in the newspaper, like many other locales of the time.

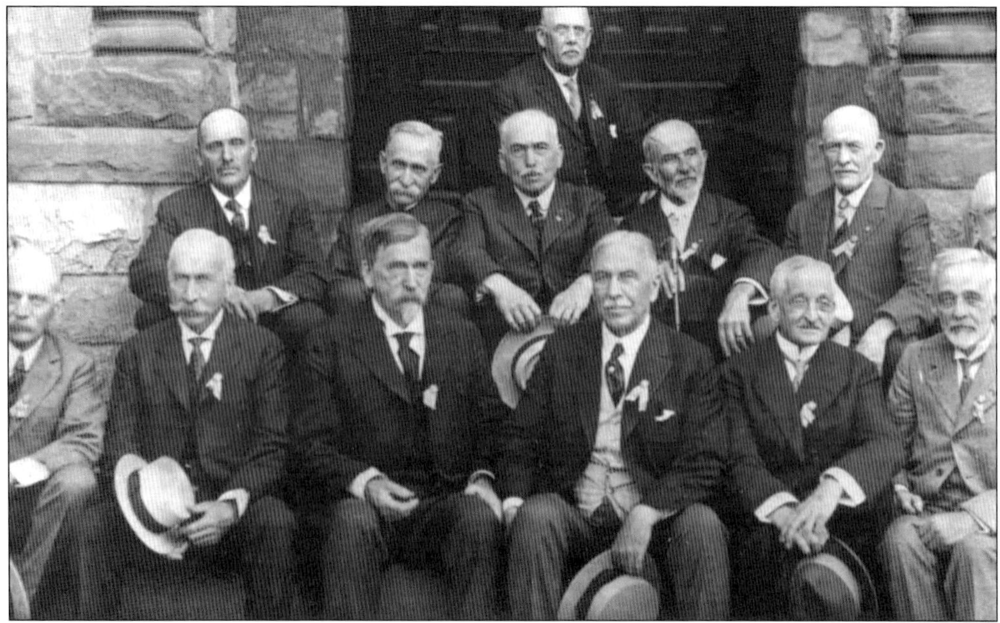

Josiah Littlefield (top left) is pictured at a reunion of his University of Michigan classmates. Education was important to the Littlefield family and something Josiah Littlefield supported in the community during his lifetime.

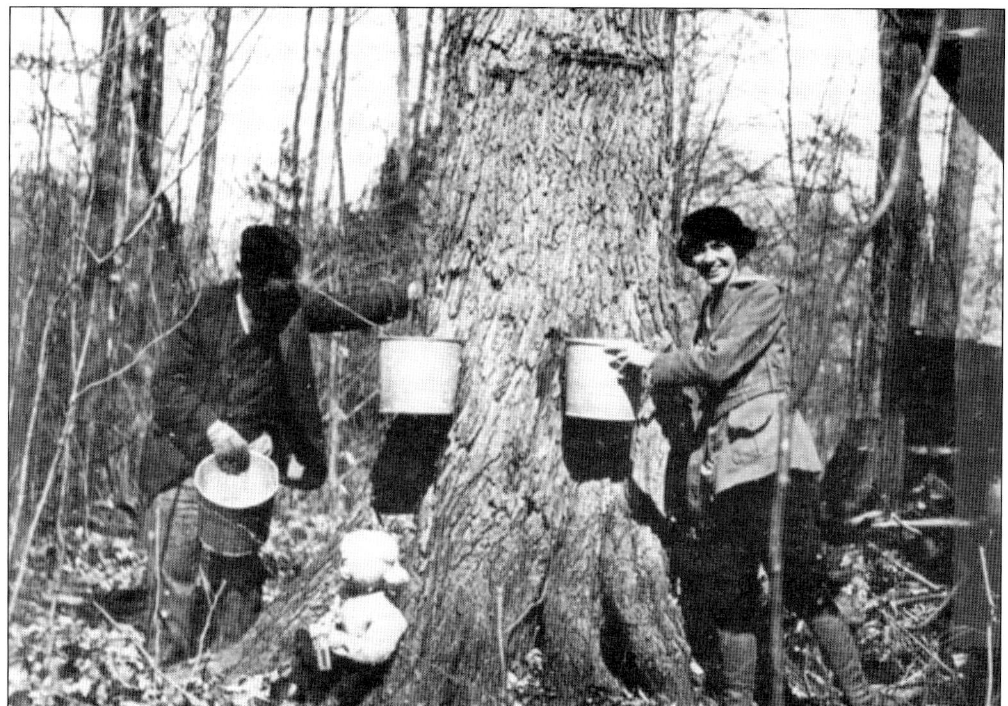

Josiah Littlefield is at left in both images collecting sap to make maple syrup near the sugar shack (right). It takes about 40 gallons of sap to make a gallon of syrup, as the sap is almost 98 percent water. Tapping maple trees for syrup making is still popular in northern Michigan. Littlefield's daughter Hazel is pictured with him above.

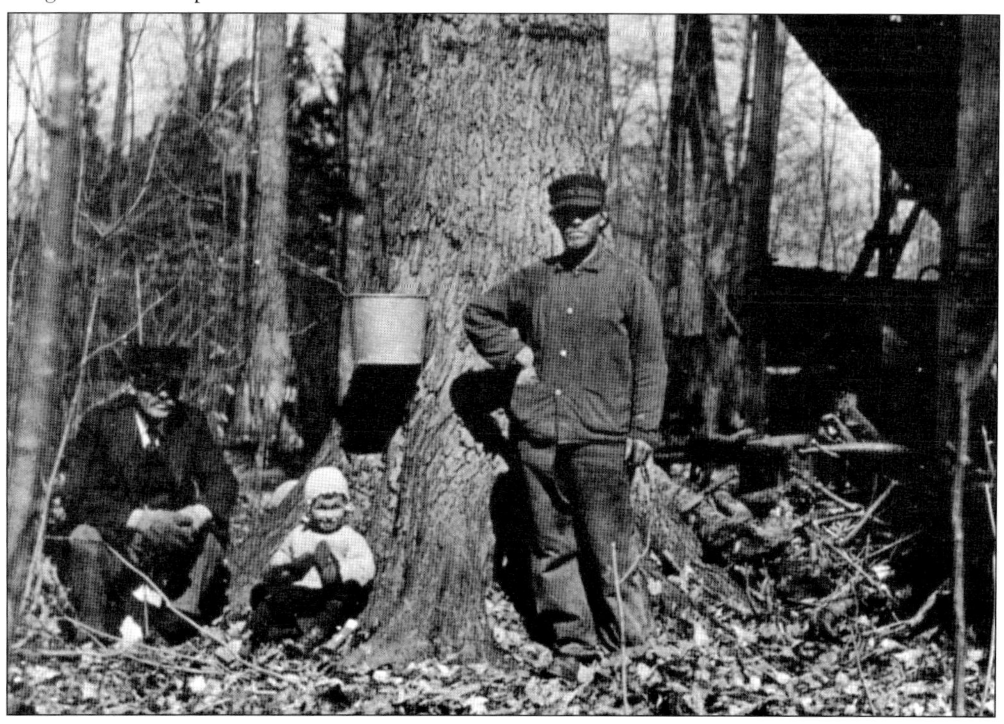

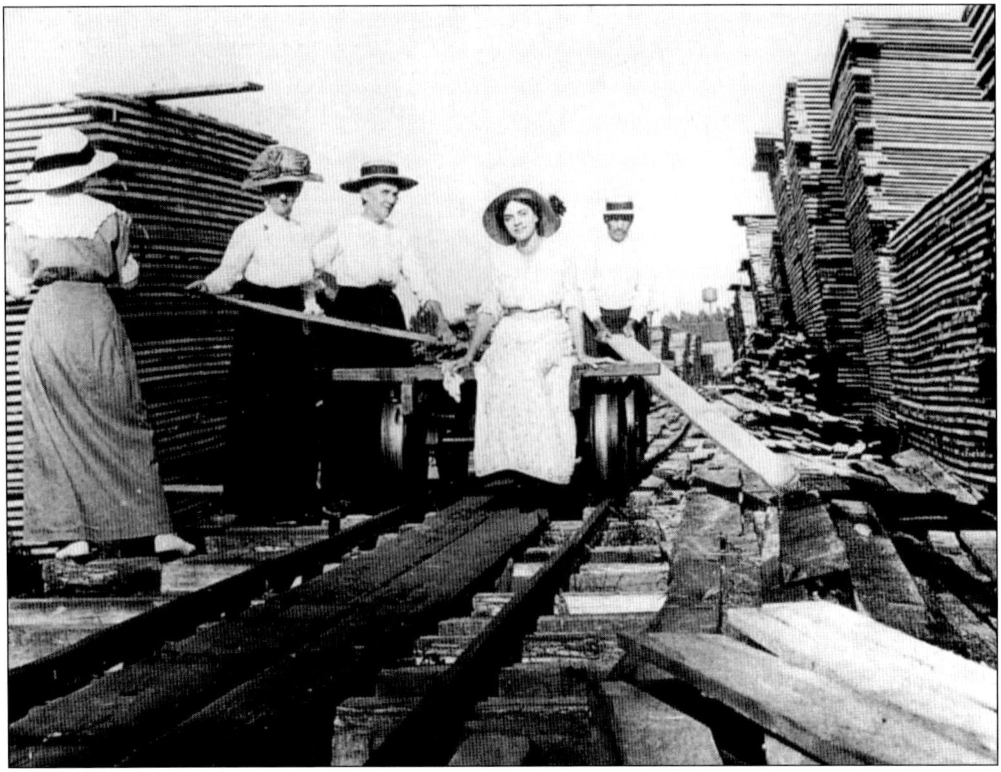

Hazel Grace Littlefield (seated, center) grew up in Farwell, the active and privileged child of Josiah and Emma Littlefield. She admired her father very much and edited his autobiography, written in 1933 and published in 1972. Hazel wrote poetry and short stories of her own as well. After girlhood, Farwell was not her permanent home, but she visited frequently. Her father is behind her on the right.

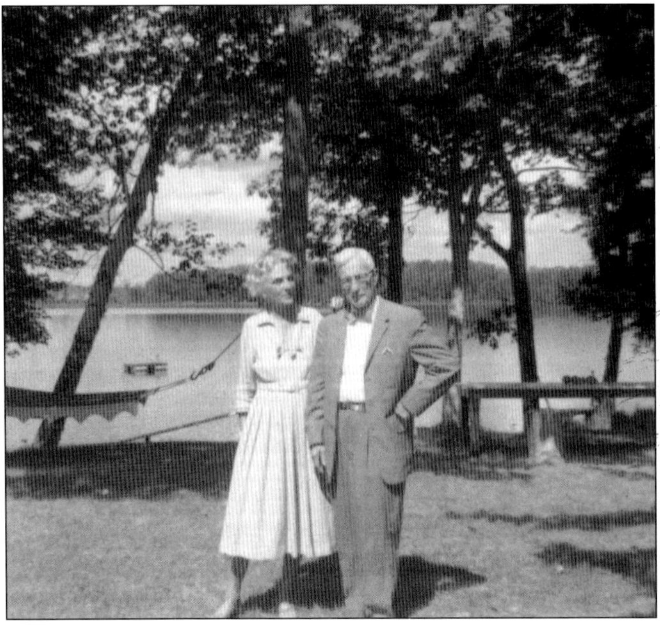

Hazel Littlefield is pictured with her husband, Dennis Smith. She met him while attending college at her father's alma mater, the University of Michigan. Smith graduated in 1909 and Hazel in 1913. He was an eye surgeon, and they spent time in China doing mission work. Her parents, Josiah and Emma, made the trip to visit her there in 1916, and since she was homesick, she returned to the United States with them.

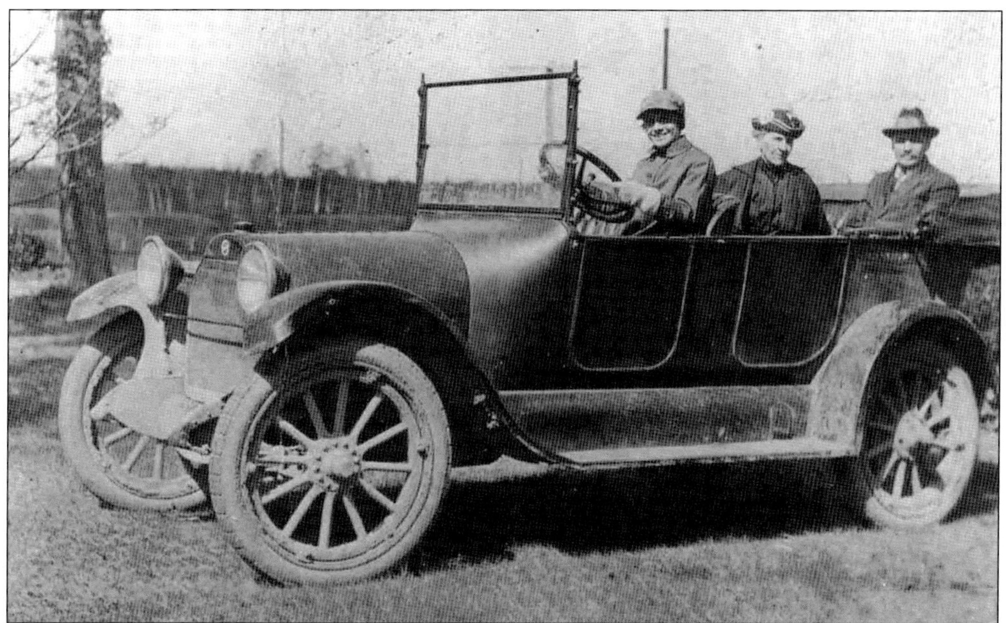

Franklin was the quieter and less obtrusive of the Littlefield children. He married Georgia Shumway in 1915. He inherited most of the Littlefield farmland and ran it himself most of his life. Much like his father, he served the community by sitting on farm program committees, bank boards of directors, the county tax commission, and many other associations and committees. Georgia passed away in 1957, and Franklin married Jennie Reed Bingham. He died in 1978. Franklin enjoyed driving cars and is pictured here driving his parents.

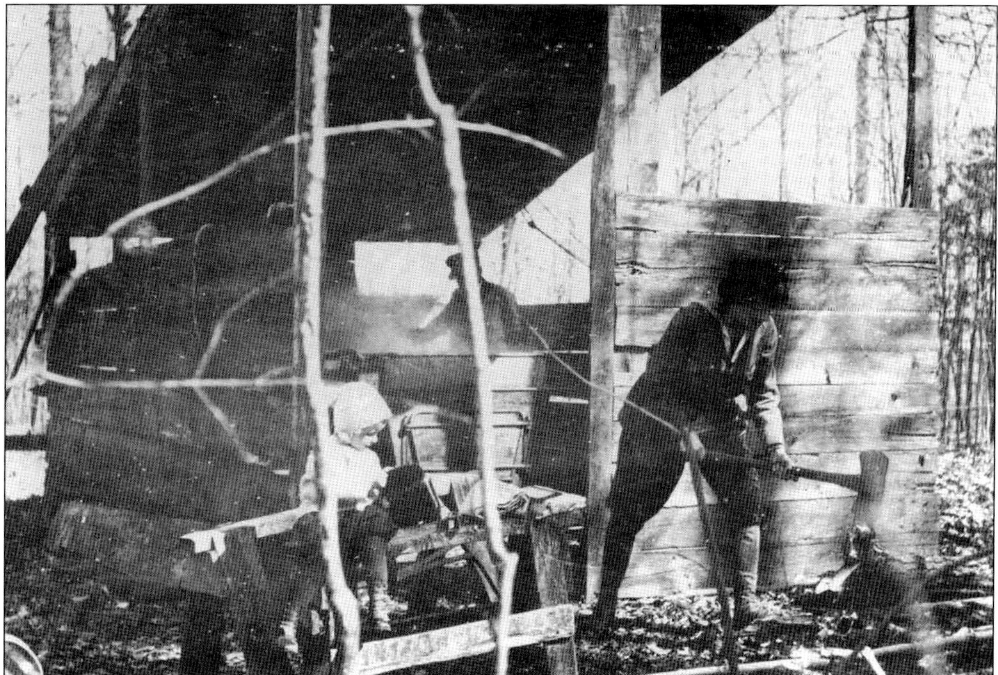

Hazel Littlefield (right) is chopping wood with an axe at Beechwood Farm. The steam and smoke from the maple sugar boiling can be seen inside the shelter.

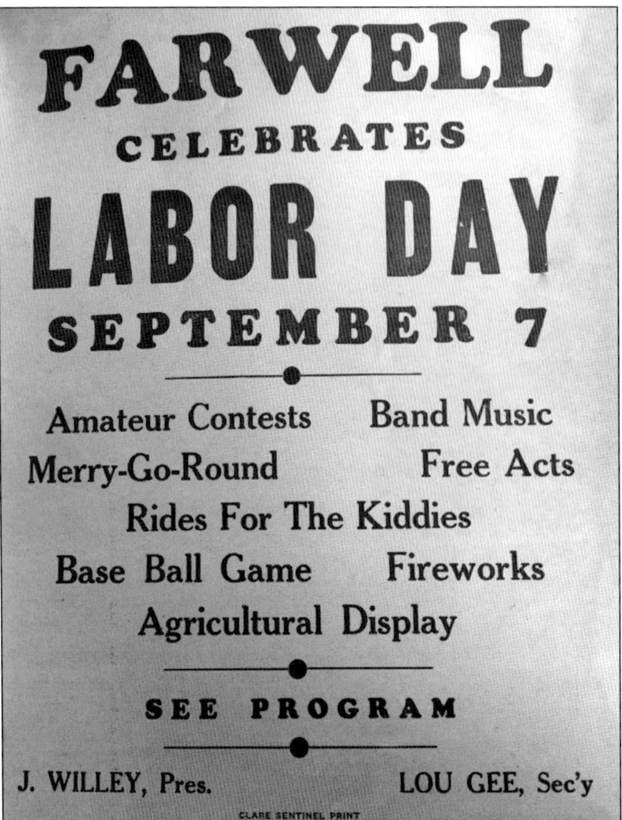

Labor Day festivities were officially called Auld Lang Syne, and the first organizational meeting was held in 1920. A weekend of festivities was held every year over Labor Day. This flyer is from 1942.

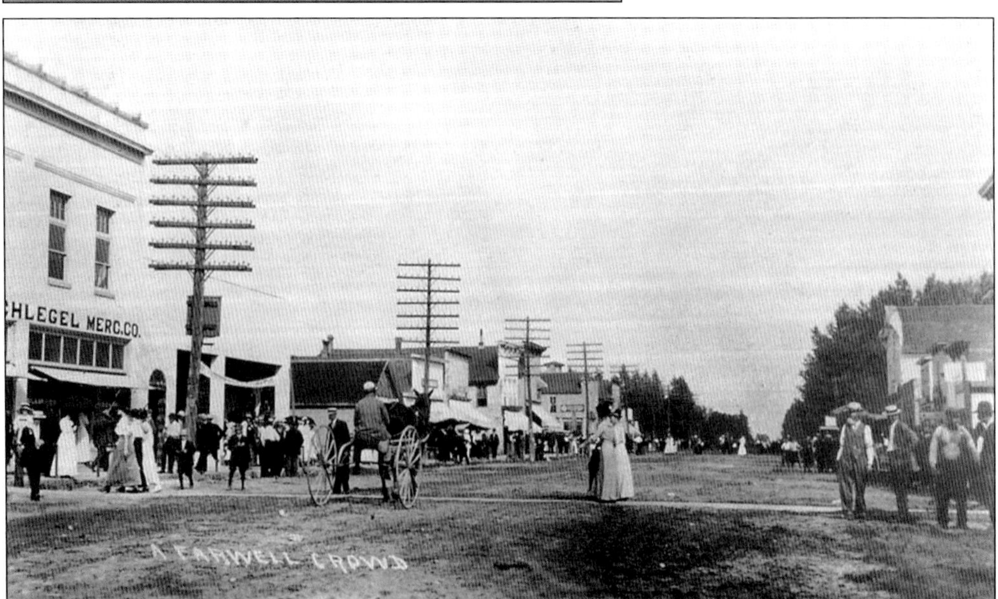

Today, Farwell's Labor Day celebration is the longest continuous festival in the state of Michigan. First begun with parades and picnics, it continues at the Farwell fairgrounds with carnival amusements, fireworks, games, and many activities. This picture postcard shows Farwell around the turn of the 20th century.

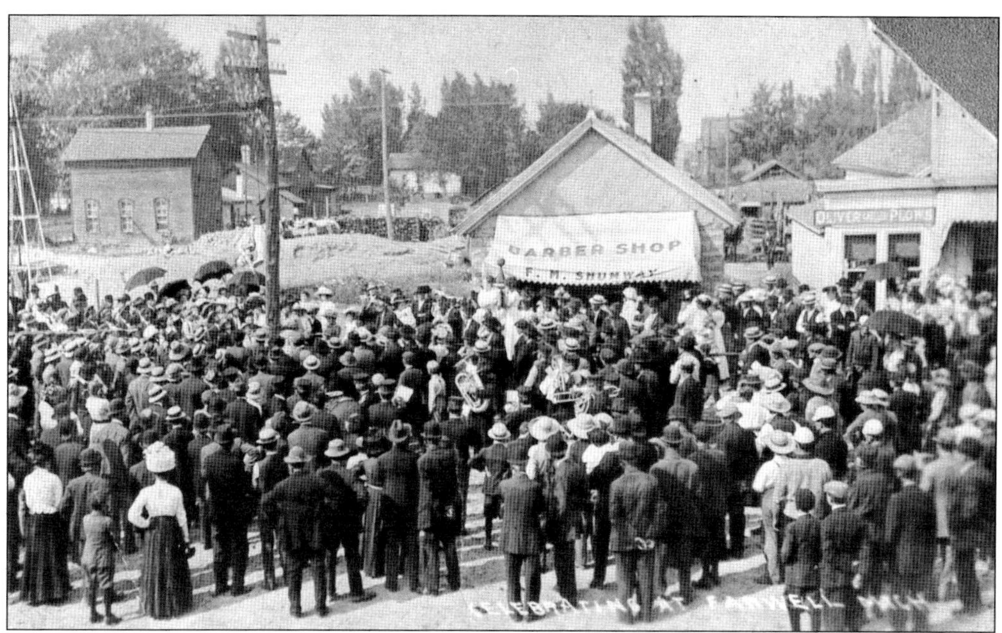

A young lady on a trapeze (to the left of the utility pole) captivates a Farwell crowd. Forest Shumway purchased the barbershop at center from Dr. Grillett and moved his business there in 1910. Shumway, along with James Gregory, held a patent in 1909 for a new and improved cuspidor (spittoon). He was a barber all his life and died in 1965. He is buried at Surrey Township Cemetery.

The Labor Day celebration of 1940 included a Ferris wheel (right) and many tents lining Main Street. Labor Day celebrations were combined with the agriculture fair, baseball games, amusements, and the annual meeting of the Auld Land Syne Society. The *Clare Sentinel* news item about the 1940 Labor Day celebration stated, "If you have never been at Farwell on Labor Day, 'you ain't seen nothin'."

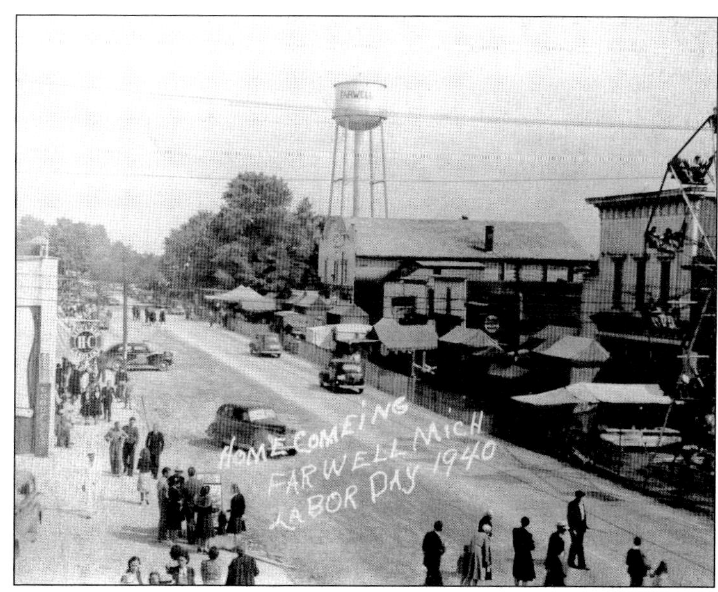

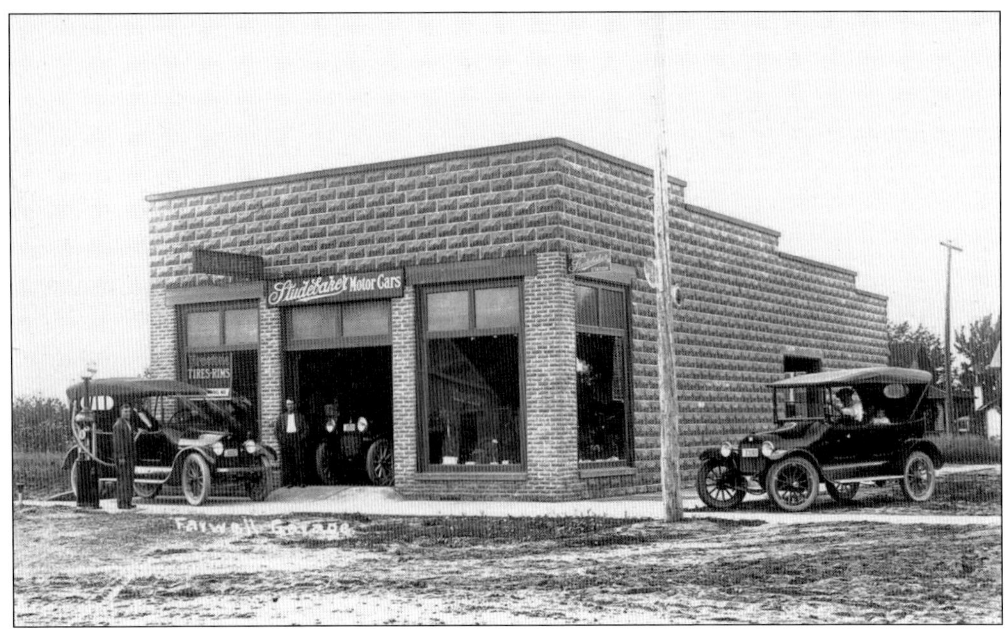

A frequent sight in many small towns, a Ford or Studebaker dealership brought the automobile to popularity in the 1920s. The Farwell Garage was a Studebaker dealership. The building still stands today as DJ's Lounge on the northwest corner of Main and Hayes Streets.

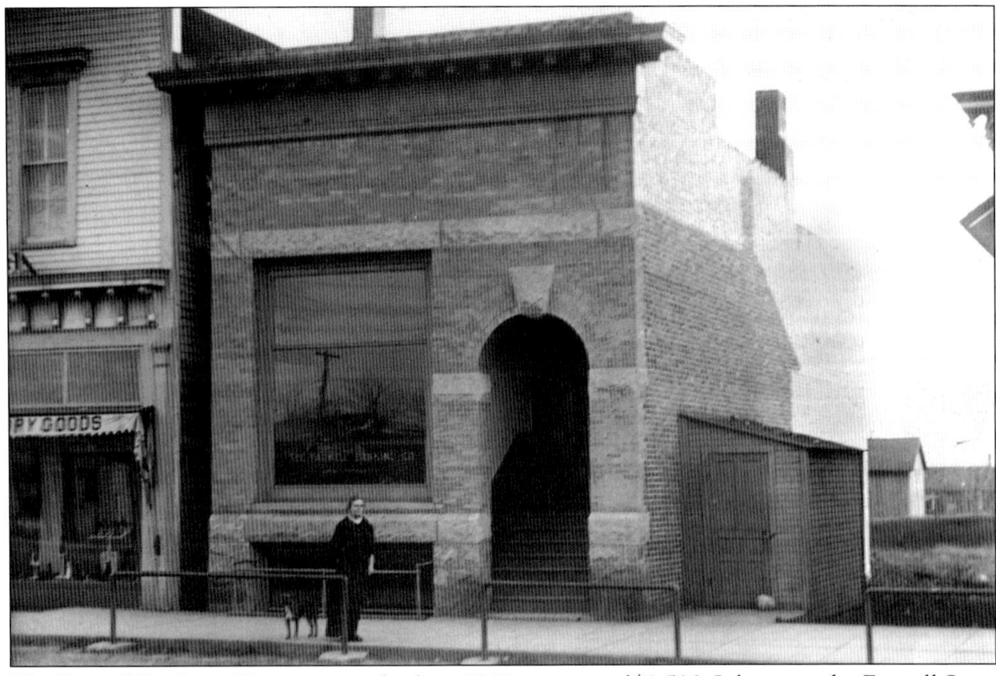

The Farwell Banking Company was built in 1903 at a cost of $2,500. It became the Farwell State Savings Bank in 1919. Note the cement sidewalks in front of the building; these replaced the wooden sidewalks in 1904.

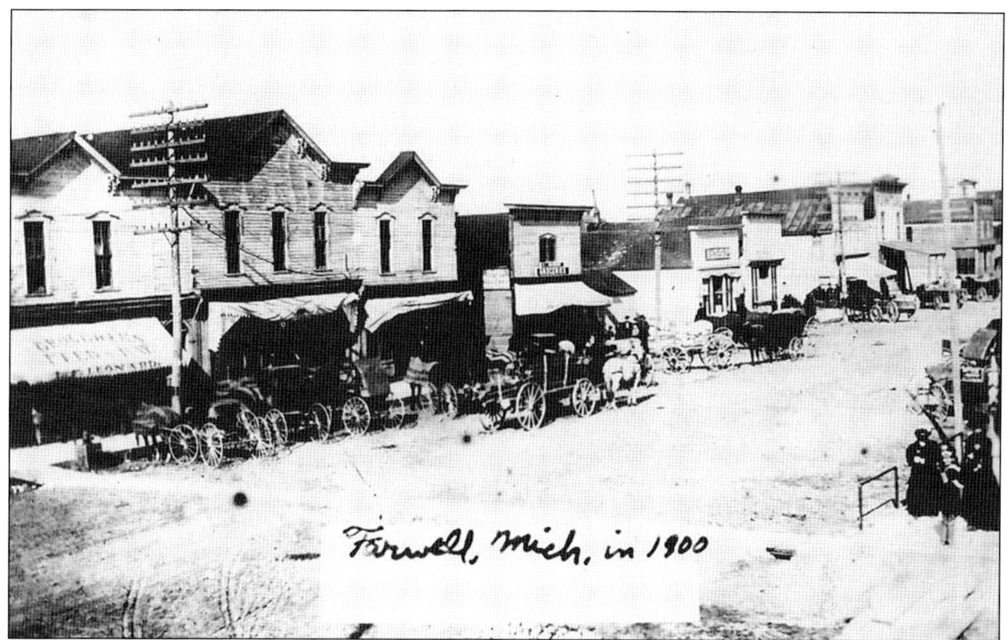

Shown here at the turn of the 20th century, this block of downtown Farwell was mostly lost in a fire in the early 1900s. The damage was estimated at over $6,000. The fire started in Leonard's general store and consumed several stores and damaged others.

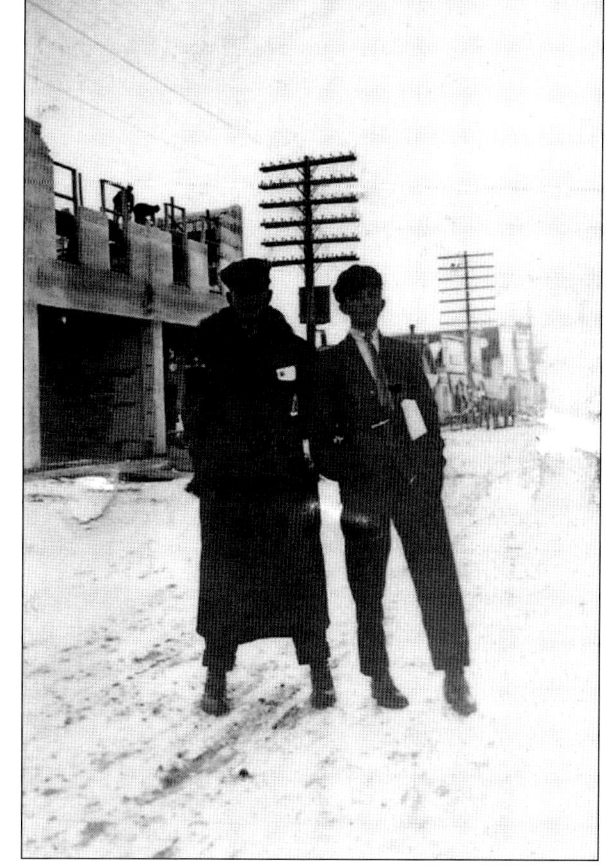

Lou Gee (right) and a friend stand downtown in front of the Littlefield building that would house the Calkins Schelgel Merchantile. Gee was born in 1895. His father was George Gee, and his mother was Montze (Henry) Gee. His family, as longtime Farwell residents, contributed many photographs to the Farwell Area Historical Museum.

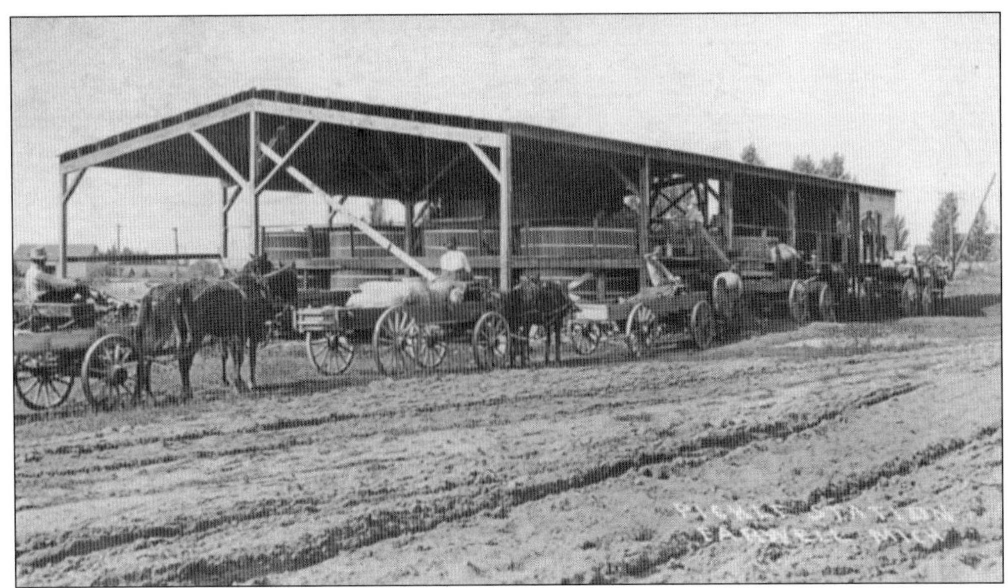

Over the years, several pickle stations were run in the Farwell and Lake areas. Farmers received cash on delivery for raising cucumbers for pickling. In the 1940s, the C.C. Lang & Son Company of Fremont, Michigan, contracted over 100 acres and raised cucumbers for pickling in Farwell.

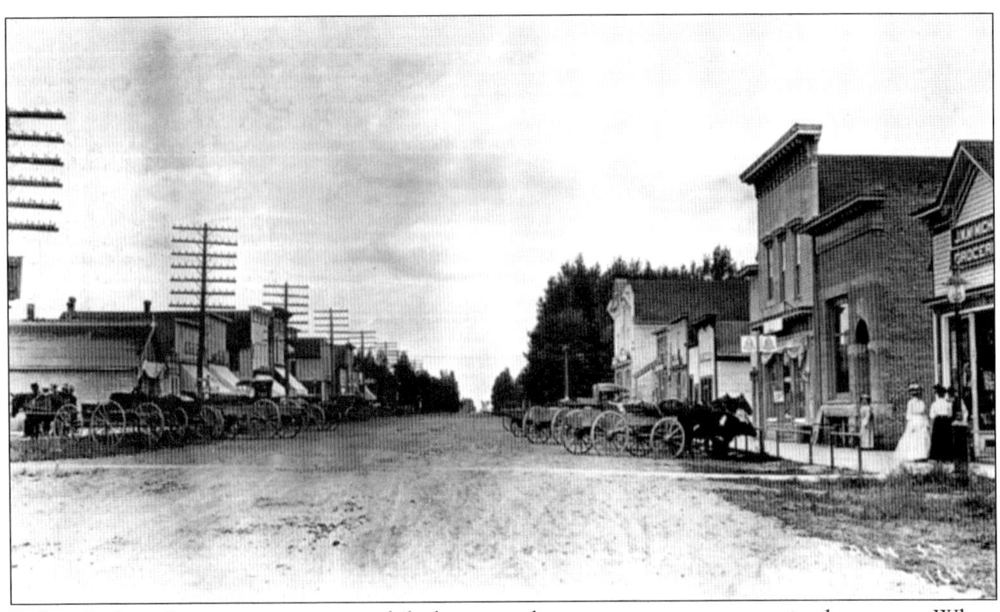

Before the horseless carriage or automobile, horses and wagons were a common site downtown. When the first cars did come roaring into town, a speed limit of 10 miles per hour was quickly set.

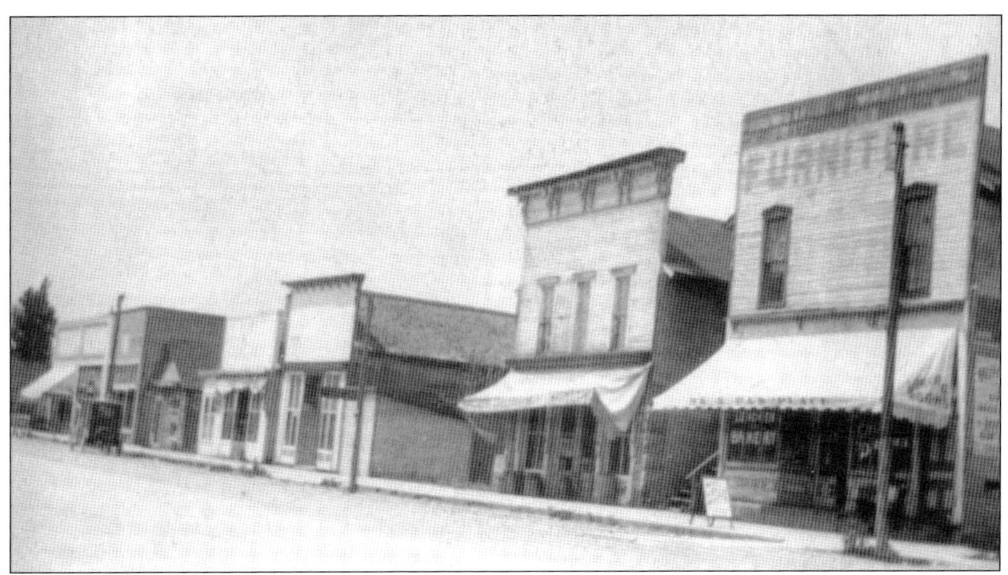

This view shows a quiet block of downtown Farwell, which included Ma and Pa's Place at far right.

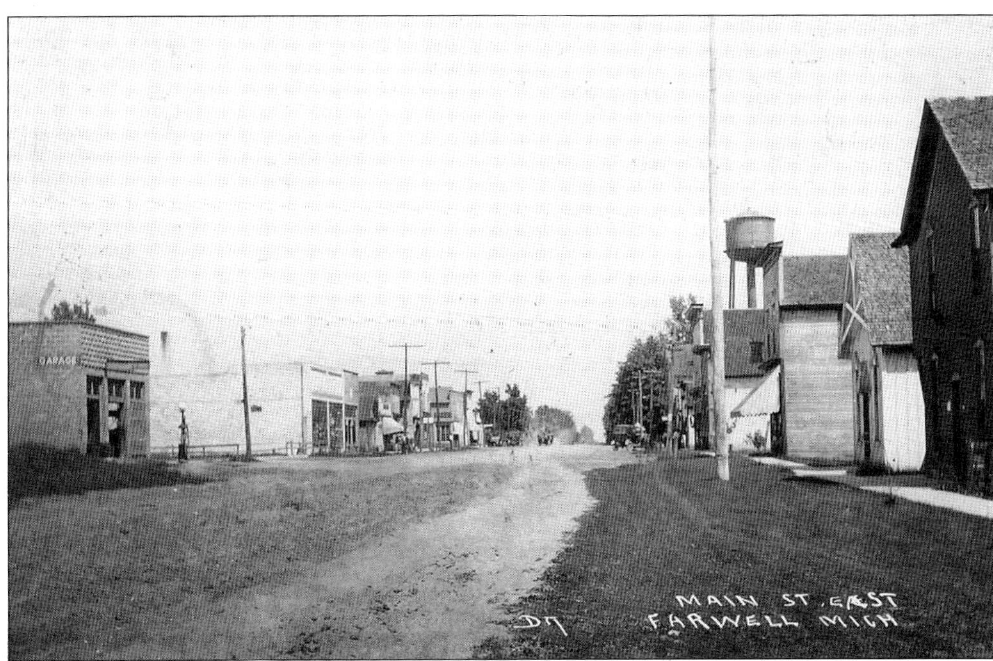

There were unpaved streets throughout downtown Farwell before the Great Depression. Main Street through Farwell is also M-115. It was designated an earthen highway during the 1930s, and it was not until the 1940s that it was paved.

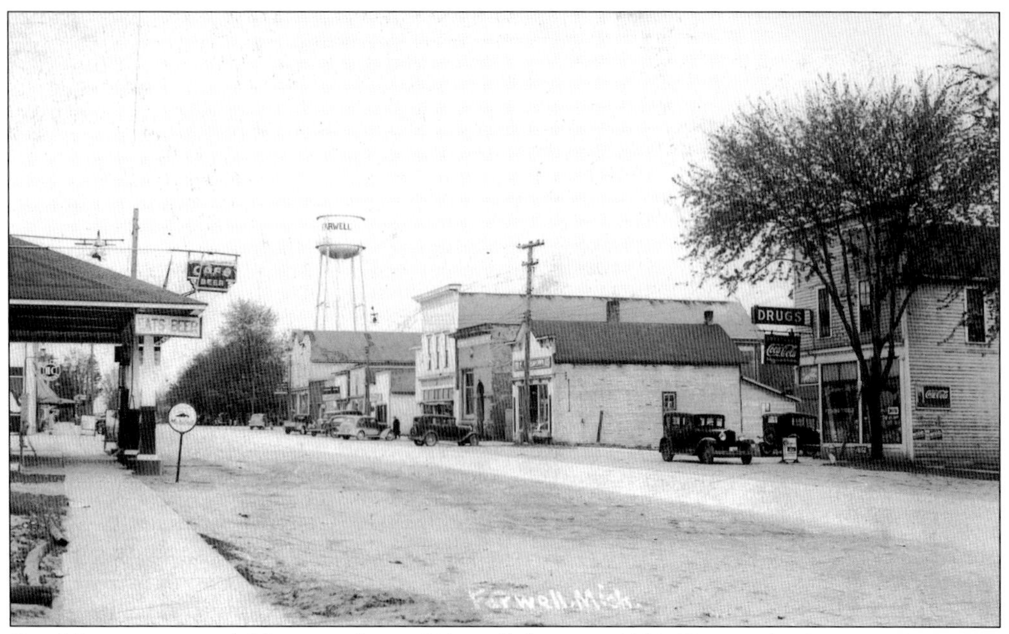

Cecil Davison was a lifelong resident of Farwell, born in 1904. He ran the Davison Garage, a Standard gas station, from the 1930s through the 1960s. He worked at this Mobil station (left) as a young man. He was an active community member, a Mason, fire chief, and the chamber of commerce president at one time. His daughter Marilyn Davison Pitchford was an active and well-loved member of the Farwell Area Historical Museum.

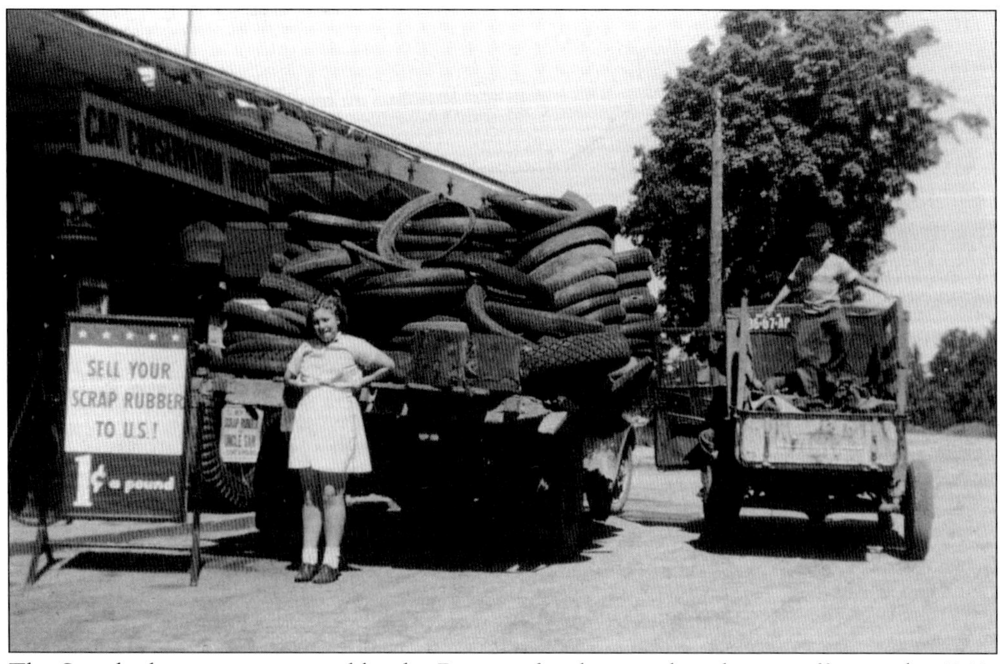

The Standard gas station, owned by the Davison family, joined in the war effort in the 1940s with a scrap rubber drive. A penny per pound was given for used rubber tires.

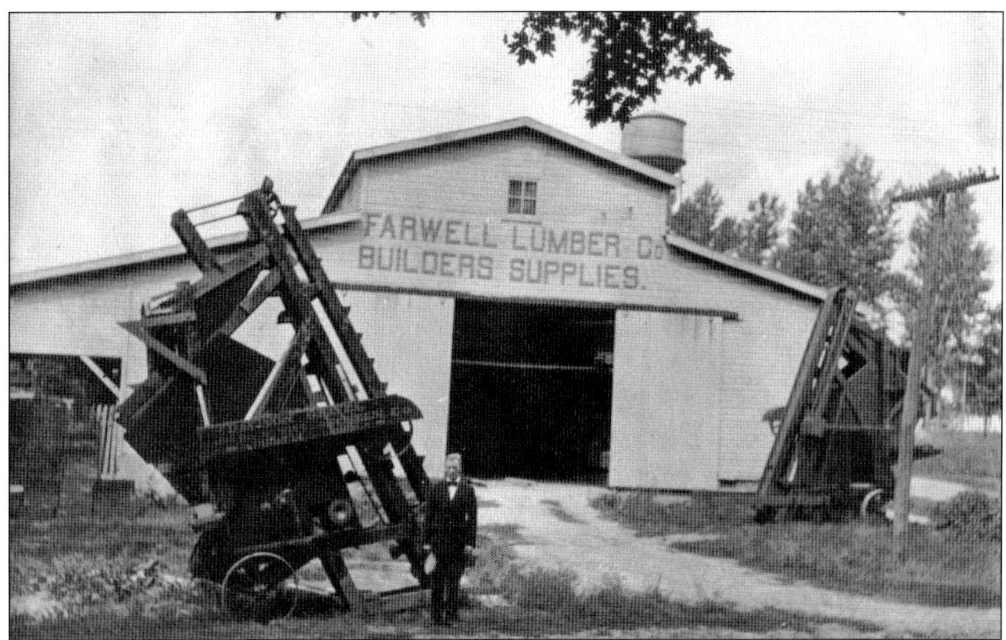

The water tower is behind the Farwell Lumber Co. The gravel-screening machine in the foreground is marked "Davison Gravel & Screen Co., Farwell, Michigan." James Davison, Merle Davison, Elmer Schofield, and Bert Graham created a new way to screen gravel suitable for road making, built the machines, and sold them throughout the state.

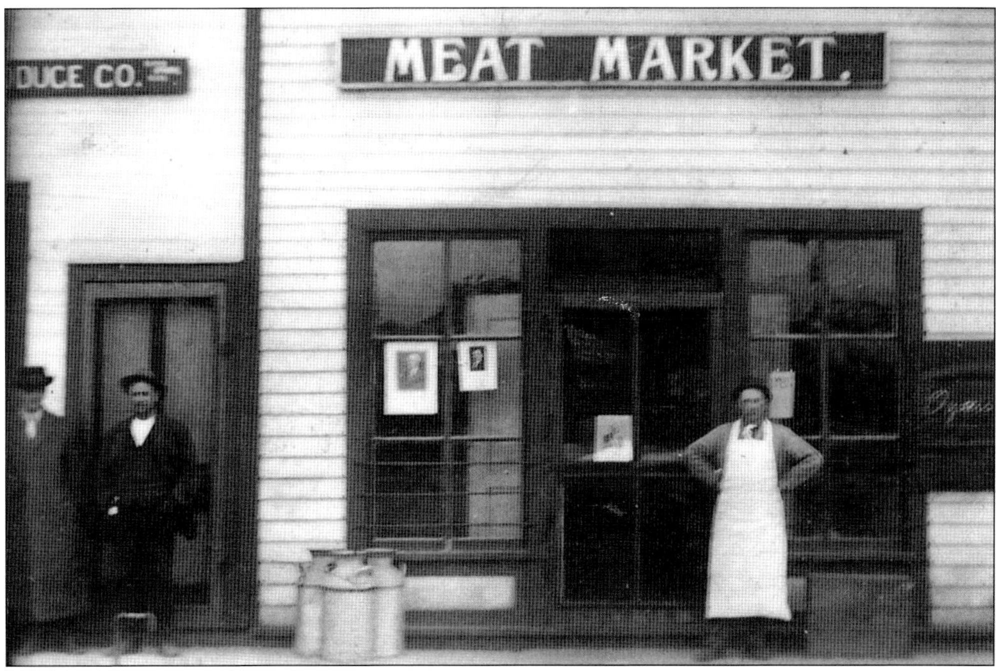

The meat market of Lon Schenk is on the south side of Main Street. Note the sign at right advertising oysters.

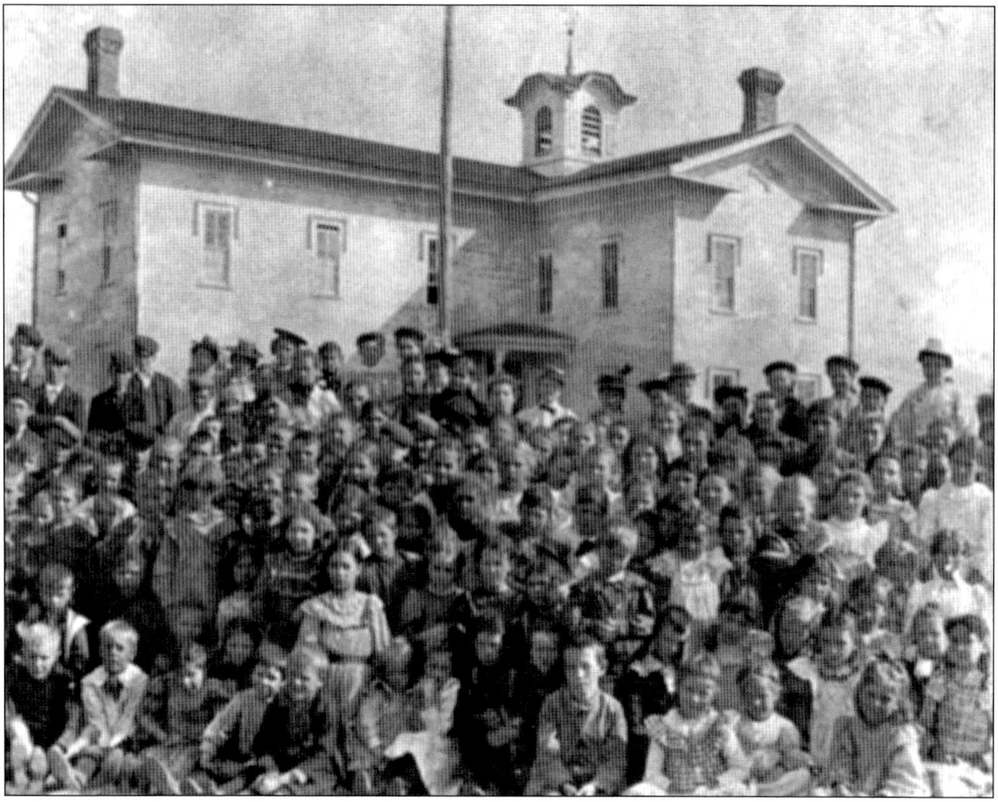

The second school in Farwell (pictured) was built in 1873 with only four rooms. It later had an addition that expanded the school and added a library, six more rooms, and school offices. No photographs of the first school are known to exist.

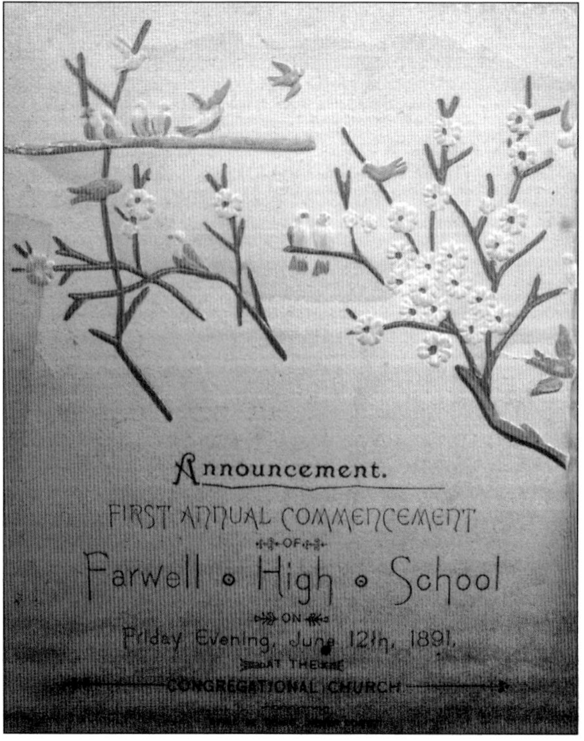

Announcement.

FIRST ANNUAL COMMENCEMENT

OF

Farwell High School

ON

Friday Evening, June 12th, 1891.

AT THE

CONGREGATIONAL CHURCH

This Farwell school commencement announcement is from 1891. Many school events were held at local churches until the 1930s, when the gymnasium was added to the school.

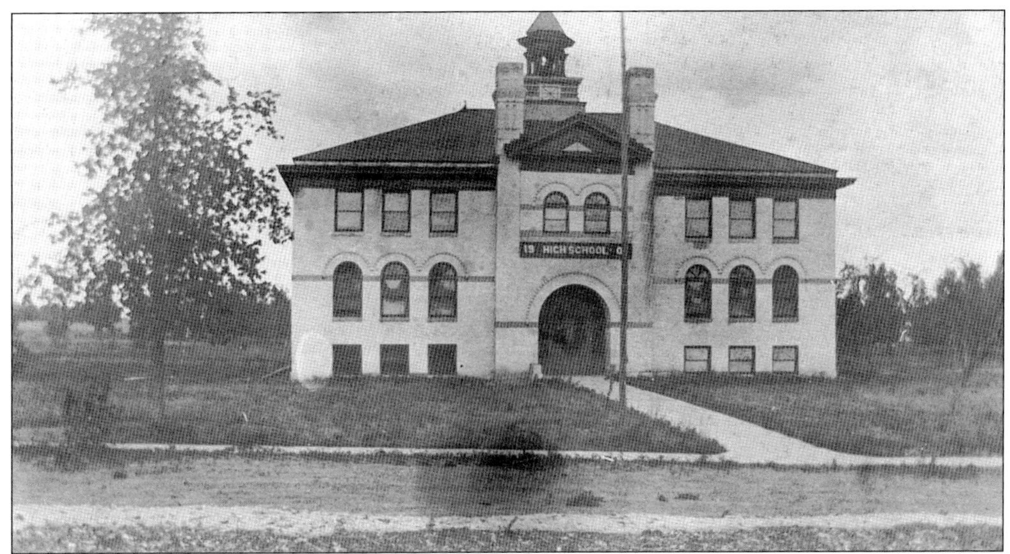

The Farwell school was built in 1907 and dedicated in April 1908. The attached community building/gym was added in 1934. It was the third school to be built in Farwell. It had two floors and a basement. In the 1920s, the official name of the school was Surrey Township Agriculture School. After 1939, it was known as the Farwell Rural Agricultural School. This building was used until 1963.

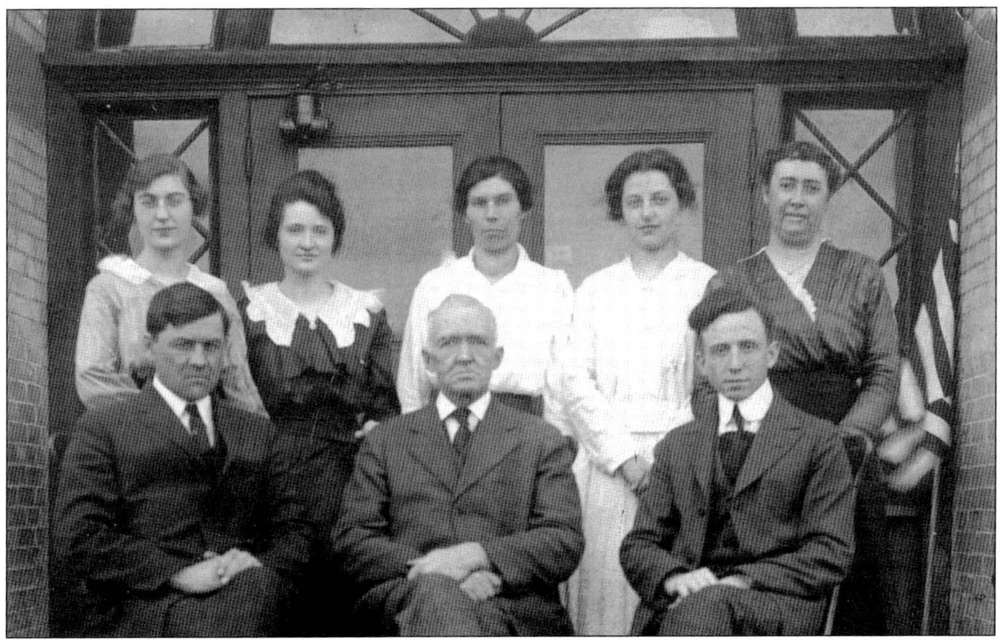

The teachers at the Farwell school are seen here in 1917. From left to right are (first row) Mr. Blackledge, Albert J. Chappel, and Hugh Naldrett; (second row) Leona Rowe, Bernice Schaaf, Ella Carpenter, R. Phelps, and Madge Lamb. Albert Chappel was the superintendent of schools for many years.

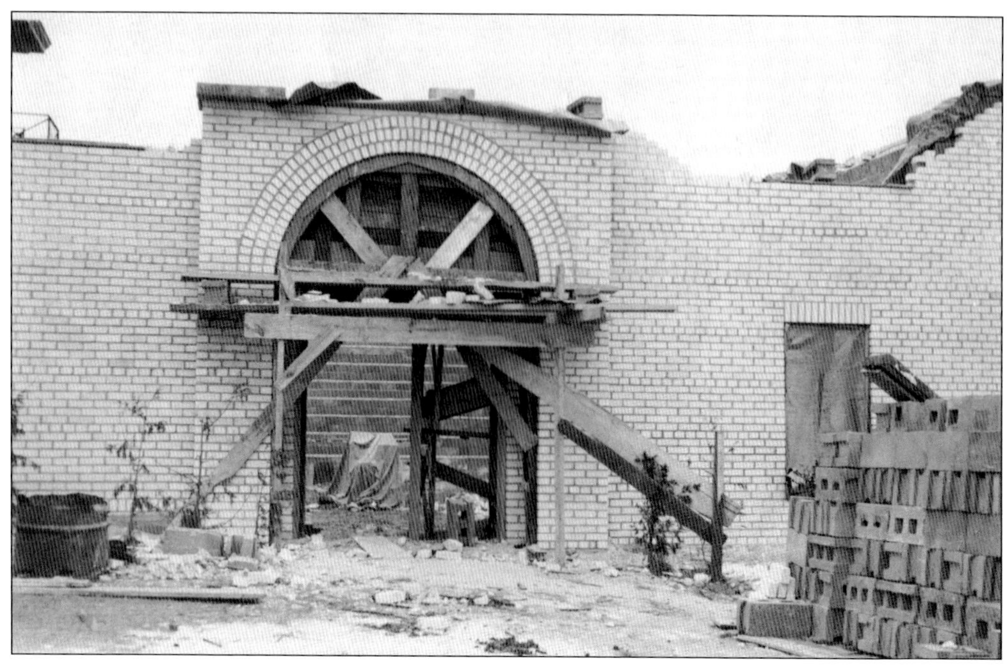

The addition to Farwell High School is shown here under construction in 1934. The gymnasium also served as a community center and meeting place for graduations, banquets, dances, and other gatherings. It was dedicated in 1939 to Madge B. Lamb for her efforts to benefit the community. She was active with the Red Cross and the Order of the Eastern Star, and was a music teacher for 26 years. (Both, courtesy of the Moore family.)

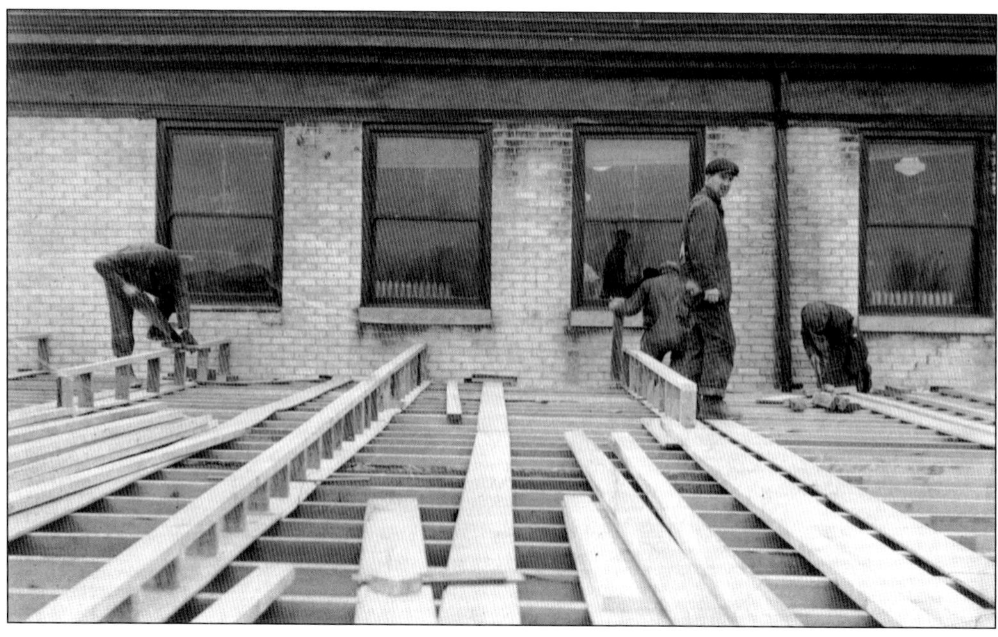

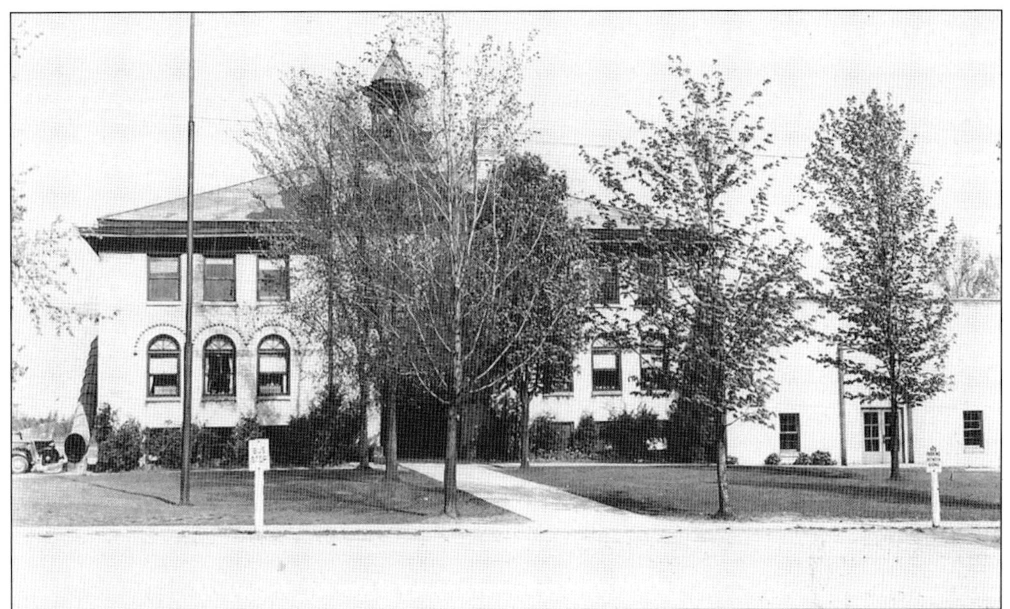

The school was a sandstone brick structure and was finished at a cost of $12,000. The metal slide visible at left was a fire escape and emergency exit for the upper floor. The slides were probably viewed by the children more as playground equipment than fire safety.

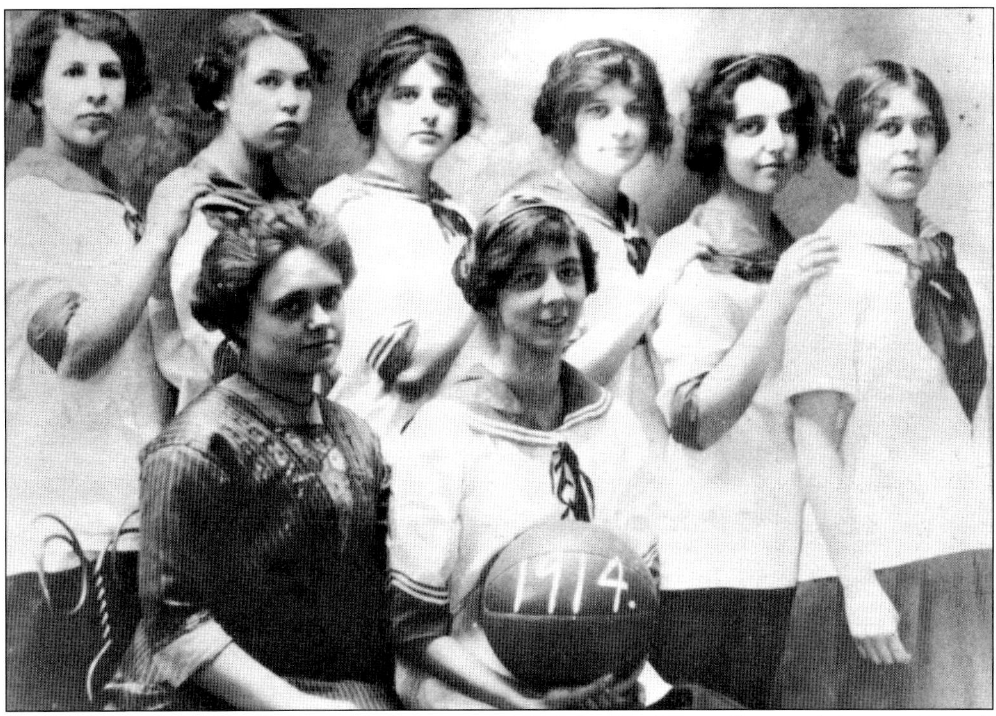

The girl's basketball team is pictured in 1914. From left to right are (first row) Juanita Cuvrell and Georgia Shumway; (second row) Inez Parker, Fleda Richmond, Ruth Hinds, Anna Sherman, Ruth Milliken, and Bess Brown. (Meek.)

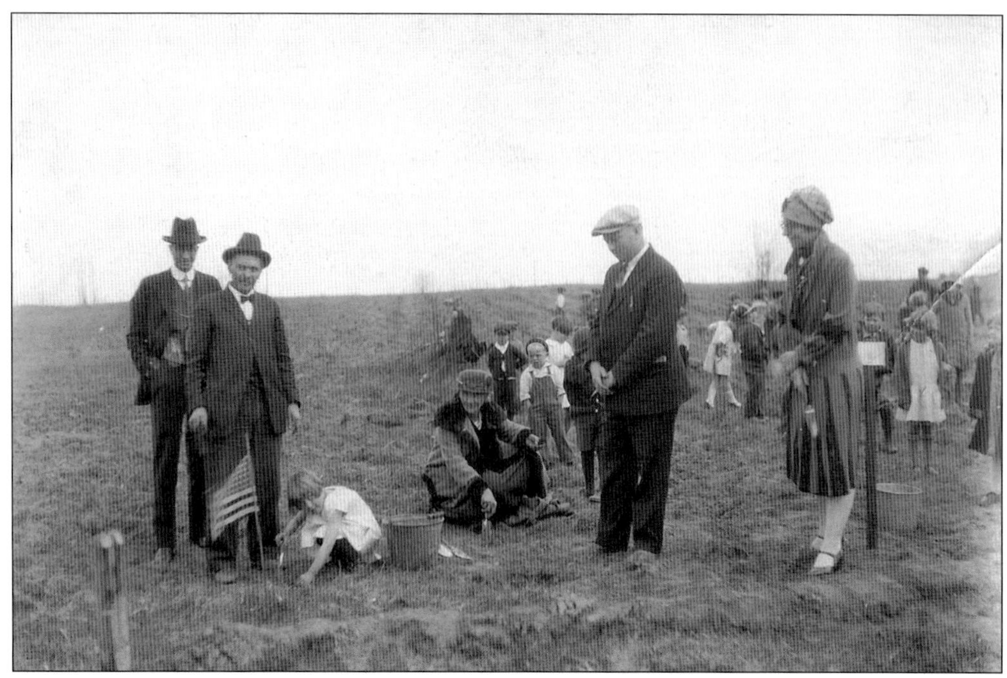

The school forest was started in the 1920s with the first plantings on 10 acres of land donated by the Littlefield family. The school forest was later expanded by 40 acres south of Farwell. The school forest fit in with Littlefield's philosophy of land conservation and his feeling of loss for the big forests cut down during the lumber era. Pictured in the foreground are, from left to right, Reverend Smith, J.L. Littlefield, Thelma Putnam (planting the first tree), Emma Littlefield (kneeling), C.L. Barnard (superintendent of Farwell Schools), and teacher Mae Campbell.

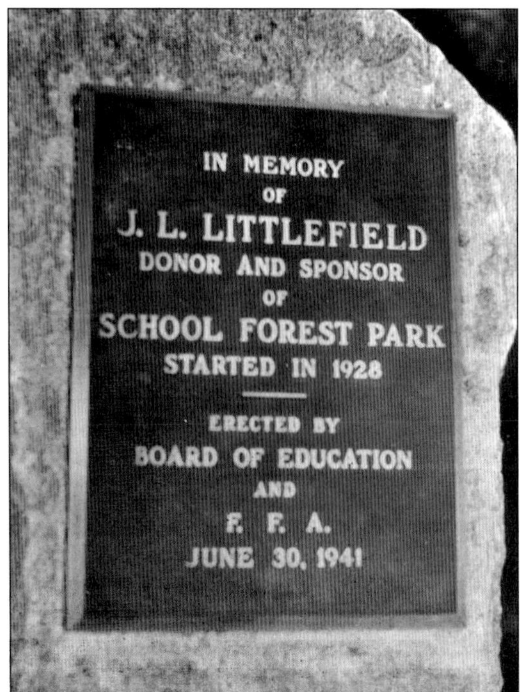

In 1941, a plaque was erected at a ceremony dedicating the forest in the memory of J.L. Littlefield. The monument was five feet tall and made from granite taken from Lochabar Ranch at Littlefield's own property, Beechwood Farm.

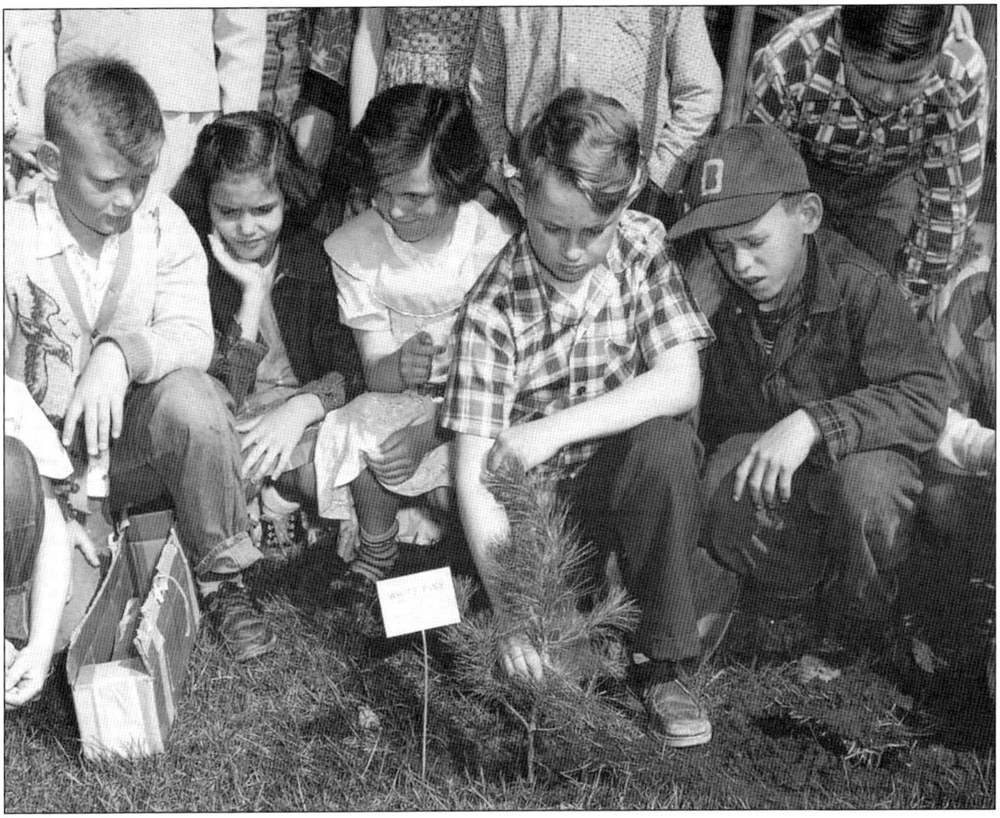

The school forest dedication was attended by Littlefield family members including son Franklin Littlefield, grandson Layle Littlefield, and wife Emma Littlefield. Many complimentary things were said about Josiah Littlefield's dedication to the community. By the 1940s, the forest had almost 25 years of growth.

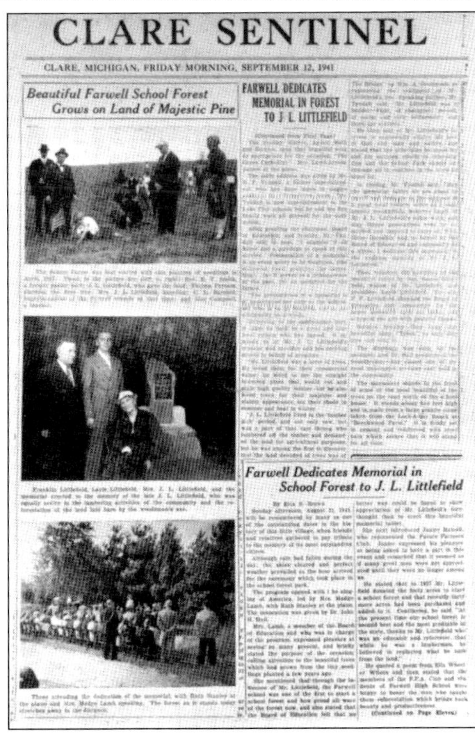

CLARE SENTINEL

CLARE, MICHIGAN, FRIDAY MORNING, SEPTEMBER 12, 1941

Beautiful Farwell School Forest Grows on Land of Majestic Pine

FARWELL DEDICATES MEMORIAL IN FOREST TO J. L. LITTLEFIELD

Farwell Dedicates Memorial in School Forest to J. L. Littlefield

A total of 16,000 seedlings were part of the first planting of the school forest. Its intentions were to create an observatory for students to learn about forestry and actively practice reforestation. The *Clare Sentinel* devoted space to the dedication of the school forest.

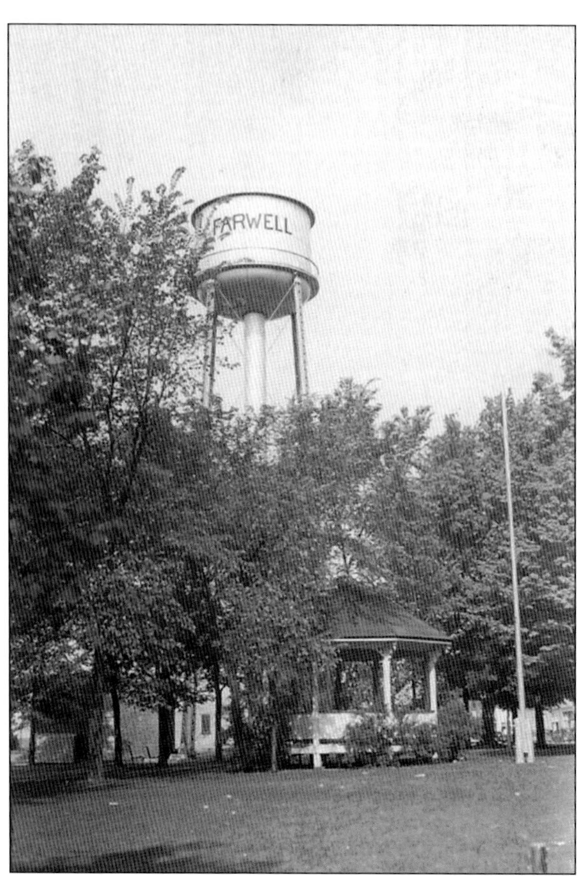

Josiah Littlefield donated a lot for a park, and it was named in his honor—Littlefield Park. Lot 28 on Main Street was suitable for a park, as Littlefield had already started planting trees on the property to improve it. The gazebo was a longtime feature in the park.

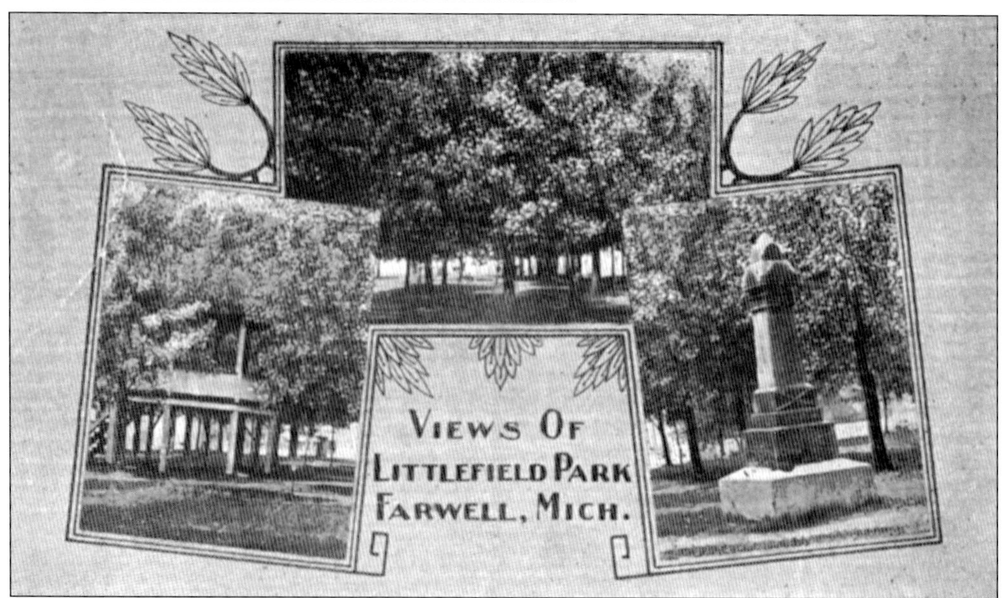

This early 1900s postcard of Littlefield Park shows the Grand Army of the Republic (GAR) memorial statue. The GAR was a fraternal organization of honorably discharged Union veterans of the Civil War. By 1890, over 400,000 veterans were members of the GAR.

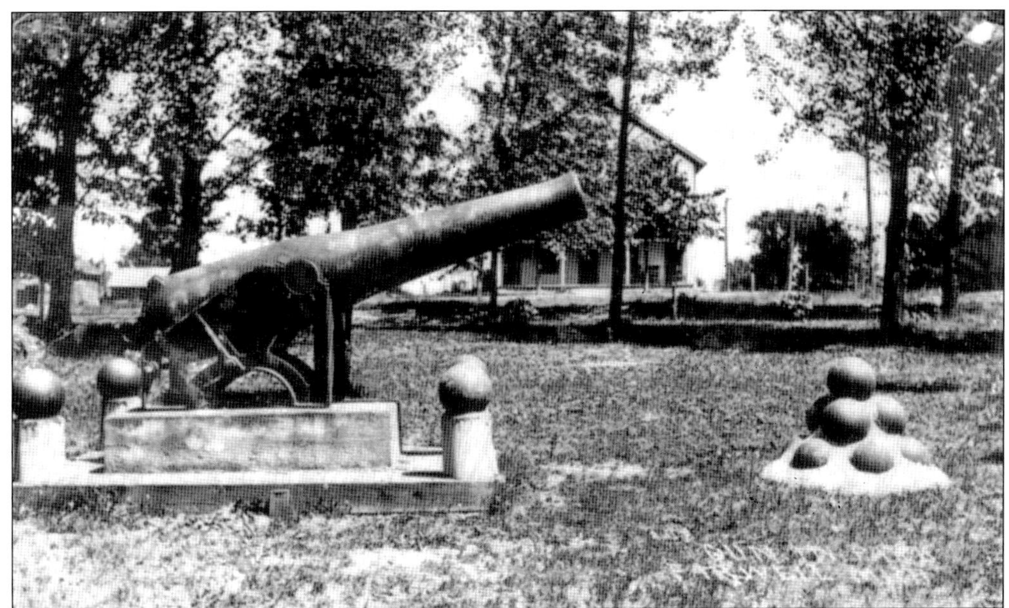

A decommissioned Civil War cannon located in Littlefield Park most likely came from the efforts of the GAR chapter active in Gilmore Township. For several years, it was fired and caused windows to shatter when the charge was too great. Many veterans took advantage of land grants from the Homestead Act of 1862, and after the Civil War, Union veterans could deduct the time they served from the residency requirements.

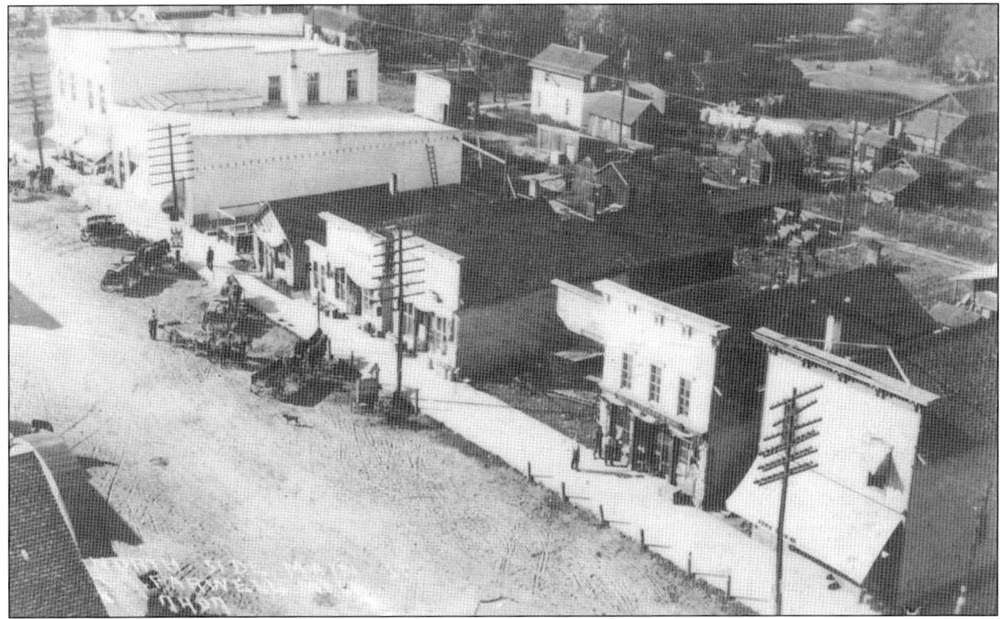

This view looking northwest of Farwell from the water tower near Littlefield Park shows the general store of George Palmer, second building from the right. He came to Farwell with his parents in 1870 at only five years of age. He worked at the sawmill at Slab Town in his younger years. He married Alice VanFleet and had three children. Palmer was a mail carrier for many years and retired in 1932.

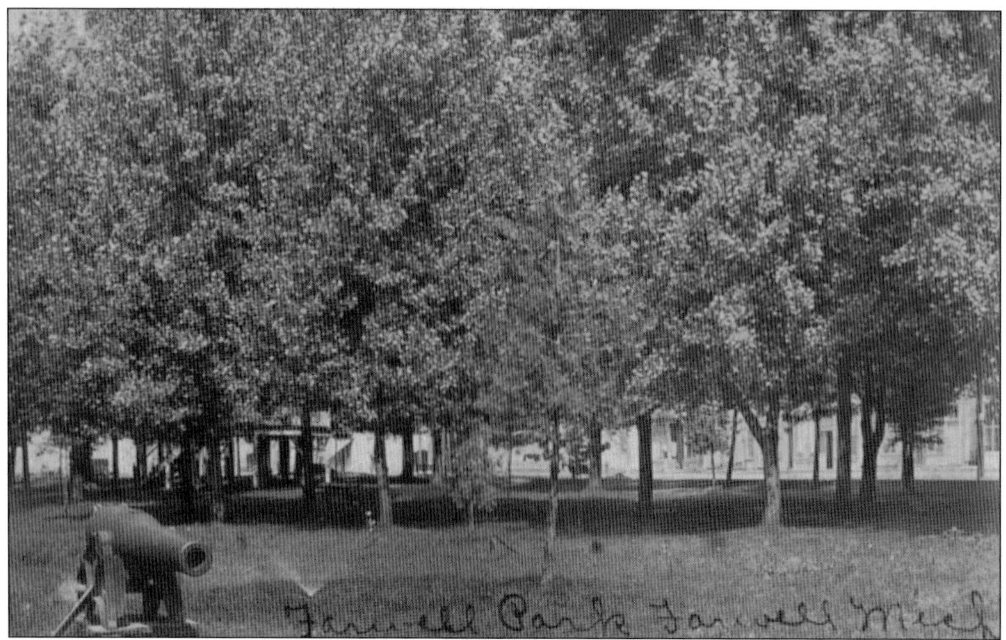

A popular new festival, the Lumberjack Festival, is held each July in Littlefield Park. The festival honors the lumber era heritage of the area and is full of family fun. The cannon in Littlefield Park is pictured at far left.

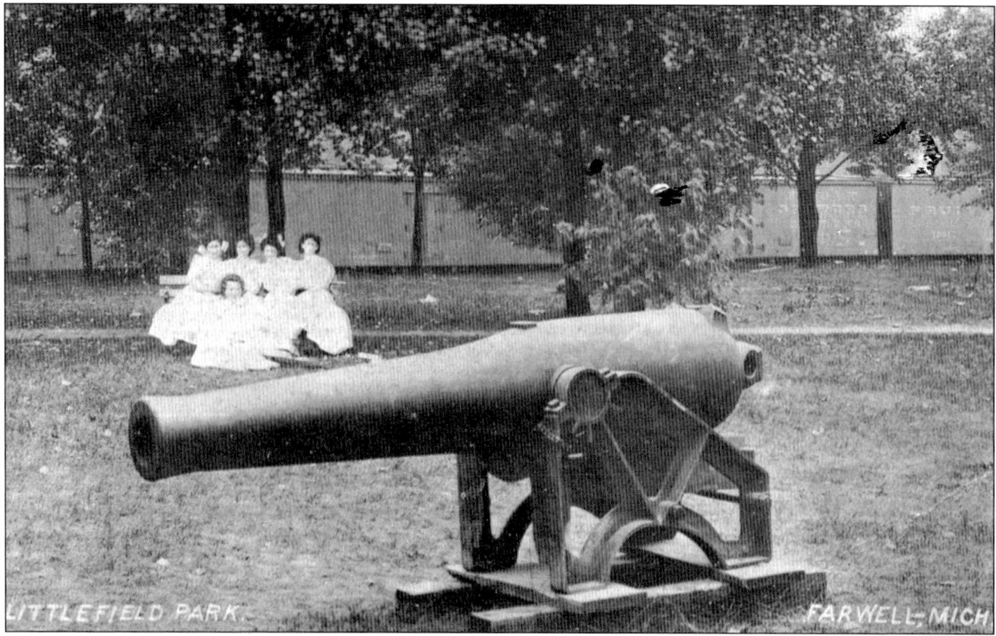

Young ladies create a ghostly illusion posing near the cannon in Littlefield Park. Train cars sit on the tracks in the background. In addition to the GAR memorial, the park now has a memorial to local veterans, which is located along the Main Street side of Littlefield Park. Veterans Day services are held each year at the memorial.

The town fire bell used to hang from the water tower and would ring when a fire broke out. It was the signal for the waterworks to begin stoking the fire for extra steam so the pumps could put out more water. Fires were a serious hazard and could ruin an entire town, so they were taken very seriously.

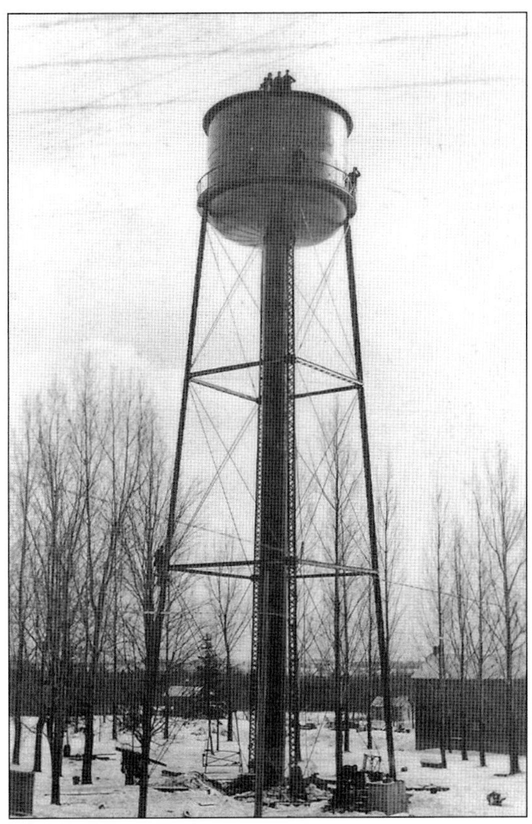

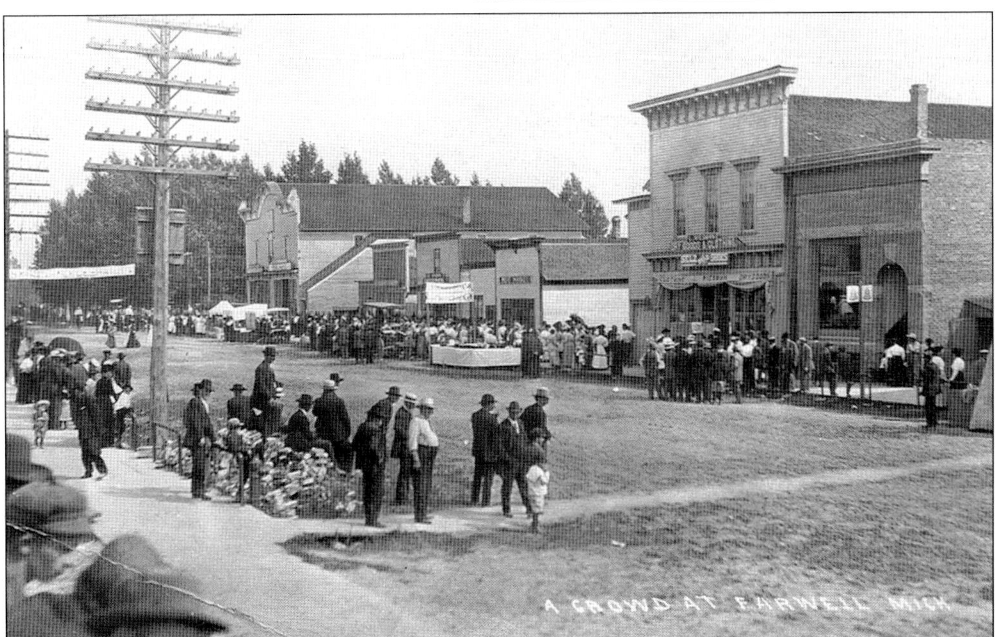

A crowd of all ages gathers downtown. Hitching posts and a fire hydrant (center) are pictured near the boys sitting on piles of wood. Louis Wiesman's dry goods store sits second from right, next to the bank.

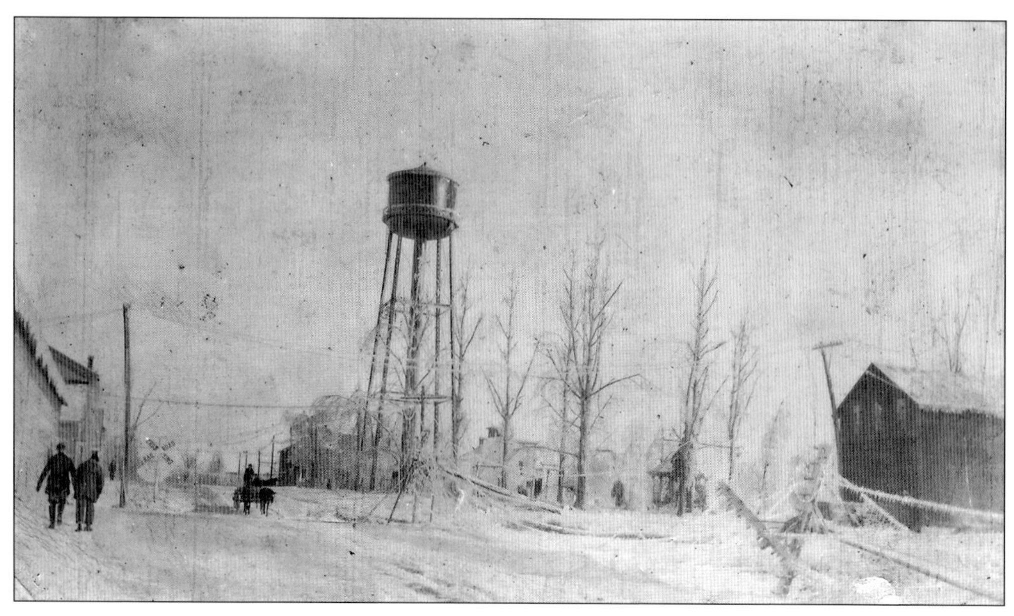

An ice storm in February 1922 affected the entire county and most of the state. It was well documented, and these photographs show views of Littlefield Park and a home in Farwell. Rain poured down, along with thunder and lightning, and ice soon brought down telephone, telegraph, and electric wires. Schools and businesses were closed, and it was deemed the worst ice storm in memory. (Both, CCHS.)

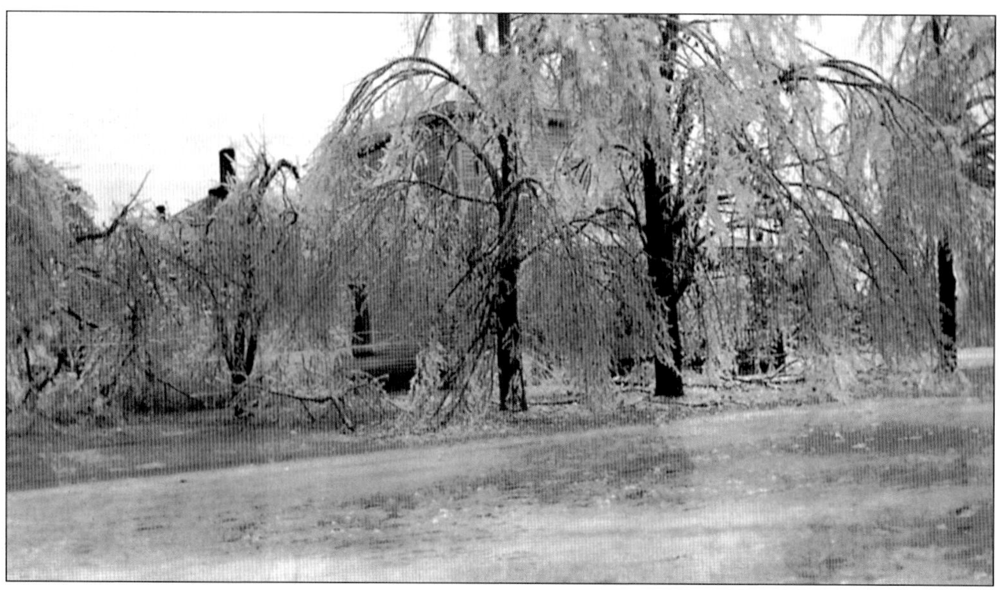

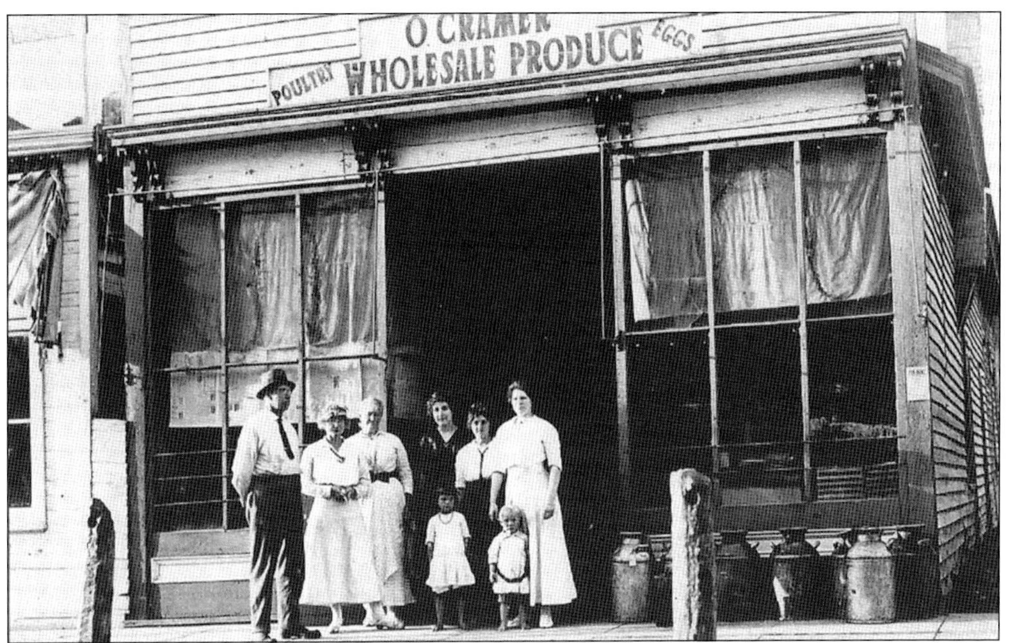

The Cramer store on Main Street is featured in this photograph. Cramer eventually leased his cream station and this produce business to Elias Sias.

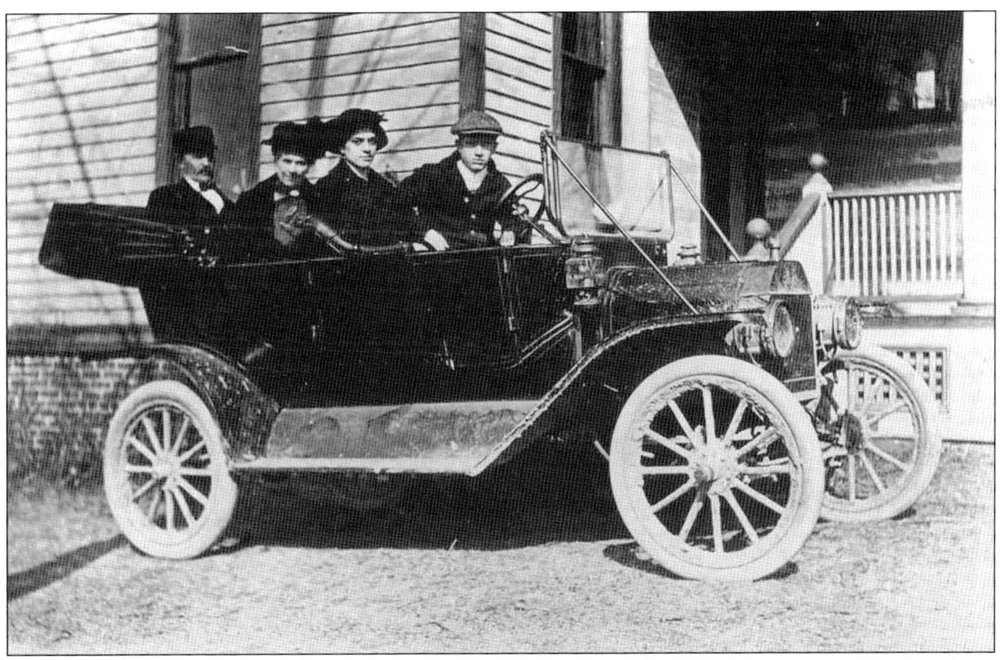

Of all the founders of Farwell, Josiah Littlefield made Farwell his lifelong home and had perhaps the most influence. He first fell in love with the large tracts of virgin forests and then became committed to the land and the people who lived there. Son Franklin Littlefield drives the family car with his sister Hazel in front and his parents in back.

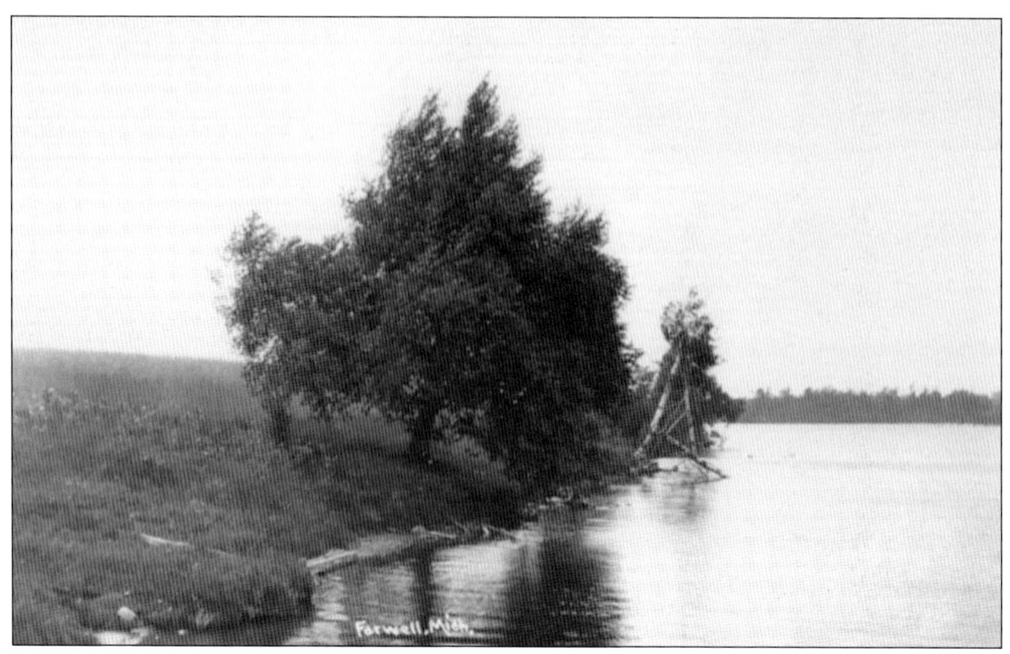

In April 1909, an earthen dam gave way at the millpond due to spring flooding. Water, logs, and debris rolled down the river. Clare prepared by lowering Dewey Lake, but the dam there was saved by the slowing of the flood due to logs and debris accumulating along the way. The Farwell dam was rebuilt with cement at a cost of over $2,500.

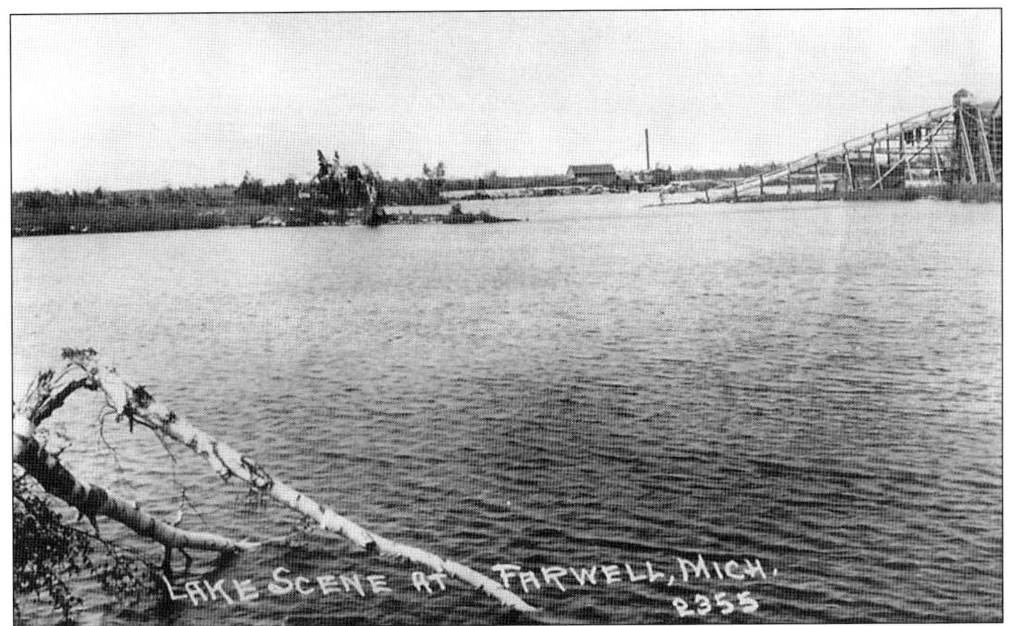

Both of the main industries on the millpond are shown here. Littlefield's mill (center) and the ice works of the Flint & Pere Marquette Railroad (right) kept the millpond and the men of Farwell working for many years.

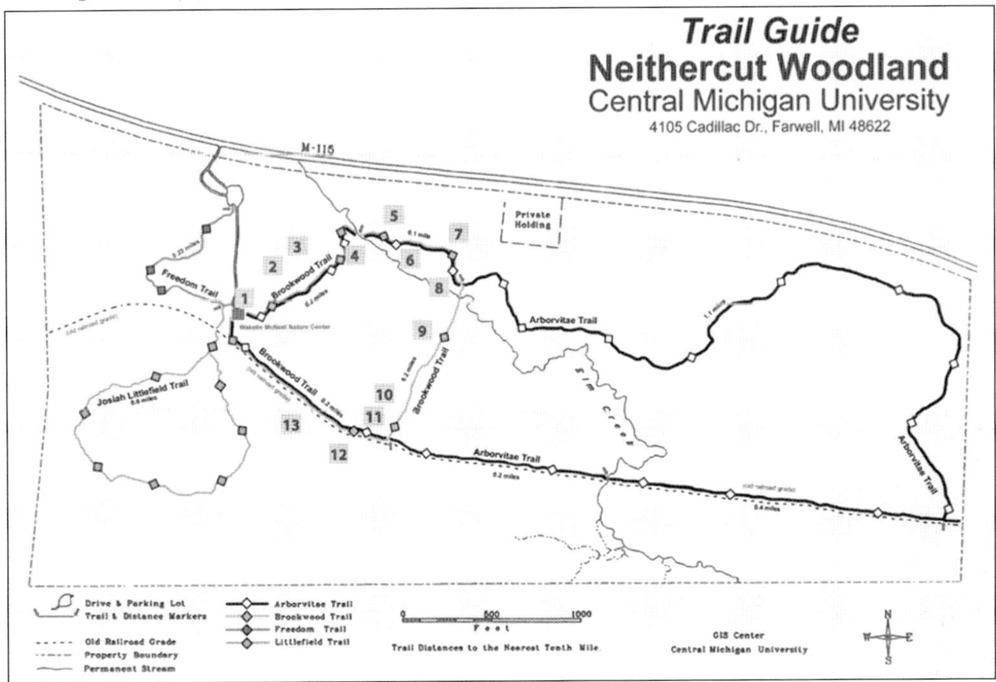

Today, a part of Josiah Littlefield's dream exists in the Neithercut Woodland on part of Littlefield's original property. Acquired by Central Michigan University with the help of William Neithercut, the 252-acre Neithercut Woodland has 80 acres of Littlefield's land he so carefully protected. Neithercut Woodland features hiking trails, a boiling station for maple syrup, and many types of trees featuring a diversity of habitats.

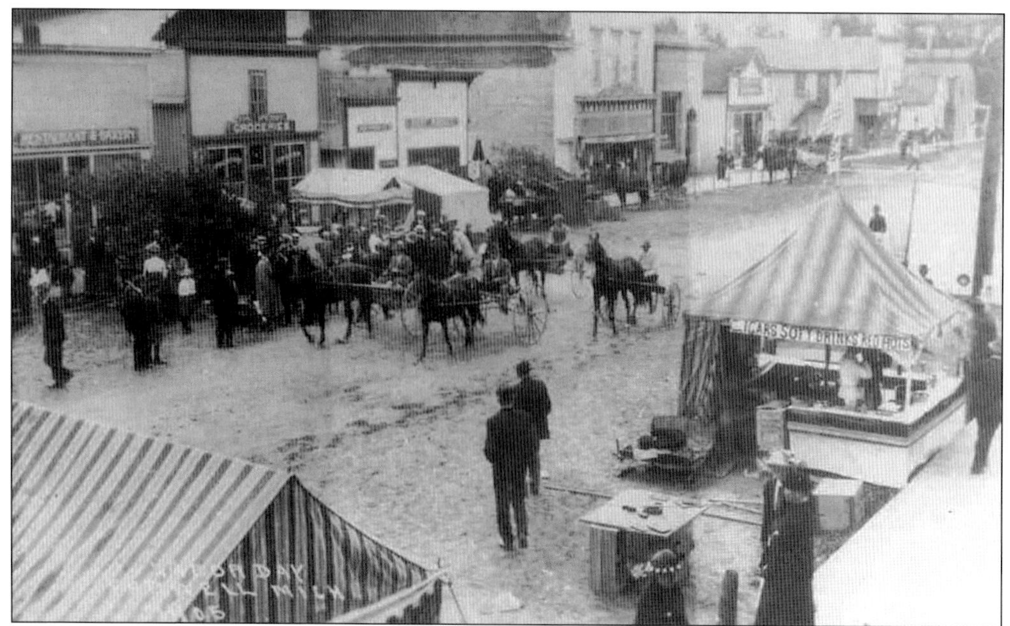

The streets of Farwell are at their finest for a celebration. The tent at right advertises cigars, soft drinks, and red hots, an early version of hot dogs. The streets are lined with street fair booths and with trees, presumably for decoration.

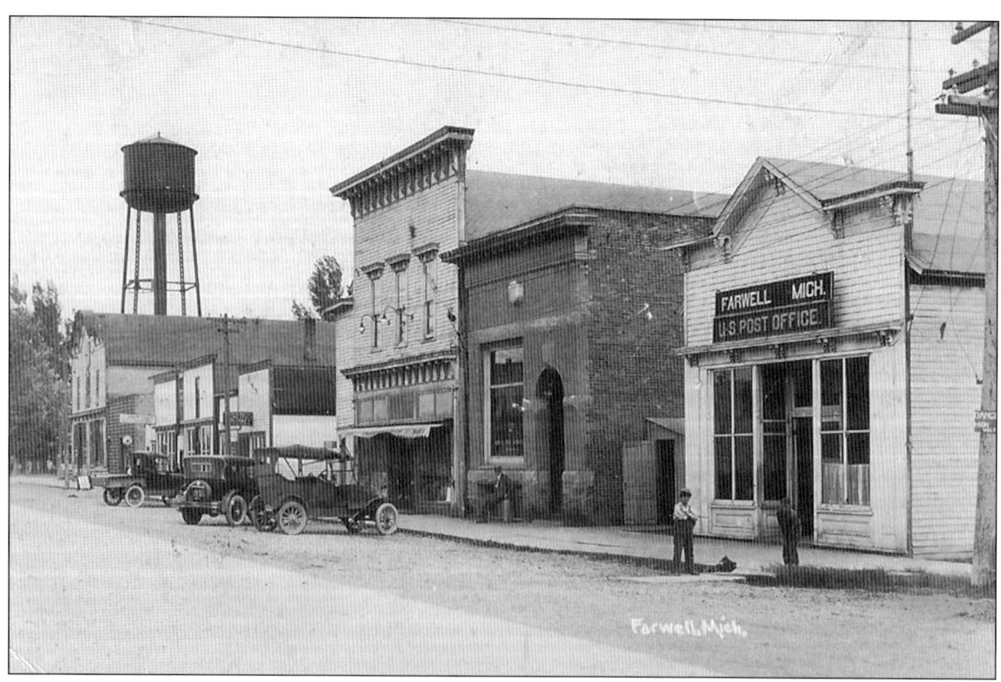

Farwell has always had many strong civic organizations—a Masonic Hall, Daughters of the American Revolution, Rebekah Lodge, Eastern Stars, Farwell Women's Club, Rotary Club, Independent Order of Odd Fellows, and the Ladies' Library Association, which was among the oldest. Small boys play in front of the post office (right), and the water tower looms in the background.

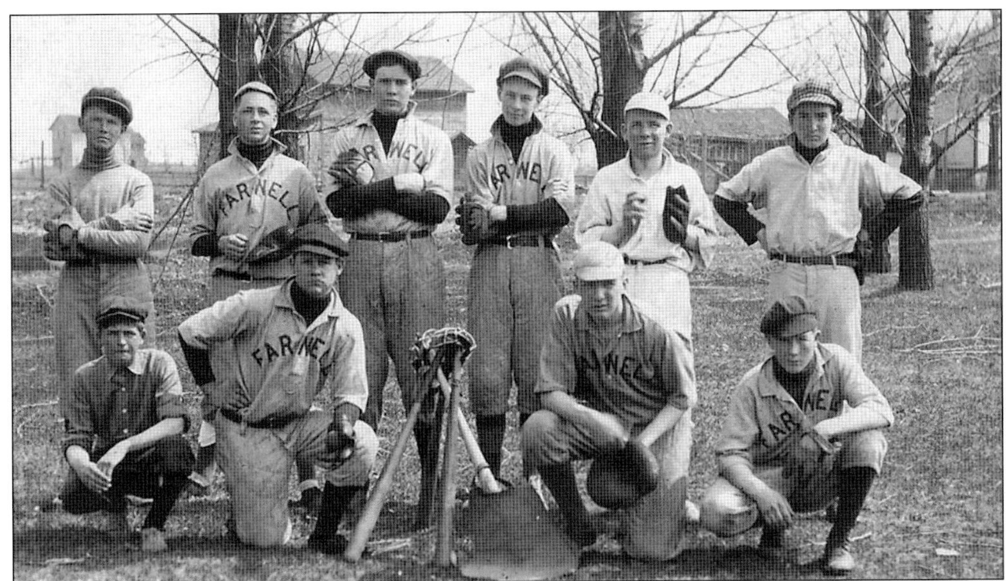

Baseball was very popular, and teams traveled to play other towns. The Farwell baseball team in the 1920s included Guy Perry, Milward Rogers, Paul Goltry, William Stevens, Floyd Graham, Alger Cline, Walter Clock, Willie Sherman, Frank Graham, and Walter Moore.

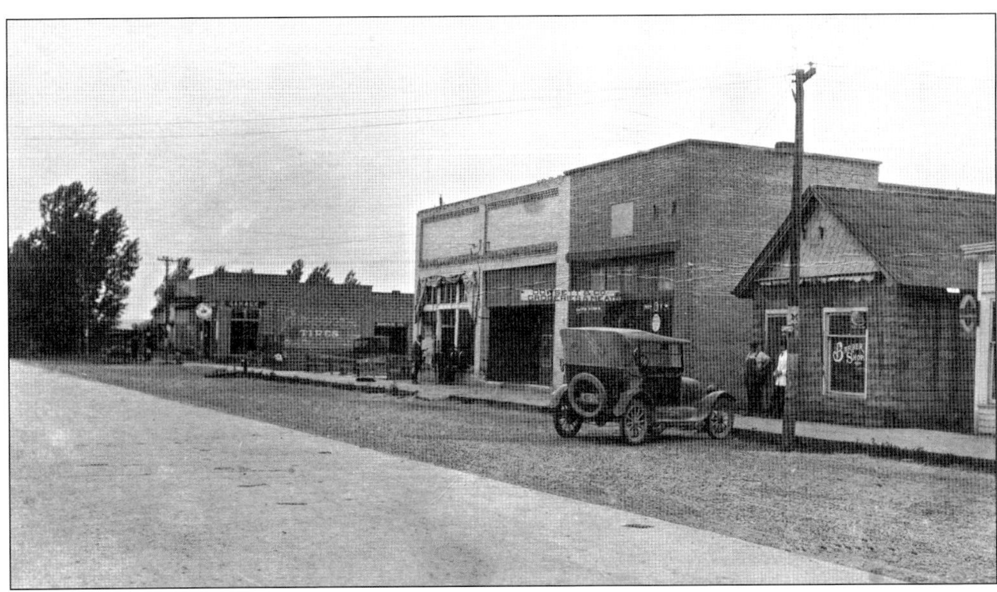

Downtown Farwell in the early 1920s was probably a pretty quiet place. By this time, less than 450 people lived in Farwell. The garage (left), Dowsett and Company groceries (center), and a barbershop (right) are businesses shown in this postcard of Farwell.

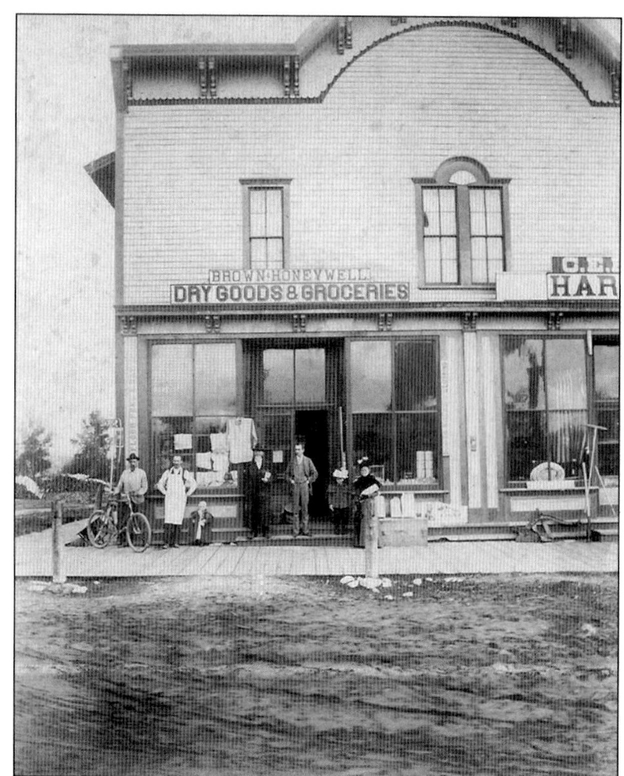

Pictured here is one of the earliest buildings—and one of the oldest remaining structures—in Farwell. Currently the site of Eagle Pharmacy, it has seen a host of general merchandise, grocery, restaurant, hardware, and other businesses throughout its more than 100 years of useful life in downtown Farwell.

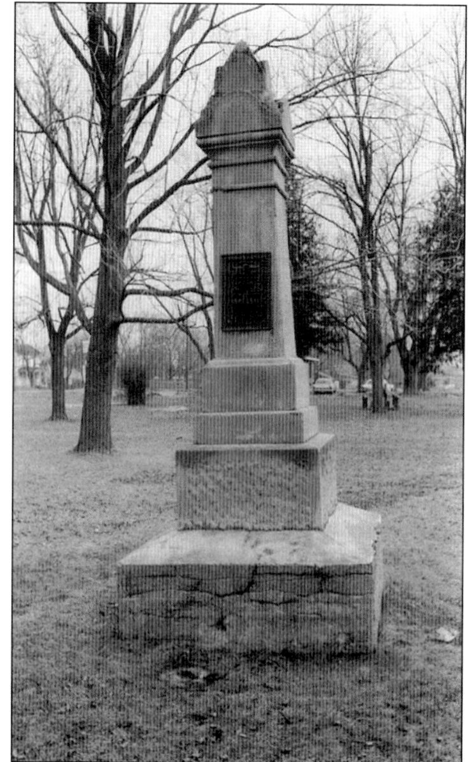

Littlefield Park was given to the village in 1894 by Josiah Littlefield. The GAR monument in Littlefield Park is shown here in the 1970s. (Meek.)

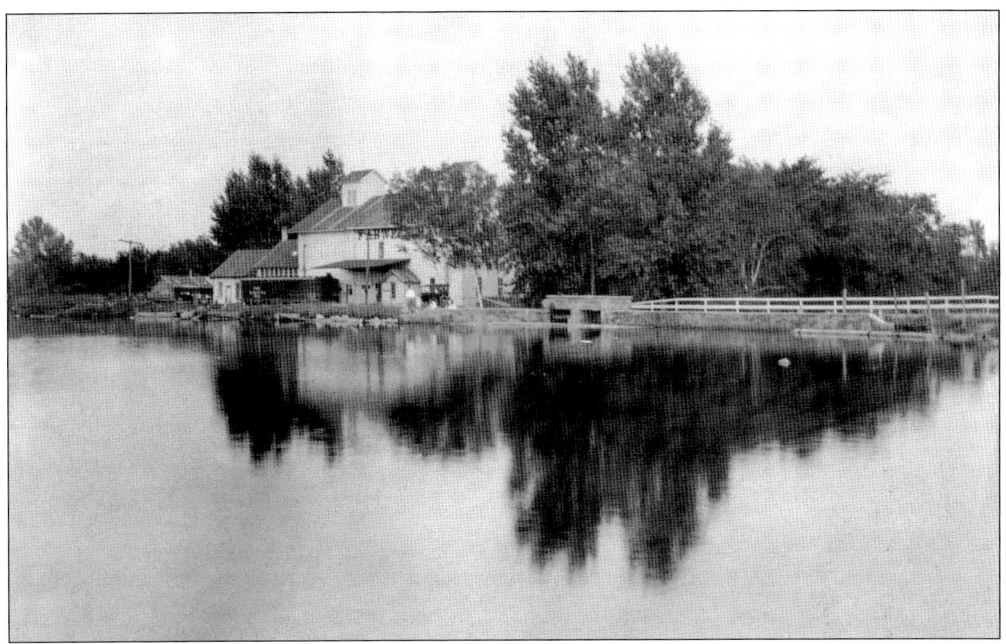

The dam on the millpond was rebuilt in 1909 after spring flooding. Three bridges were swept away in a flood along the Tobacco River.

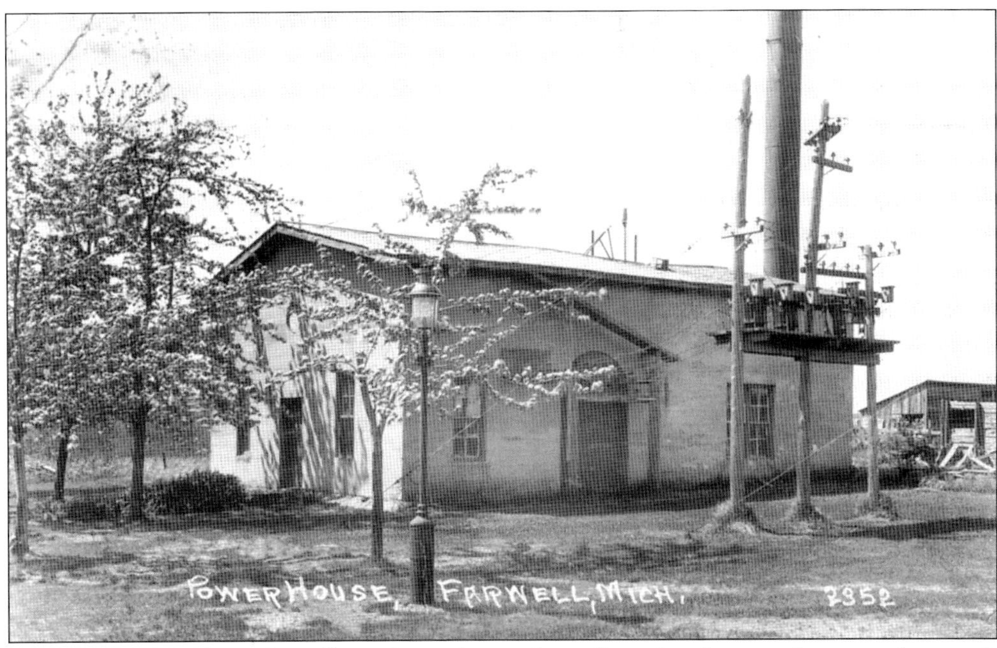

The first waterworks in Farwell was located near the millpond and pumped water to homes. A bond issued was passed in 1887 to create the first water system. The millpond was the water supply for the village, with an intake valve in the pond.

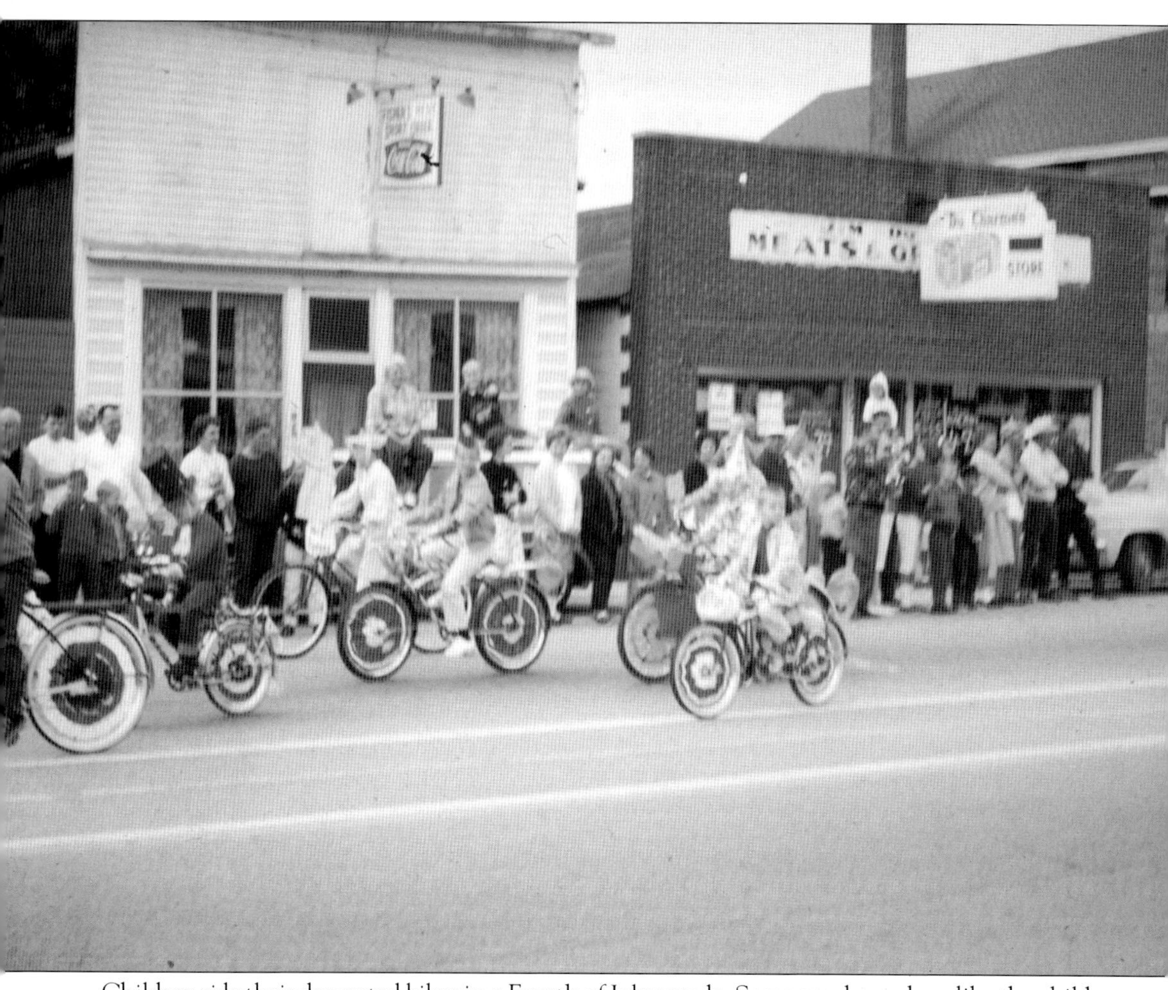

Children ride their decorated bikes in a Fourth of July parade. Some are dressed up, like the child in a stovepipe top hat second from left.

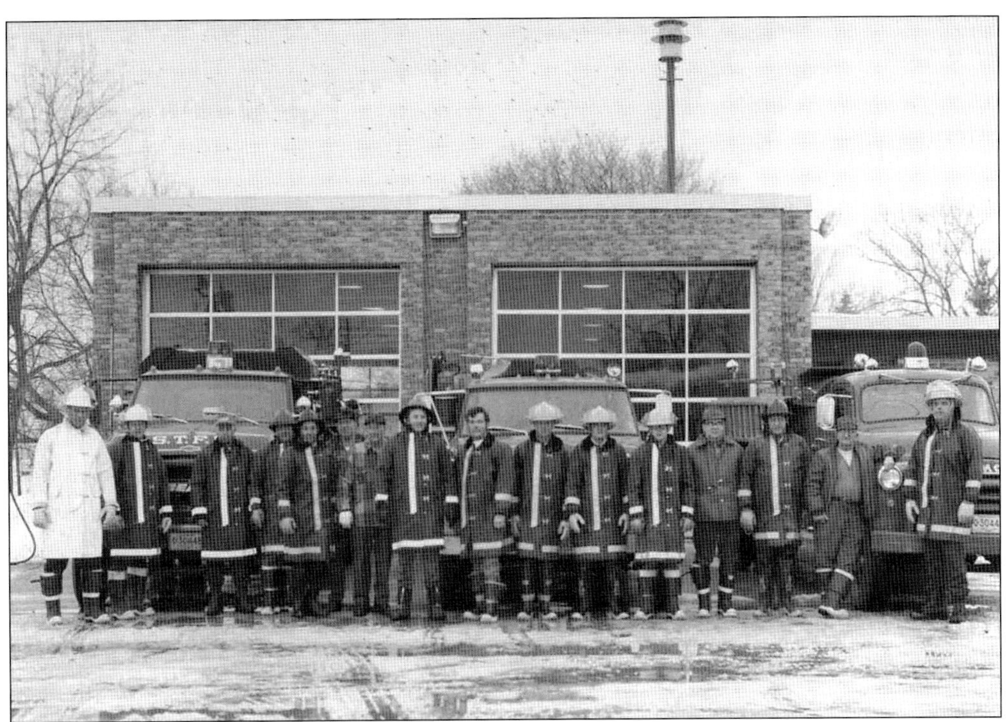

The Surrey Township Fire Department, shown here with its fire trucks, is a long way from the bucket brigades of early Farwell. A full-time fire department is now supported by volunteers and modern equipment, used to fight fires in the village and Surrey Township, and assist other local departments when called upon.

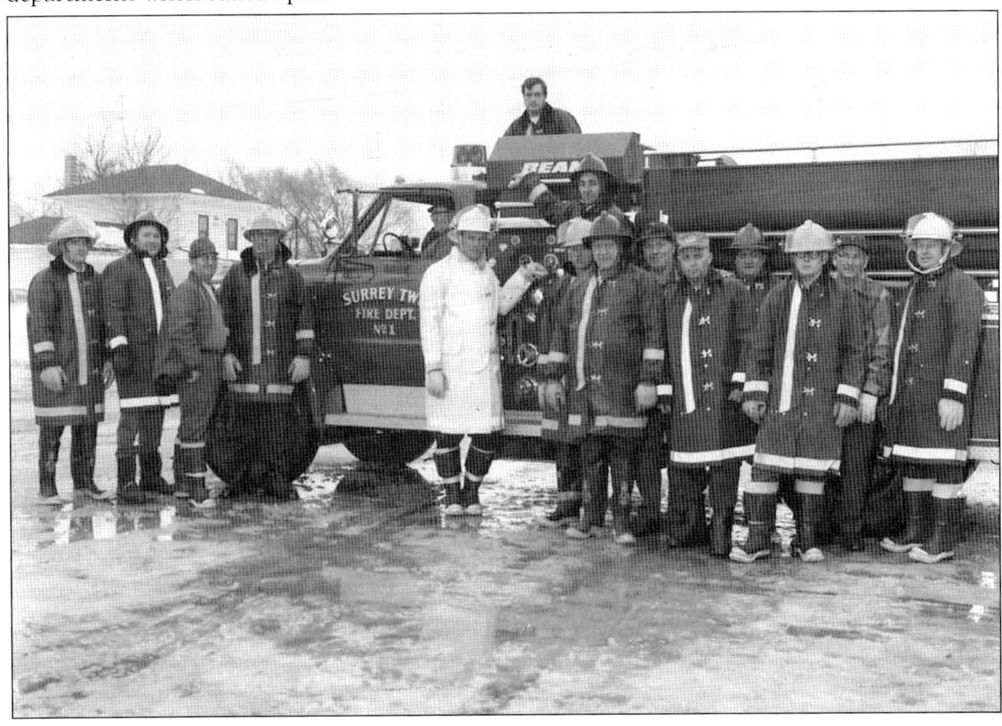

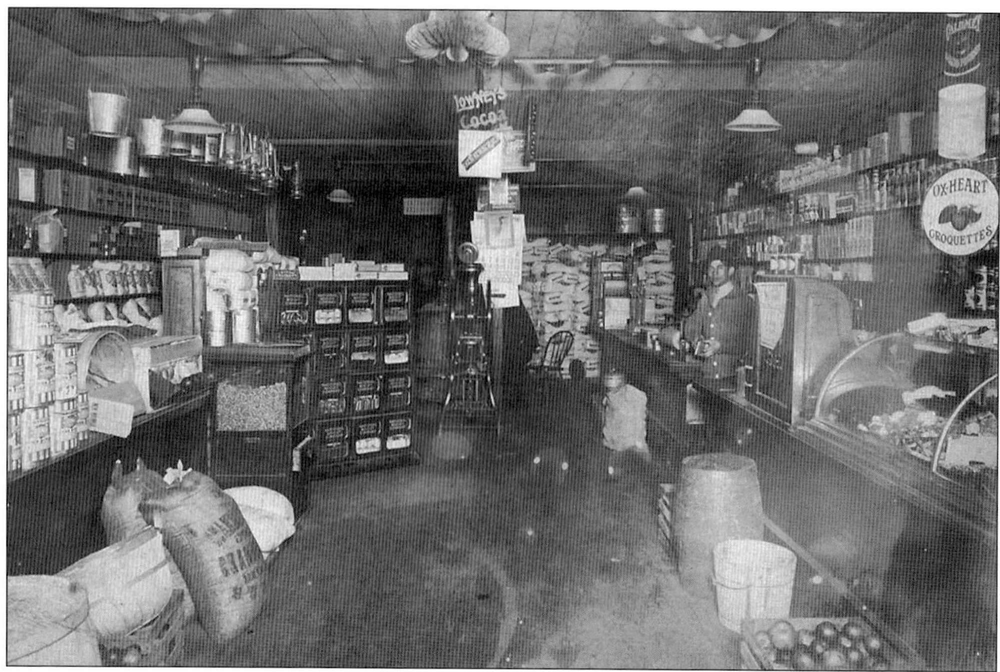

The general store was a necessity in every early American town. A large amount of merchandise with a broad selection was usually housed in a small store. Necessities and staple food items sat beside household items and hardware and a few farm supplies. Early general stores in Farwell were described as large warehouses supplying lumber camps.

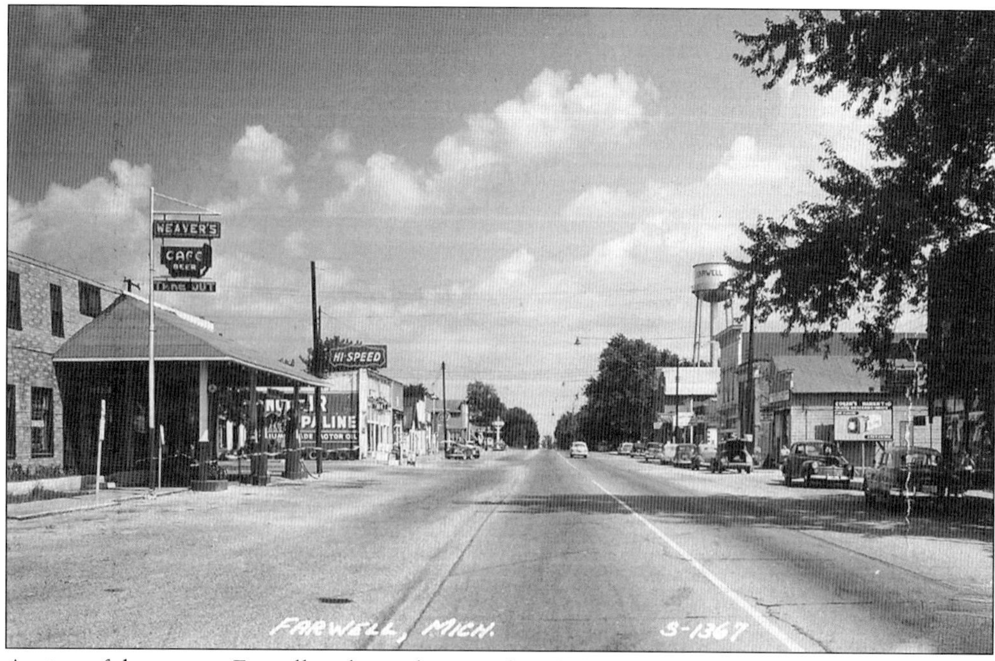

A view of downtown Farwell is shown here in the 1940s. Weaver's Café (right) was owned by Bunk Engstrom.

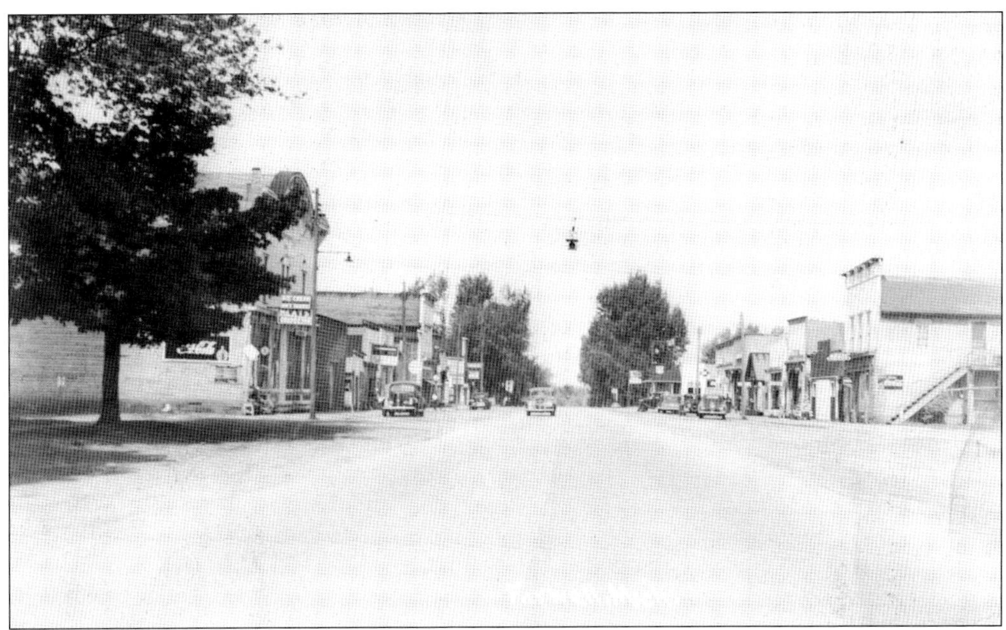

Downtown Farwell is pictured in this 1940s postcard. Today, the offices of the Village of Farwell are to the left of the tree. (Courtesy of the Moore family.)

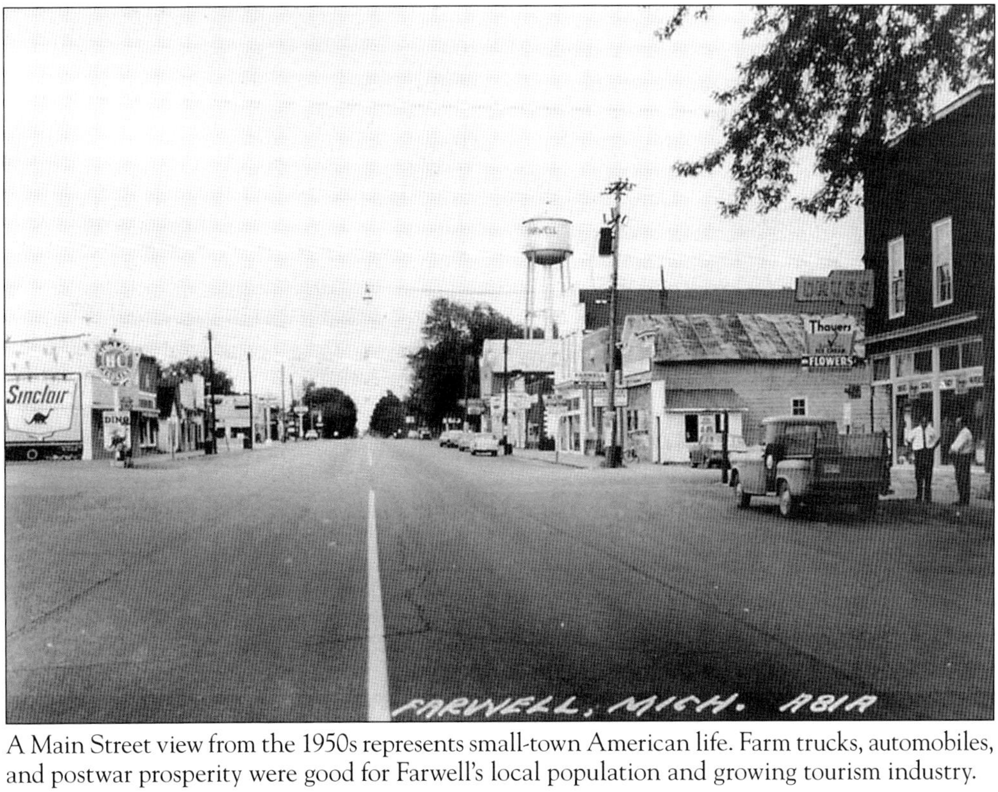

A Main Street view from the 1950s represents small-town American life. Farm trucks, automobiles, and postwar prosperity were good for Farwell's local population and growing tourism industry.

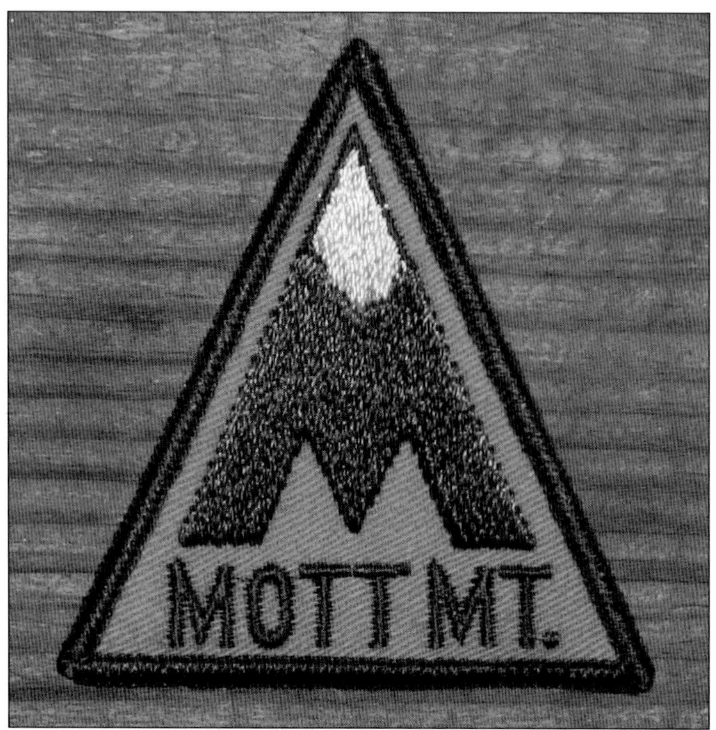

Skiing attracted hundreds of people to Mott Mountain. Winter carnivals were held, and each year, a Miss Mott Mountain would represent Farwell in pageants around the state. A ski patrol badge is shown here.

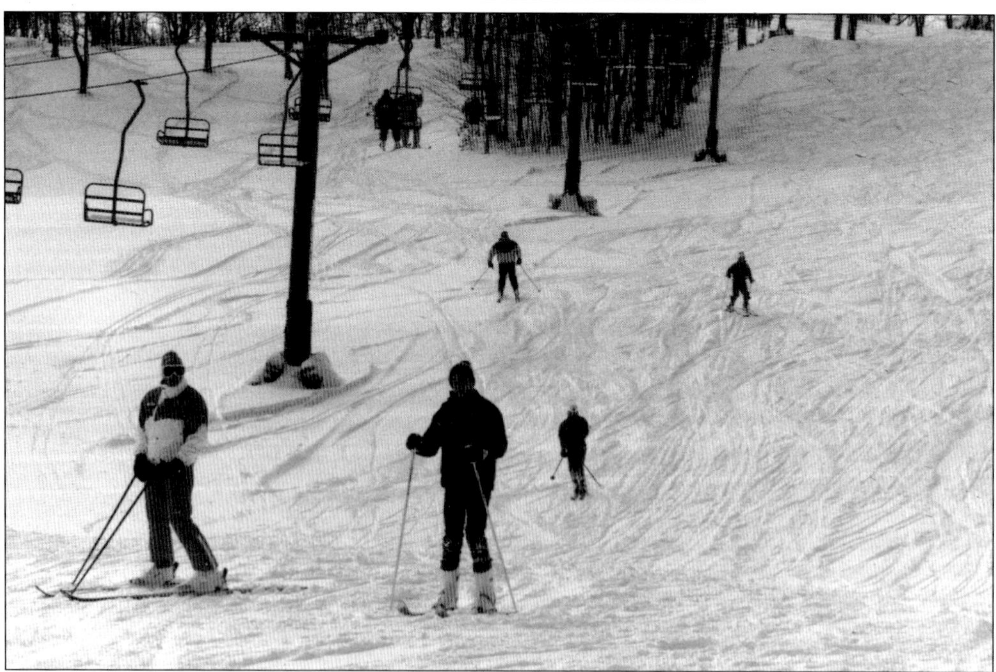

The 113-acre Mott Mountain ski resort was developed and owned by George and Phyllis Palmer in the 1960s. Earl and Phyllis Daymon owned and operated the resort from 1969 until it was sold in 1995 and renamed Jasper Ski Resort. It was later renamed Silver Ridge in the mid-2000s, and attempted plans for an outdoor concert venue were not successful. Justin Ogg (center, front) and Julia Ogg (far right) are shown here take skiing lessons. (Courtesy of the Ogg family.)

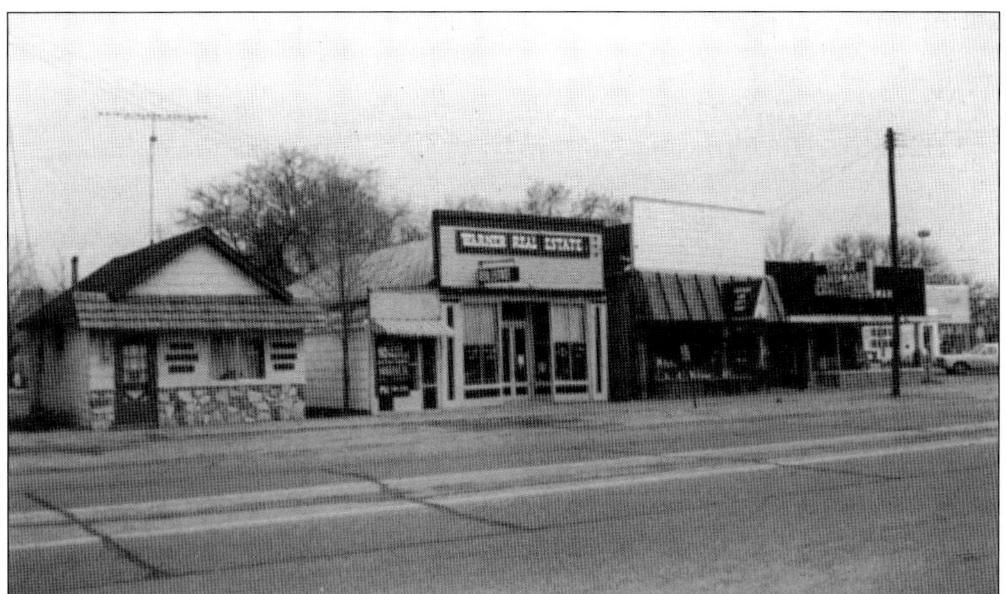

Shear Hardware was opened and operated by Leslie Roy Shear and his wife, Mable Shear. Their grandson Alvin "Bud" Loomis later took over the business. The Loomis family ran the hardware store until 1977, when it was sold to George D. Palmer from Farwell. Palmer renamed the store Palmer's Hardware, and it continues as such to this day.

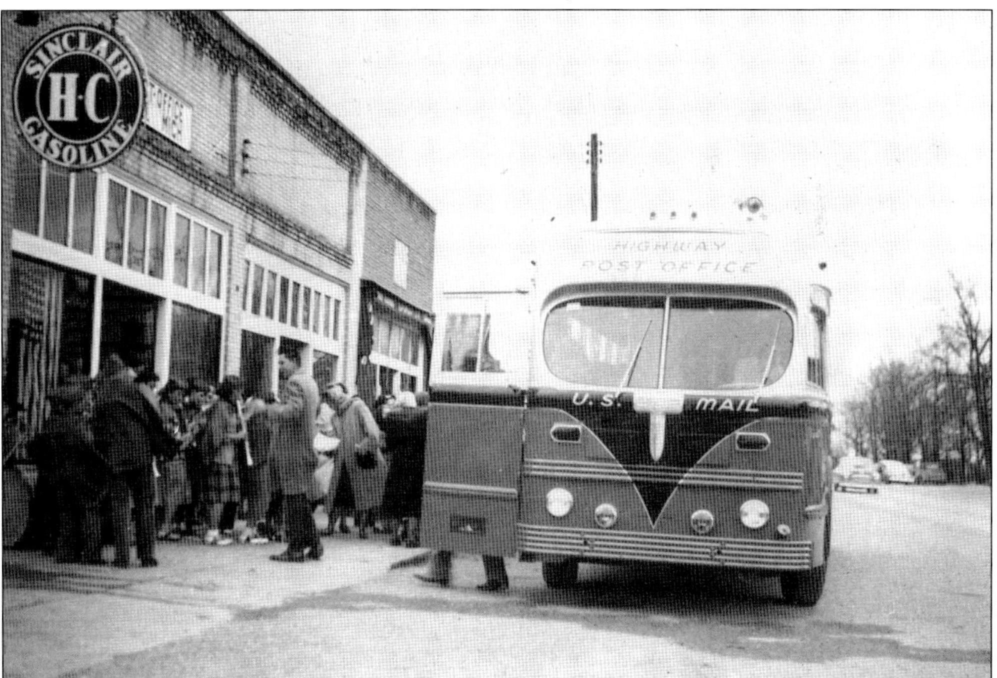

A Highway Post Office bus draws attention in front of the post office on Main Street in 1956. The postal service created Highway Post Office buses after 1941, when most of the Railway Post Office trains were decommissioning due to declining railway service. The bus routes ran until 1974. The buses were post offices on wheels; the mail not only traveled on the bus, it was sorted there too. (Meek.)

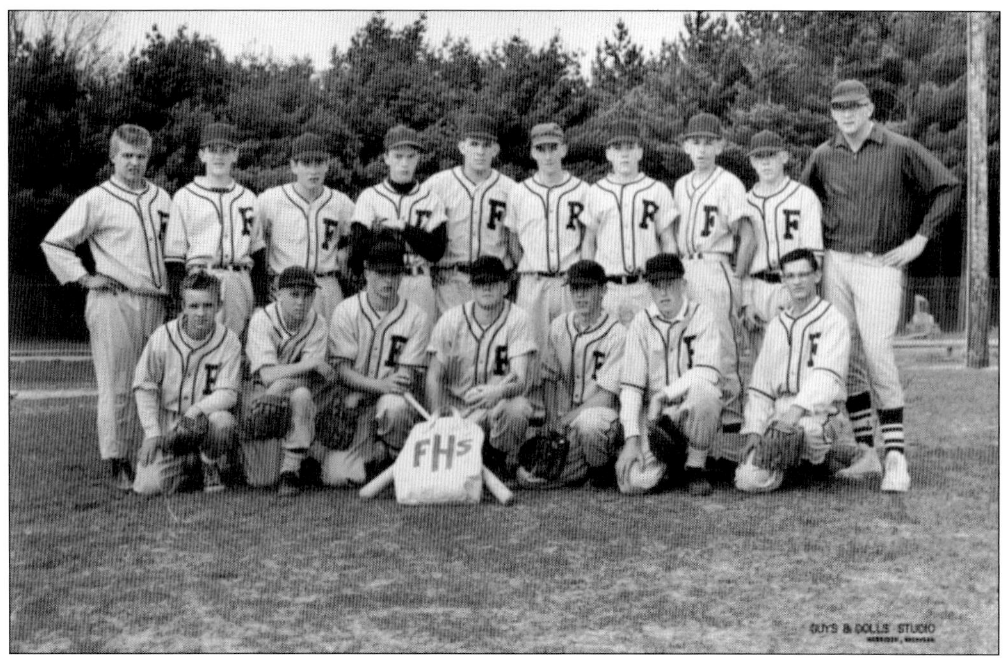

The Farwell High School baseball team is pictured in 1962. From left to right are (kneeling) John Crawford, Lenny Eastlick, Bob Embrey, Charlie Schaar, Roger Wymer, Gary Ruckle, and Joe Manley; (standing) Ed Bergey, John Pratt, Barry Henry, Velvin Borden, Ted Penny, Dewey Barber, Jim Pratt, Terry Hose, Jerry Spicer, and Coach Banoff. (Courtesy of the Henry family.)

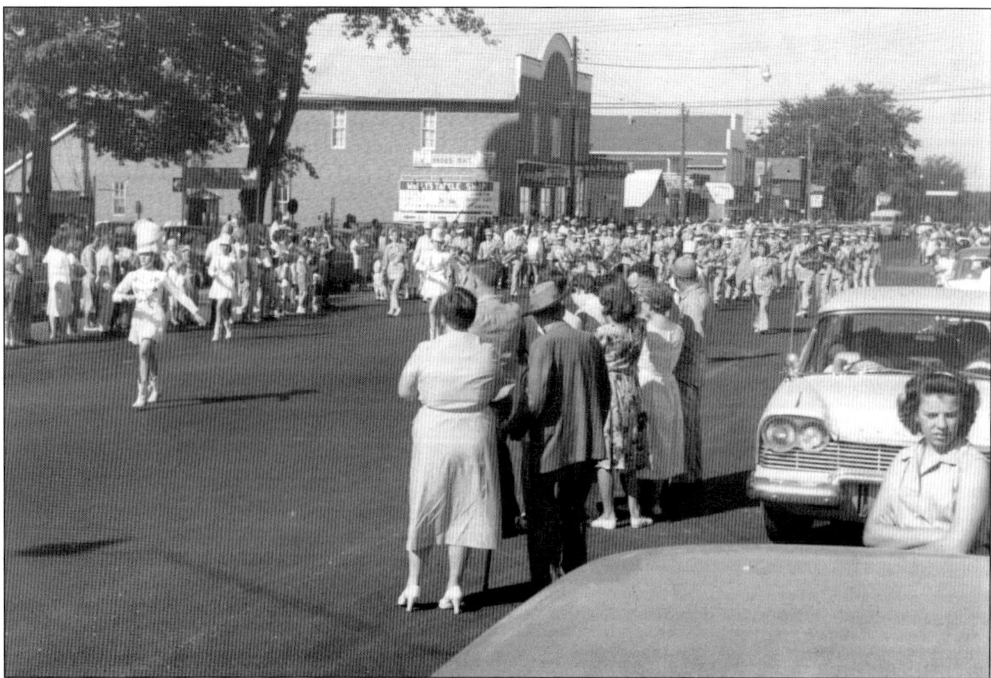

The band marches through town in a parade. Farwell has endured, adapted, and succeeded at providing generations with a small town to grow up in and call home. Many young people stay, and many leave knowing they always have a place to come home to.

Two

Lake George

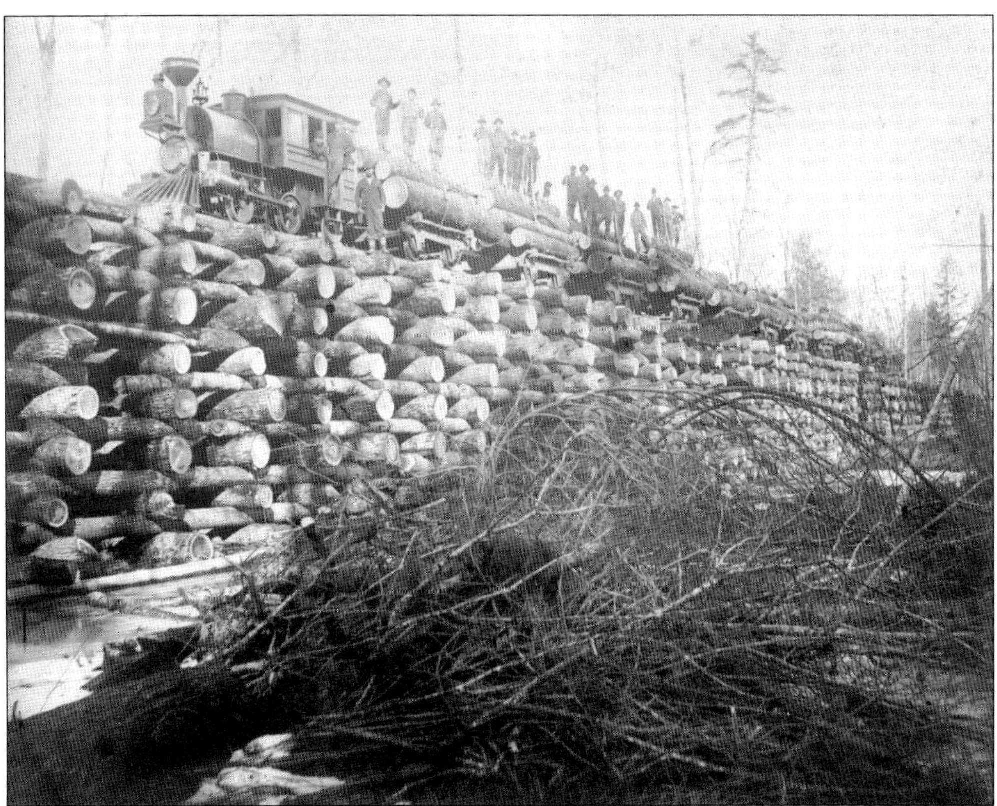

This train trestle is one of the many feats of engineering by the Lake George & Muskegon River Railroad. The LG&MRR long held the folklore title as the first logging railroad. Though not the first, it did revolutionize logging by rail. With few outgoing streams or rivers, Clare County was ideal for the concept of replacing streams and tributaries with rails and trains. In this manner, Winfield Scott Gerrish, a lumberman, was able to cut prized timber that was inaccessible by traditional logging means and take it to the Muskegon River. (Courtesy of Cody Beemer.)

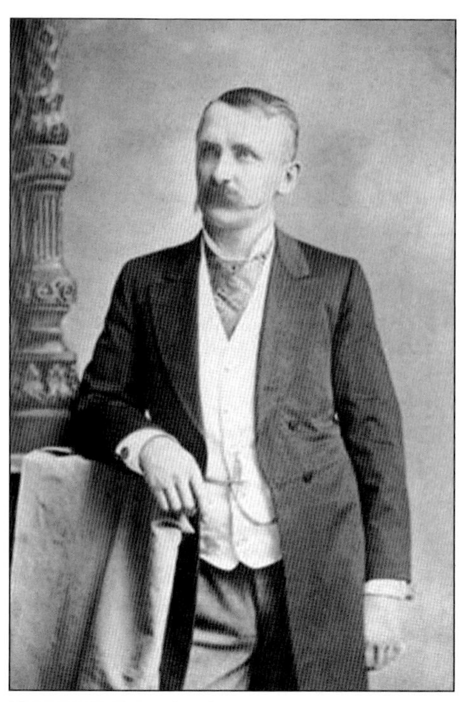

Winfield Scott Gerrish was born in Maine, where he grew up learning the lumber business from his father. His logging operation, Lake George & Muskegon River Railroad, received a lot of attention and profits from the 7.1-mile route from Lake George to the Muskegon River, with spurs of all sizes in between. Gerrish passed away in 1882 in Evart, Michigan, at only 33 years of age.

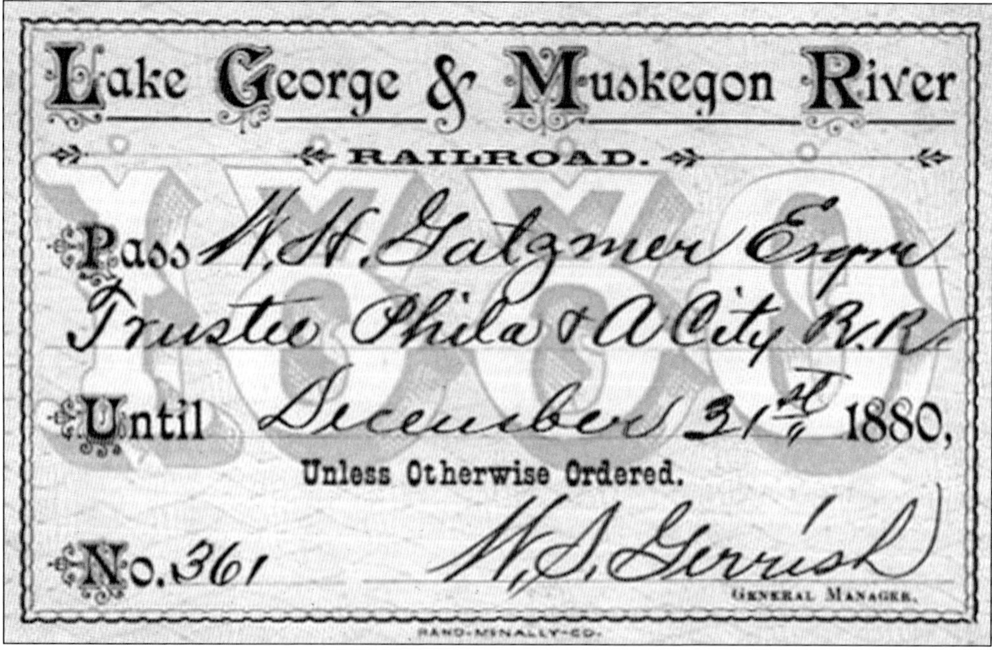

Lake George & Muskegon River
RAILROAD.
Pass W. H. Gatzmer Esqr
Trustee Phila & A City R.R.
Until December 31st 1880,
Unless Otherwise Ordered.
No. 361 W. S. Gerrish
General Manager.
RAND-McNALLY-CO.

Gerrish adopted the idea of bringing narrow-gauge Porter locomotives to northern Michigan after attending the Philadelphia Centennial Exposition in 1876. Coincidentally, his first year had a mild winter, which makes for a bad season of logging. Snow and ice made it easier to log in the woods, and the melt in the spring had to be large enough for water to flow and to dam the water for proper flooding and floating of the logs. With the railroad engines and cars, that was not necessary, and logging was not as dependent on the weather or a particular season. A Lake George & Muskegon River Railroad pass signed by W.S. Gerrish is shown here.

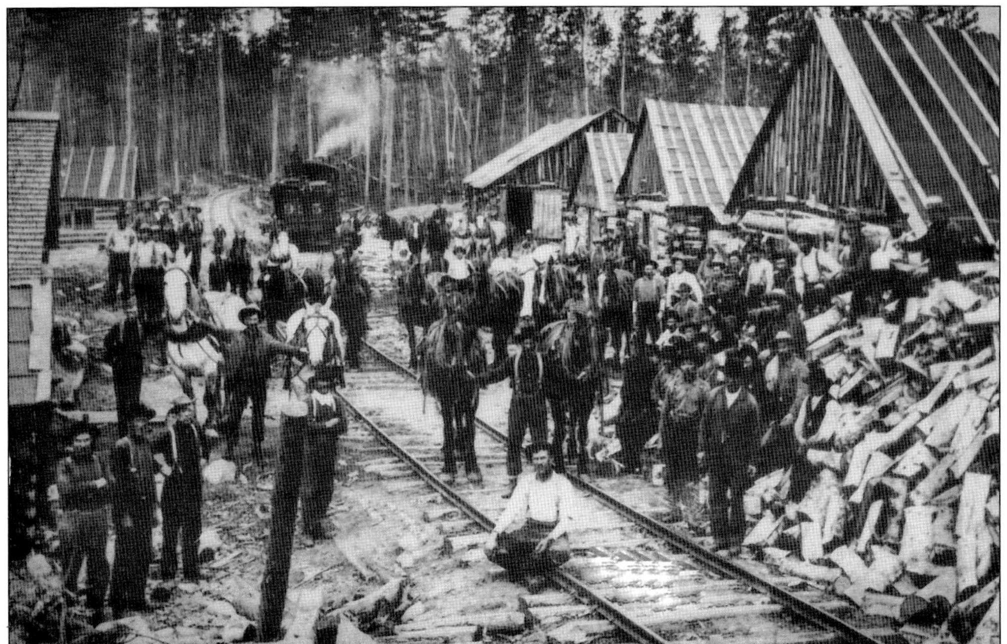

An unidentified lumber camp near Farwell about 1878 demonstrates perfectly the nature of a small lumber camp. Hastily built, its proximity to the tracks was useful for easy loading and unloading of logs, supplies, and people. Many times the buildings themselves would be loaded after the season and reconstructed at another camp the next year.

REPORT

OF THE

LAKE GEORGE & MUSKEGON RIVER RAILROAD COMPANY,

For the Year Ending December 31st, 1878.

CAPITAL STOCK.

1.	Capital stock authorized by charter or articles of association,		$100,000 00
2.	Par value of shares, ...	$100 00	
3.	Average price received per share, . . .	100 00	
4.	Number of stockholders at date of last election,	7	
5.	Number of stockholders in Michigan at same date, ...	7	
6.	Amount of full-paid stock held in Michigan, . . .		
7.	Capital stock issued (number of shares 985), amount paid in, ...		$98,500 00
8.	Capital stock paid in on shares not issued (number shares——), ...		
9.	Capital stock paid in, common, ...		98,500 00
10.	Capital stock paid in, preferred, ...		
11.	Capital stock, total amount paid in as per books of the Co.,		$98,500 00
12.	Capital stock, total amount realized in cash, . . .		
13.	Capital stock, total amount realized in property, . .		
14.	Capital stock paid in per mile of road owned by Company (14.21 miles), ...		6,861 36

ASSETS—CORPORATE PROPERTY.

1.	Estimated value of the road bed, including iron and bridges, ...	$90,000 00
2.	Estimated value of rolling stock, ...	18,500 00
3.	Estimated value of stations, buildings, and fixtures, .	2,500 00
4.	Estimated value of all other property, including investments in stocks and bonds of other corporations, .	3,000 00
5.	Estimated value of property per mile of road (14.21 miles),	8,092 89

Railroad companies reported annually on everything from their equipment value to how many men were injured or killed. The reports are a treasure trove of information for railroad enthusiasts and historians. The 1878 year-end report for the Lake George & Muskegon River Railroad company is shown here. (HDL.)

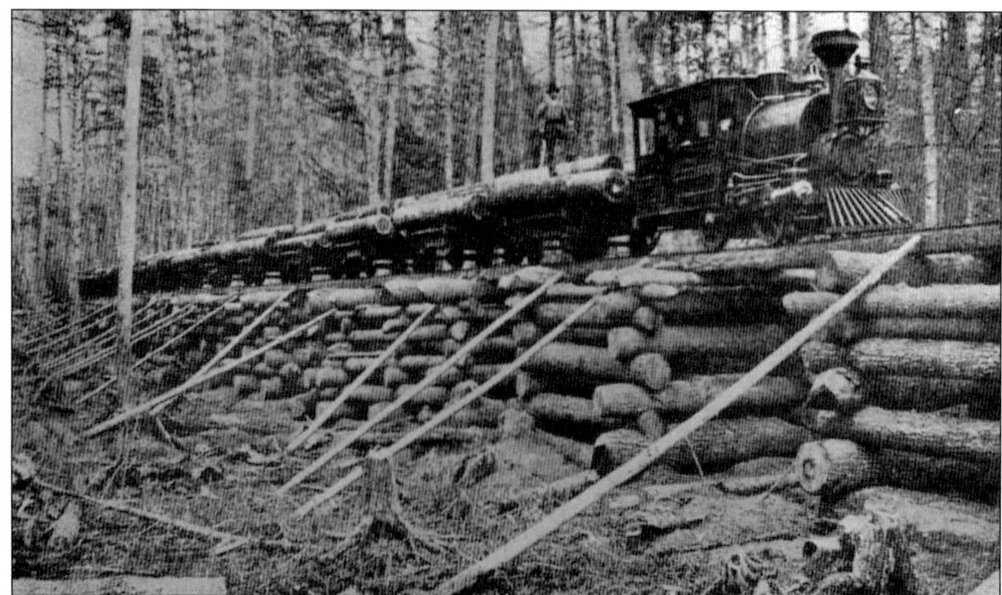

The smaller of two known trestles built by the Lake George & Muskeon River Railroad is shown here. Two trestles were built in May 1878. One was 150 feet in length, and the other was 550 feet. The valuable lumber of the trestles would not have been left behind. It would have been reclaimed and used or sold along with the fresh cut timber. (Meek.)

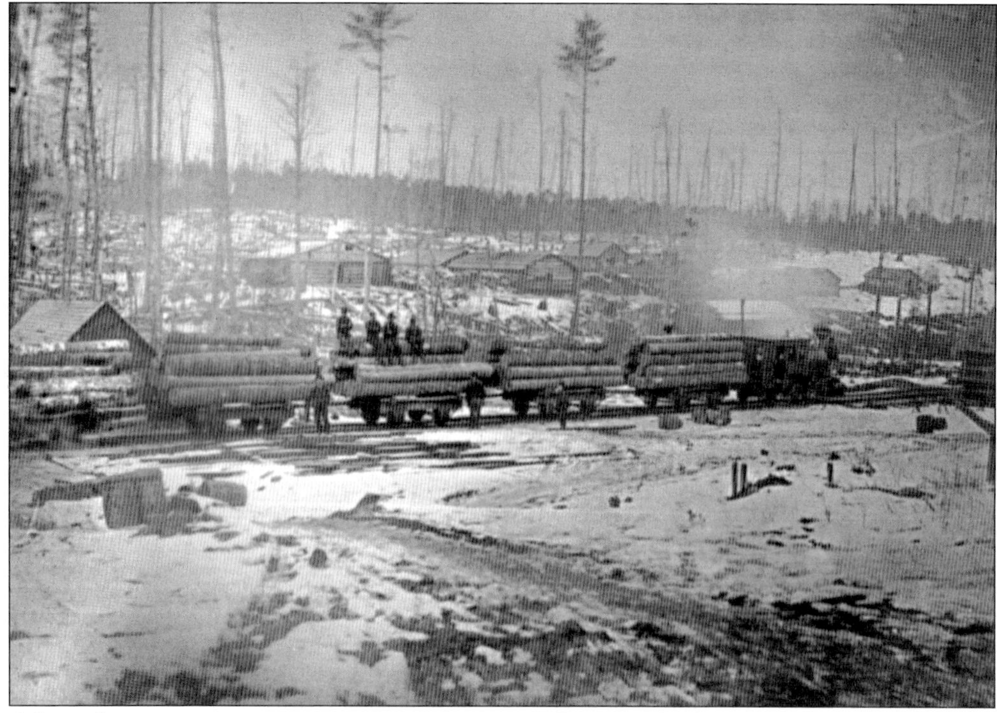

A line of narrow-gauge train cars carries its precious white pine load most likely to the Muskegon River, where it will be stacked into a rollaway and floated down the river to Muskegon and Lake Michigan with the spring thaw. The lumber camp is in the background. "L.G. & M. R. R" can be seen on the bottom of the second car from the left. (Courtesy of Cody Beemer.)

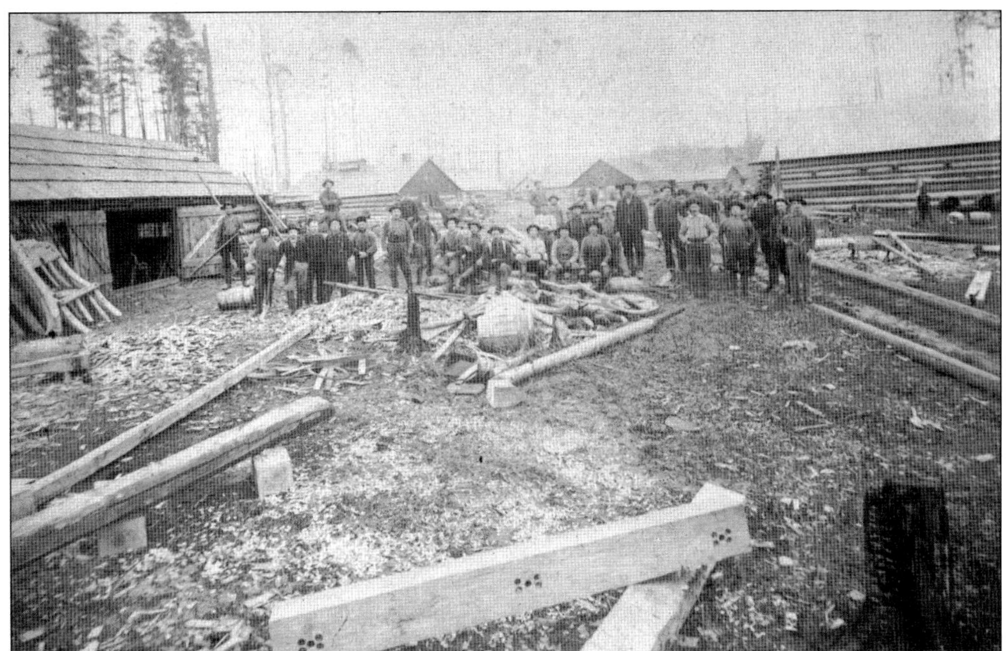

The tools and implements the lumber operation would need were often made right in the lumber camp. Woodworkers and blacksmiths produced articulated sleds (skids and parts, far left), barrels (center), beams for hitching horses (front center), and cant hook handles, and repairs were made to existing equipment. (Courtesy of Cody Beemer.)

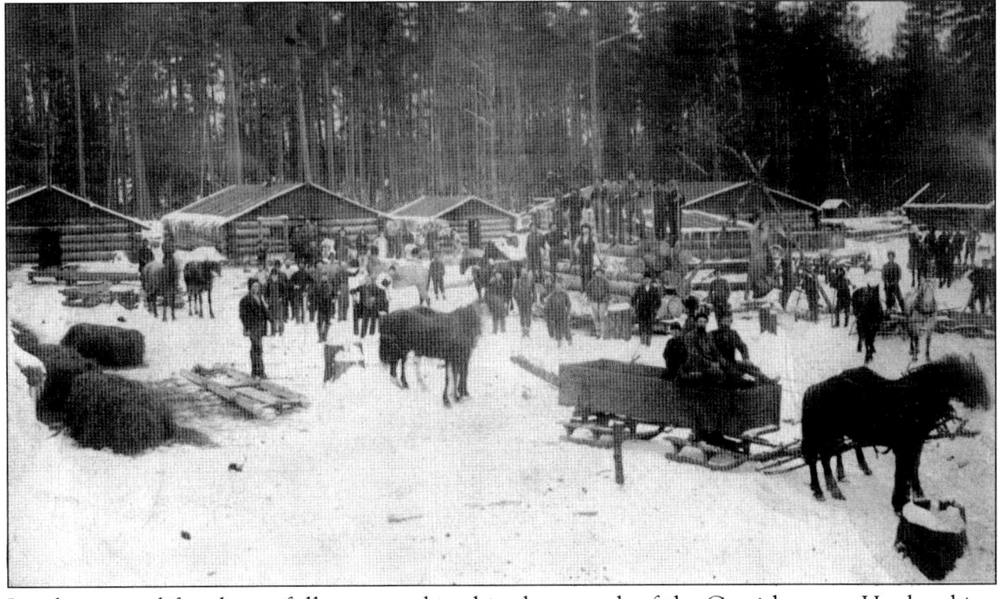

Lumber camp life is beautifully captured in this photograph of the Gerrish camp. Hardworking men each had their own specific role to play in the life of camp. A line of shanty boys pauses in a row with their cant hooks in hand (center, on logs); a deer and a larger animal (right center), which was likely a downed horse hang ready to be made into meals by the camp cook (back center in apron), hang nearby; and men with their team reins in their hands are ready to go to work. (Courtesy of Cody Beemer.)

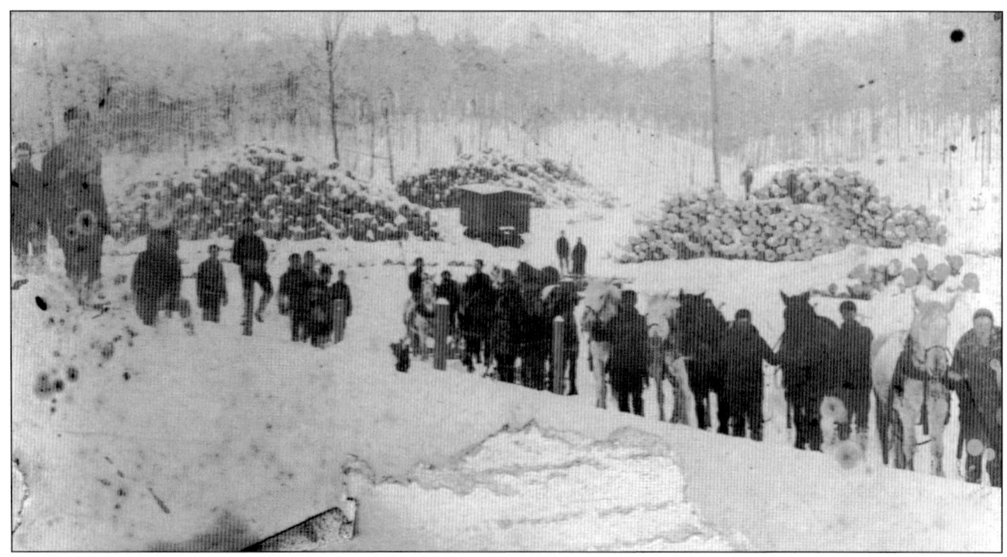

Rows of logs are banked so that when the train rolled in, it was a quick process to load them. Gerrish ordered three Porter engines for his new venture. The first two engines were poled up the Muskegon River on rafts. When the third arrived at Farwell on the Flint & Pere Marquette Railroad from Pittsburgh, it was run through the woods 15 miles on a pole road for lack of rails or other means to get it where it was needed. It was quite a sight to see a steam engine puffing through the pines followed by a team of men with a water supply. (Courtesy of Cody Beemer.)

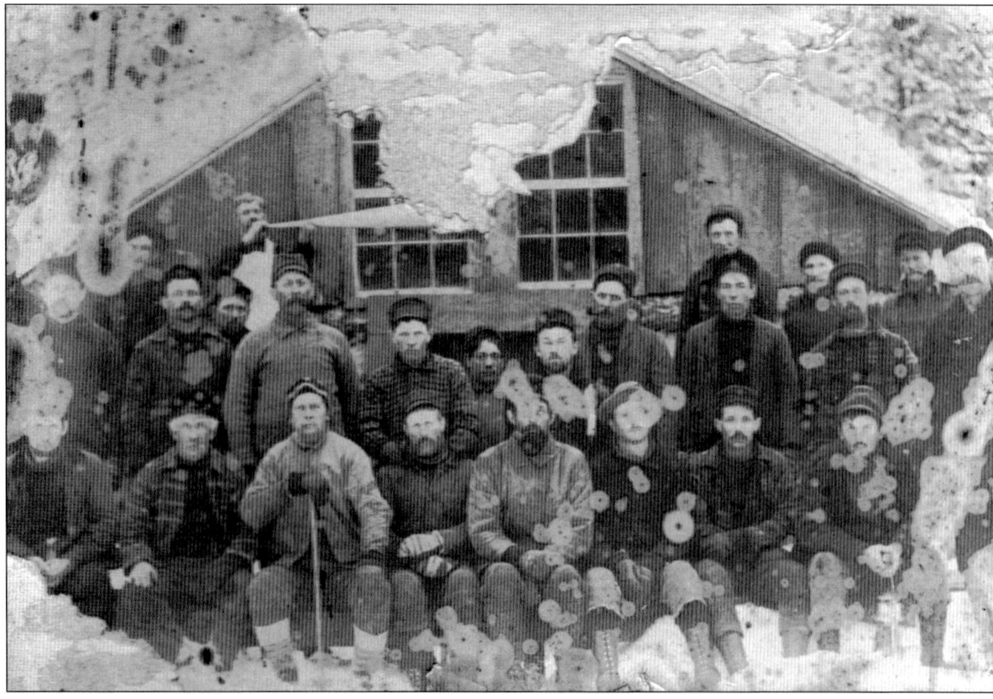

The cook or "cookee" (back left) demonstrates his Gabriel's horn, a long, thin horn blown to announce a meal was ready in the lumber camp. There were many men to feed. During the winter in Gerrish's camps, there were almost 700 men in 225 teams. In other seasons, there were up to 400 men in 70 teams. (Courtesy of Cody Beemer.)

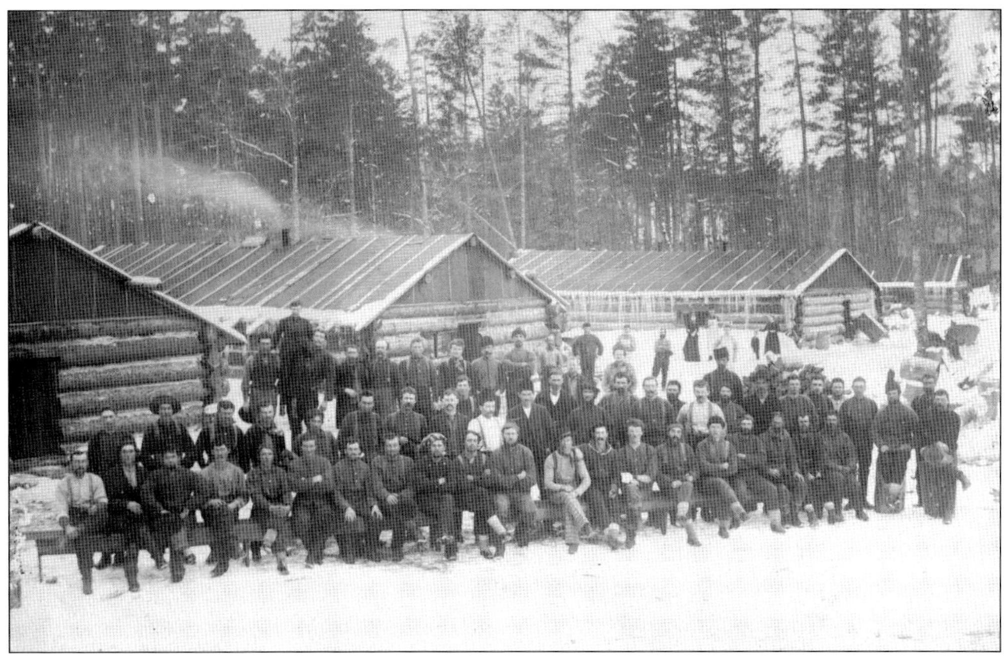

Women and children (back right) were a familiar site in many lumber camps. Cooks, foremen, or other workers would sometimes bring their families to help them keep the camp. Several men in the front row are probably recent immigrants to Michigan and dressed noticeably different in colorful hats, coats, and pants of their native home. Though alcohol was forbidden in lumber camps, tobacco was not, and several men are smoking clay pipes. (Courtesy of Cody Beemer.)

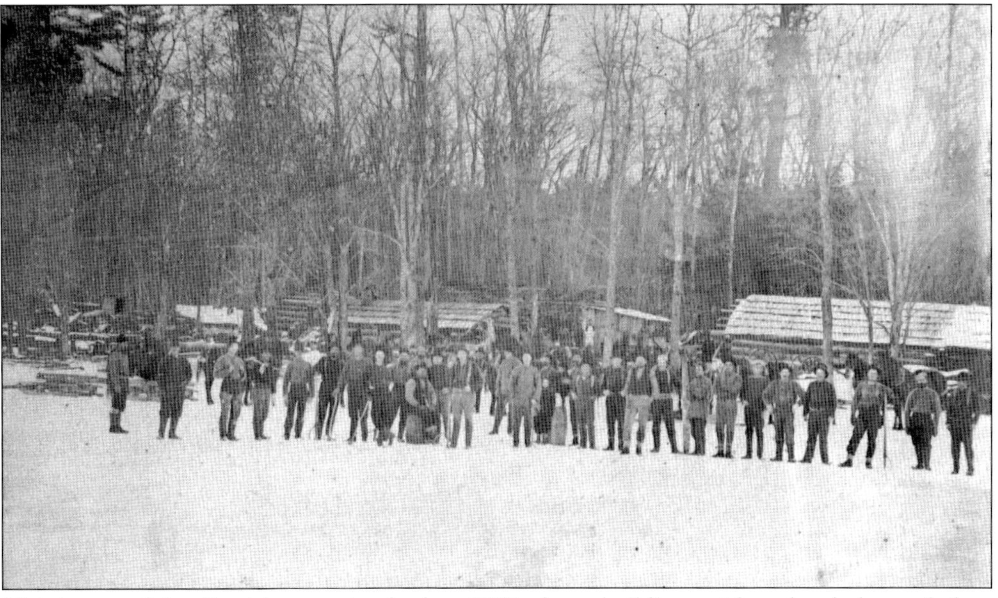

This image of the Gerrish camp in the late 1870s shows buildings with cedar shake roofs, logs piled up, and men with their tools of crosscut saws, cant hooks, and axes. The cook (back center in his white apron) was an important part of the camp. The men worked hard, and camp life was not comfortable. Keeping the men fed with more than 6,000 calories a day to keep them working was a big job. (Courtesy of Cody Beemer.)

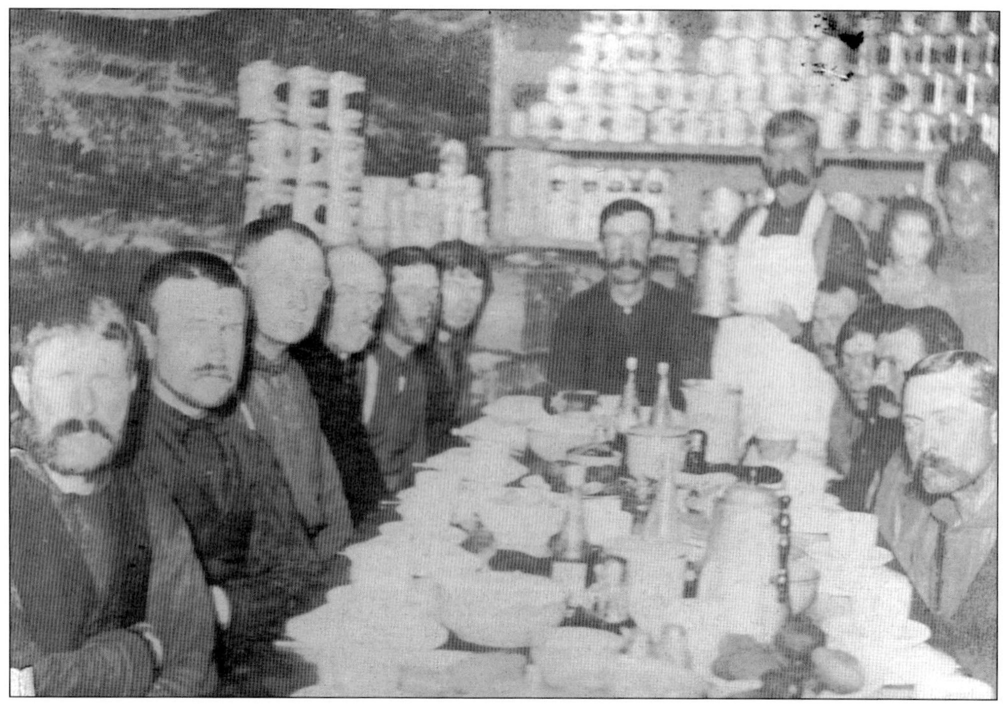

The shanty boys at the Gerrish camp sit down to eat in the cramped dining cabin. They are surrounded by supplies for their next meal (above). The cook and his family stand over the table in both photographs (above, at right; below, at left). (Both, courtesy of Cody Beemer.)

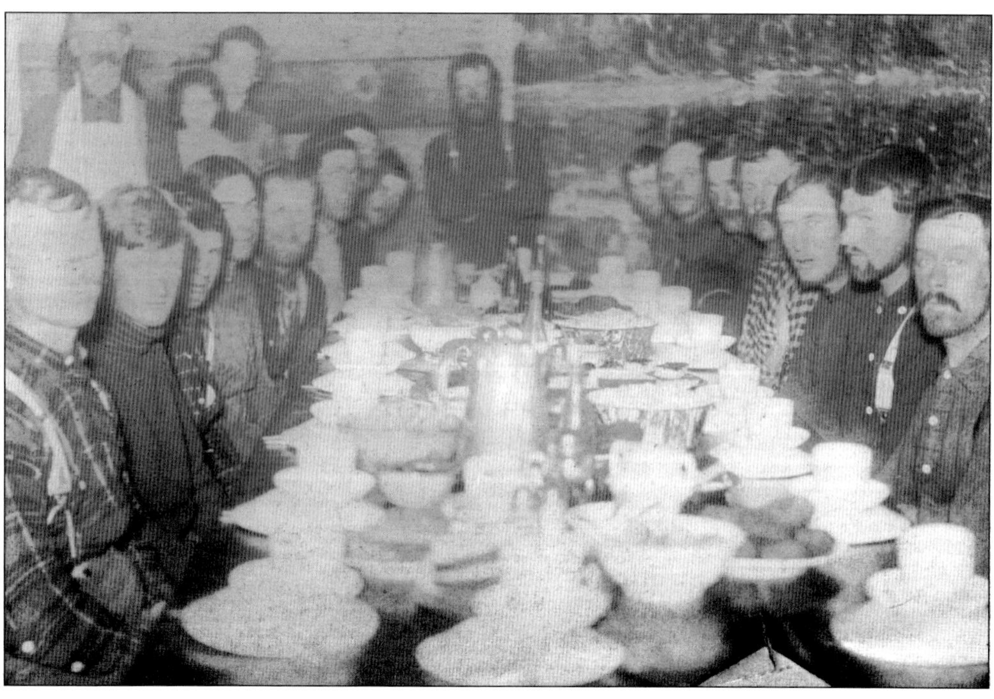

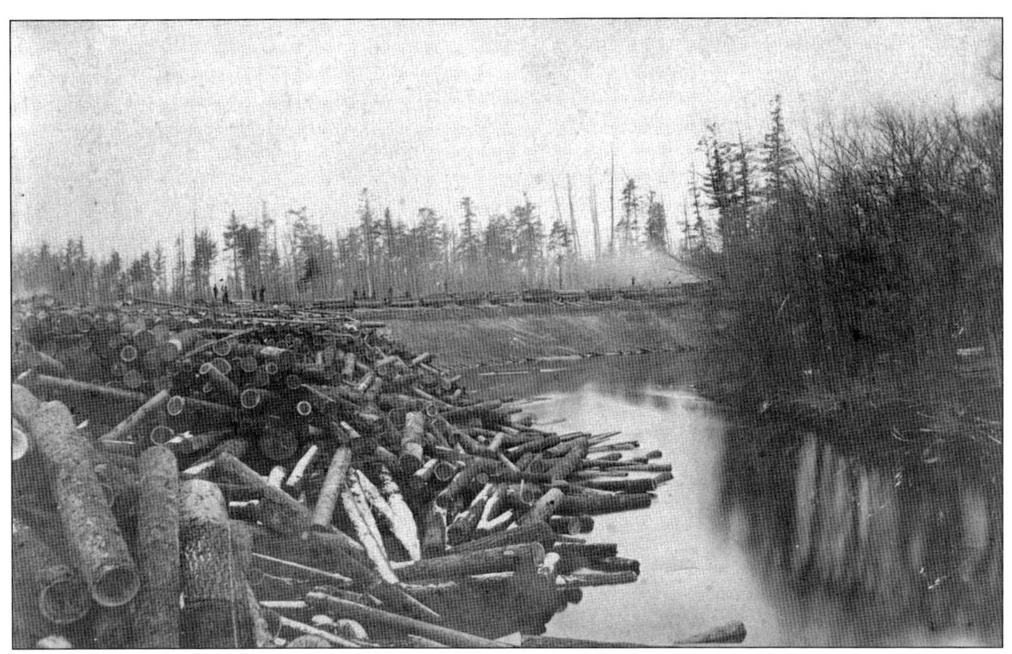

The banking grounds at Temple on the Muskegon River are shown during the lumber heyday of the Lake George & Muskegon River Railroad (above) and in 2013 (below). (Above, courtesy of Cody Beemer; below, courtesy of James Hannum.)

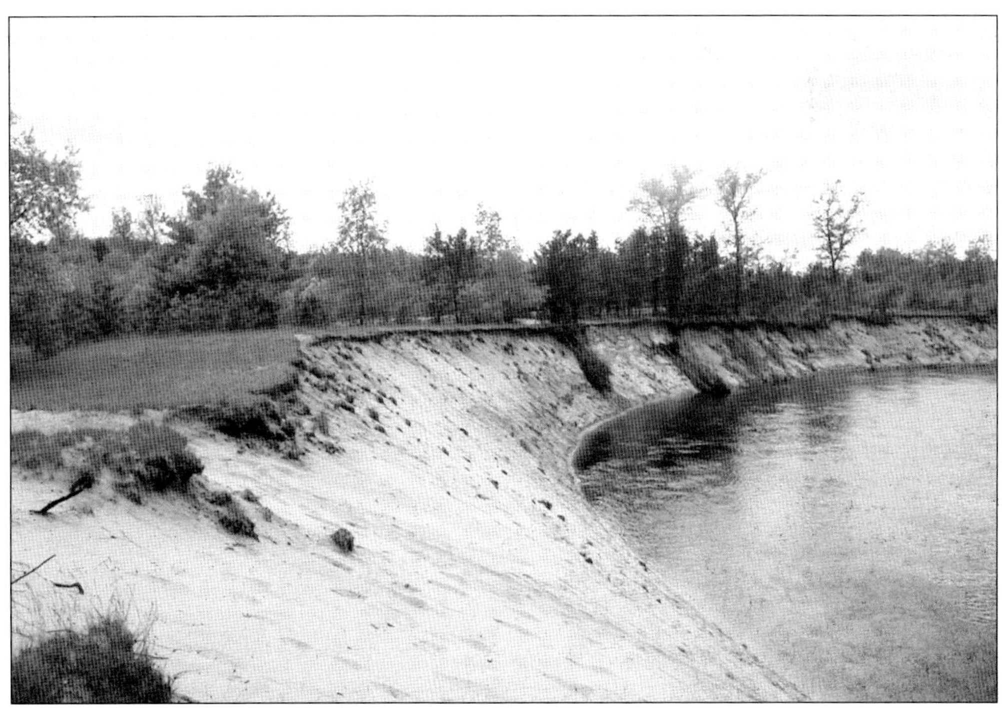

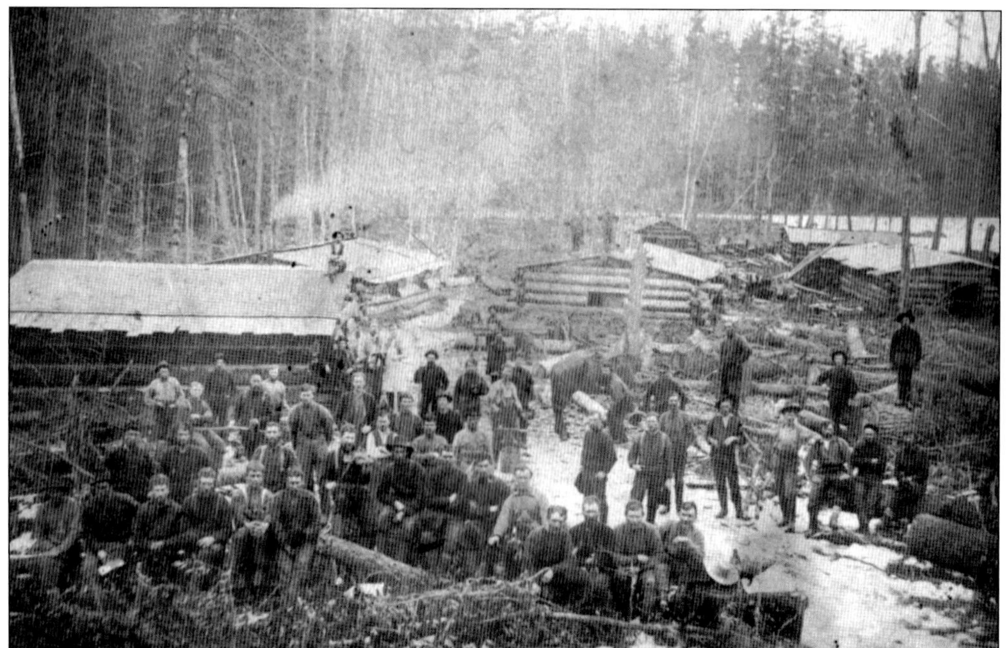

The men at the Gerrish camps worked in 12-hour shifts. Three men ran a train with 13 cars, and three men were on the riverbank to unload logs. Up to 20 men remained at the skidway to load logs. Note the man with a fiddle; one can imagine a bit of fun and distraction from the long hard days of work in the woods. (Courtesy of Cody Beemer.)

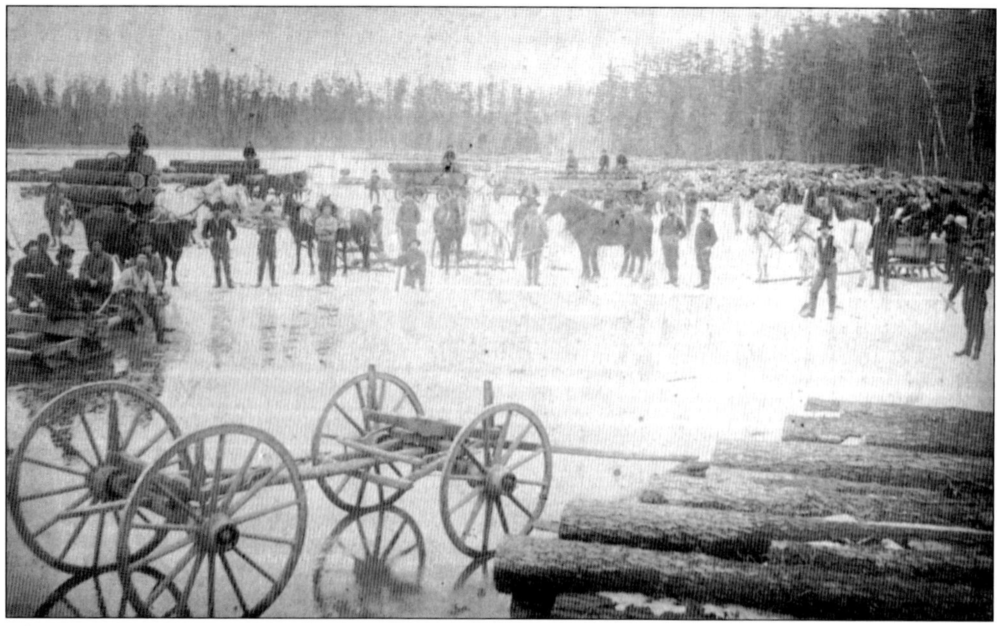

The Gerrish crew shown here is working on the ice hauling logs with oxen and horses. The Lake George & Muskegon River Railroad company was sold to John Woods in 1882. He then sold it to the large Muskegon lumber operation of C.H. Hackley and Co., which was Charles Hackley, Porter Hackley, and Thomas Hume. They also had camps in Clare and surrounding counties, operating as Hackley & Hume. (Courtesy of Cody Beemer.)

Gerrish also owned significant lumber supply stores that were successful. In Farwell, he partnered with Jacob "Little Jake" Seligman. Little Jake was a colorful figure and immigrant tailor turned successful businessman from Saginaw. He was nicknamed Little Jake because he was only 4 feet, 11 inches. He owned his own bank and, in this case with Gerrish, became a partner in selling clothing and other supplies down the line of the Flint & Pere Marquette Railroad route. He later moved to Colorado and died there in 1911 but is buried in Saginaw, Michigan. Their partnership was short-lived and sold out to W. George Emerick & Co. (Courtesy of Clare County Press.)

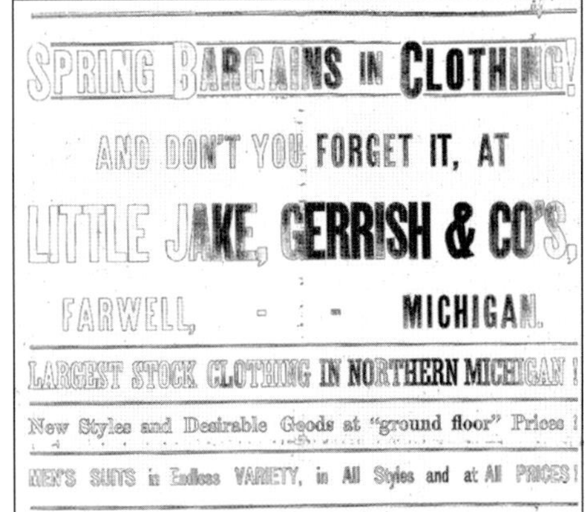

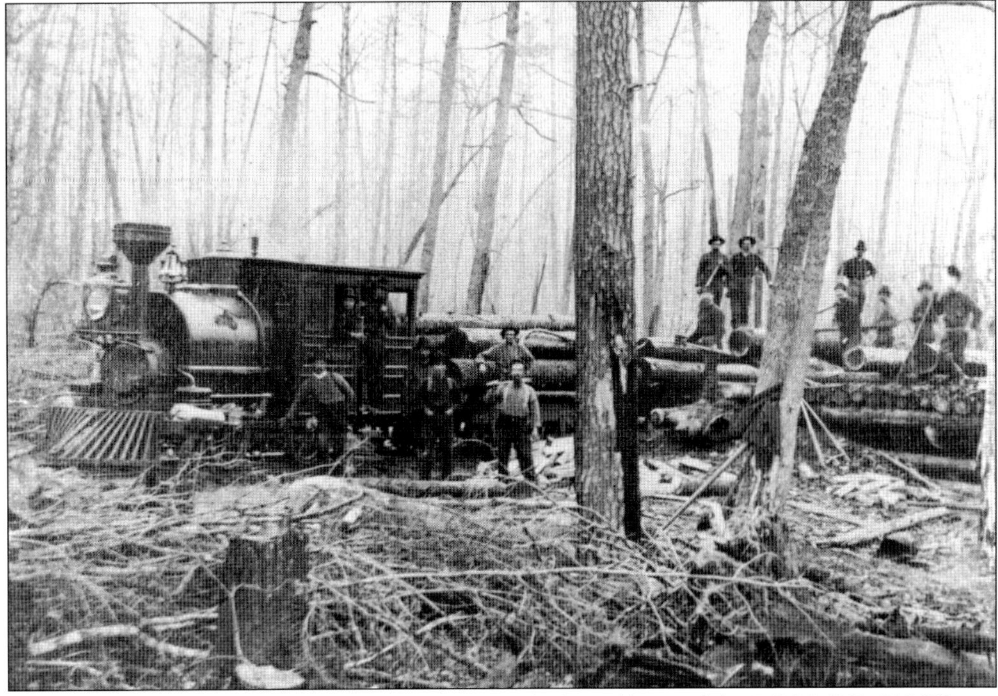

The narrow-gauge Porter locomotives were named after officers of the LG&MRR. *J.V. Watson* (shown here), *William Stafford*, and *Jos M. Gerrish* were named after James Verree Watson, William Stafford, and many members of the Gerrish family involved in the business. A forest fire burn mark on the tree at center creates the illusion that a man is hiding in the side of the tree. (Courtesy of Cody Beemer.)

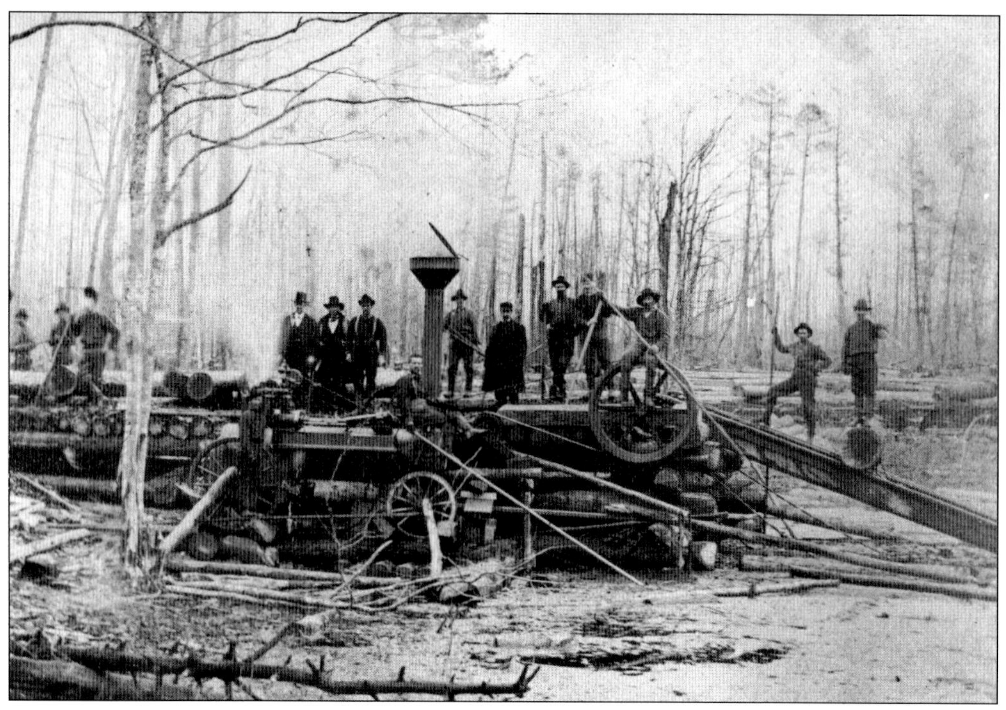

A steam engine or "steam donkey" is shown here mounted on wheels. Pulled by horses, it was a useful machine to haul logs for the camps. It was commonly used in the western states to pull logs up mountains. Possible uses of the steam donkey would be a practical means of reclamation of the trestles, and pulling logs onto train cars. (Courtesy of Cody Beemer.)

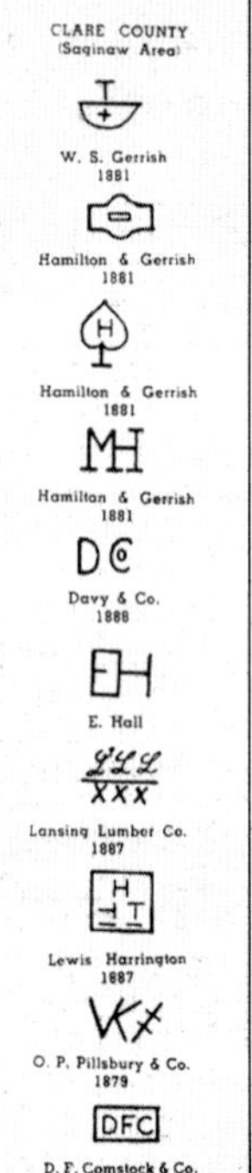

Among the Clare County log marks shown here are various Gerrish company marks and the mark of Edmund Hall. The cattle brand of the lumbering business, log marks were important outposts of law and order in pioneering communities where law enforcement was often weak. A mark on a log carried the right of ownership and was recognized on every lake and stream in northern Michigan. (HDL.)

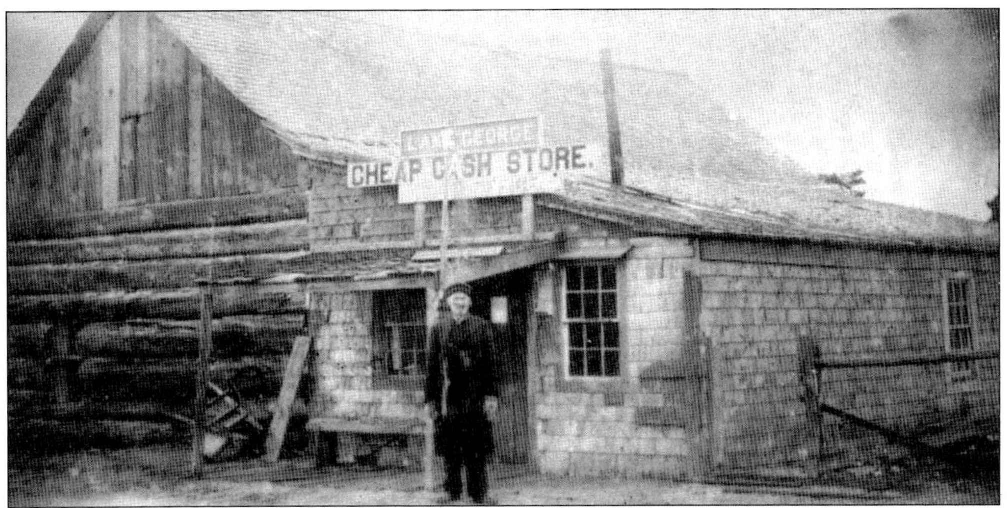

Julius Borst bought the Cheap Cash Store in 1880. It was originally the office and store of the Gerrish railroad operation, and also served as the post office in Lake George. The Lake George post office was established in 1888, with Edward J. Roys appointed as the first postmaster. It was located on Shingle Lake east of the current park location. (Meek.)

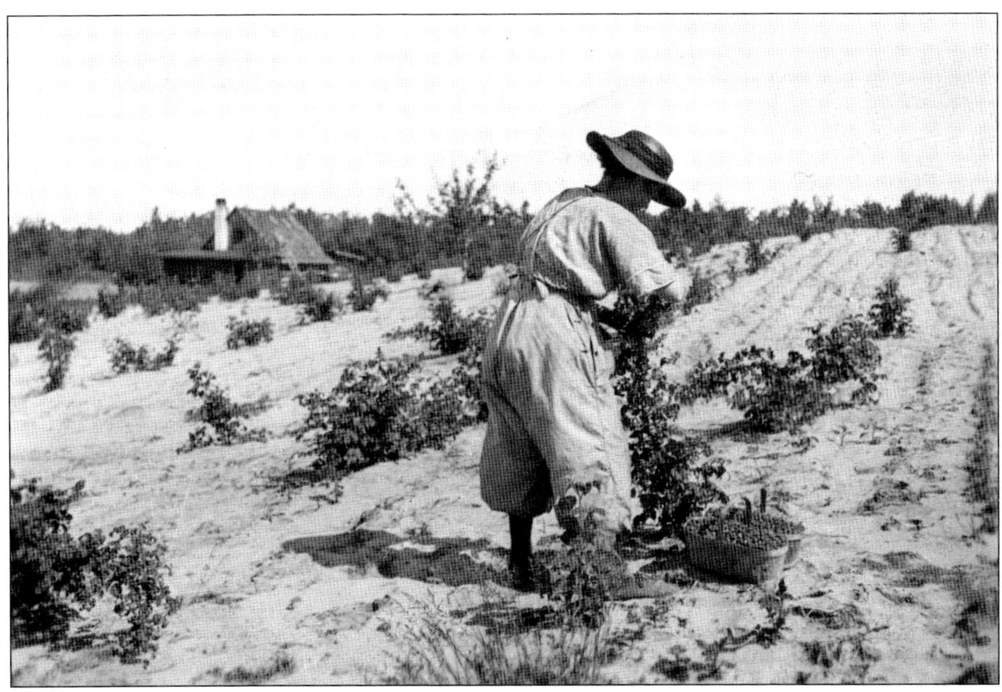

Red raspberries are shown here growing on the Dina Welty farm in 1923. The 160-acre Welty farm was just north of Lake George. The sandy soil is typical of the conditions after the lumber era. The Welty/Tolson family had a cabin on Lake George named Michalet, a combination of "Michigan" and "chalet." (Courtesy of the Welty Family.)

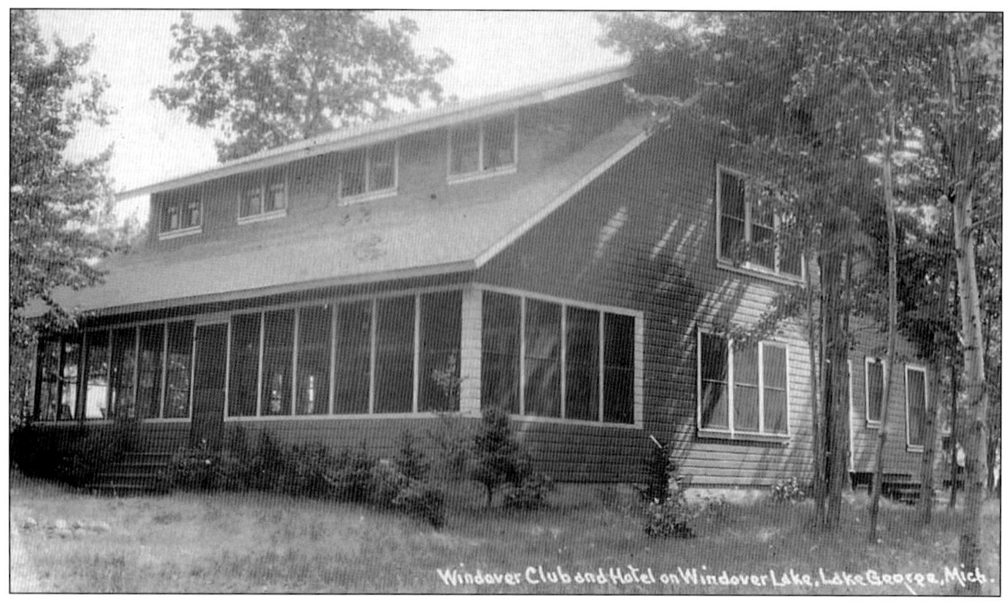

Still standing and privately owned, this home on Windover Lake in Freeman Township was built by L.R. Perkins. Perkins was involved in the Freeman Oil Company. The home was originally a summer resort with a restaurant and an ice cream parlor. The original eight-burner stove is still used today. (HDL.)

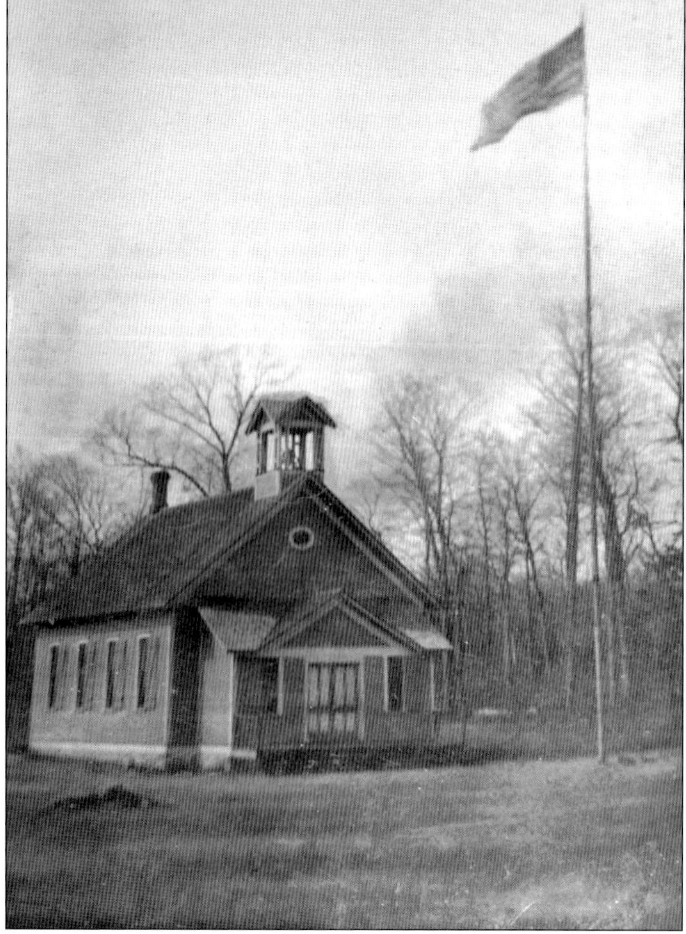

Freeman Township consolidated with the Farwell schools in 1944. Their schoolhouse was moved to Farwell, remodeled, and used as a kindergarten classroom. Many one-room schoolhouses were still in use into the 1950s.

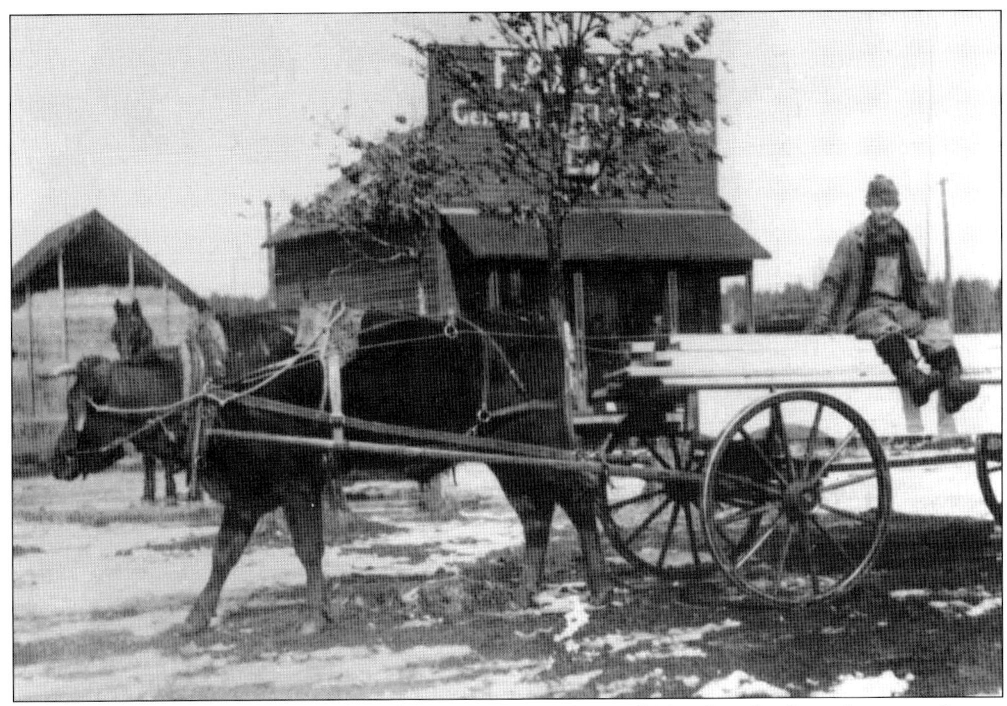

A tree partially obscures the sign reading "F. A. Luce General Merchandise" on the general store of Frank Luce in Lake George. Luce worked as a clerk in stores in Marion and Clarence before he opened his own store. He was postmaster at Lake George from 1905 to 1906. (Meek.)

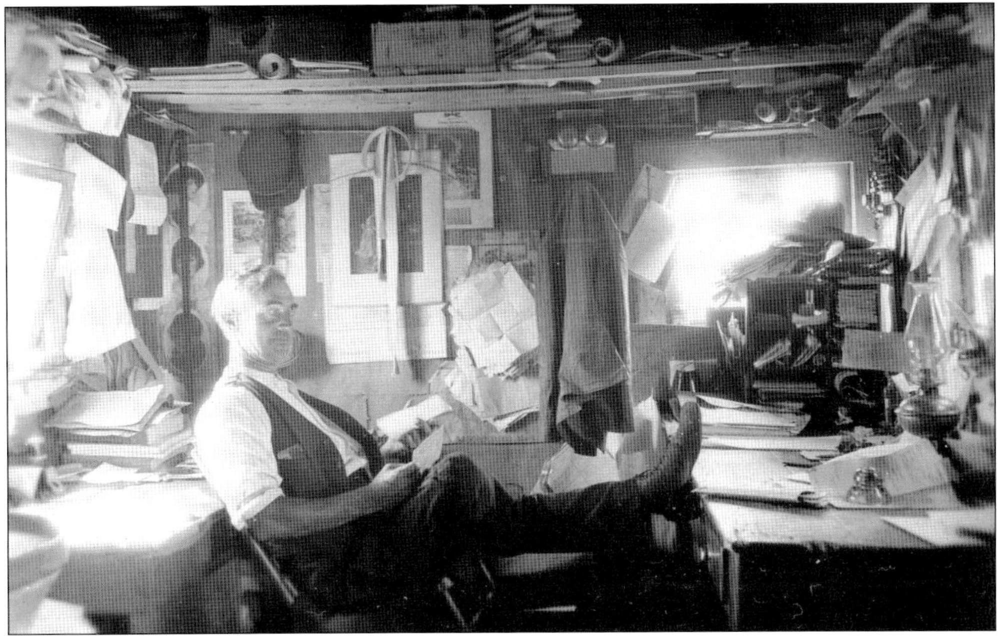

Garrett Silover is shown here relaxing in the Ann Arbor Railroad office. Silover and his wife, Emma (Spence), were Lake George residents and he was a telegraph operator. Emma had six children with her first husband, Julius T. Borst of Lake George. Garrett and Emma Silover were married in 1918. (Courtesy of the Welty family.)

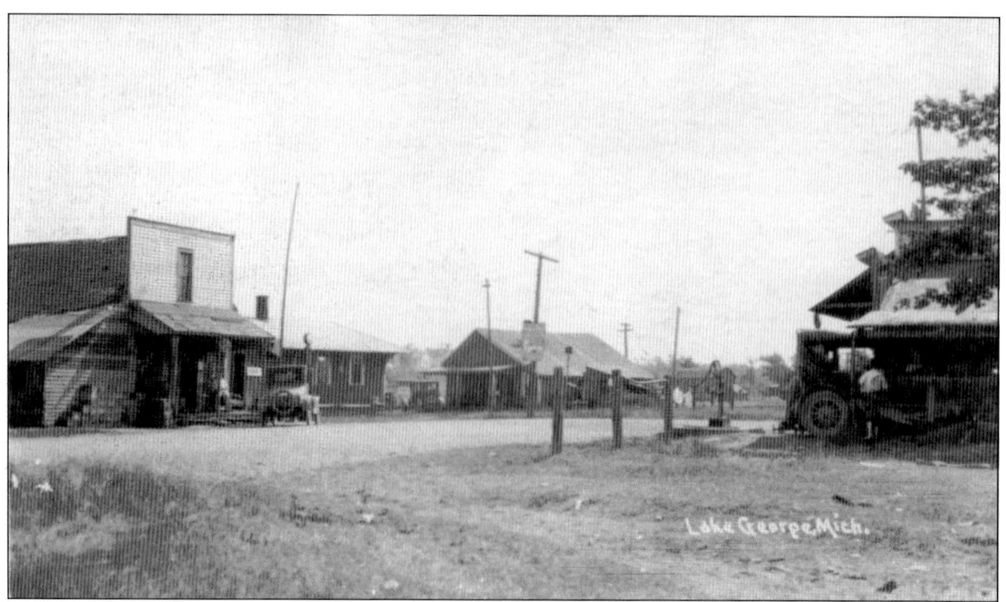

This postcard mailed in 1928 from Lake George shows a corner of the depot (center) and the store (right). Note the hand pump just off the street to the right.

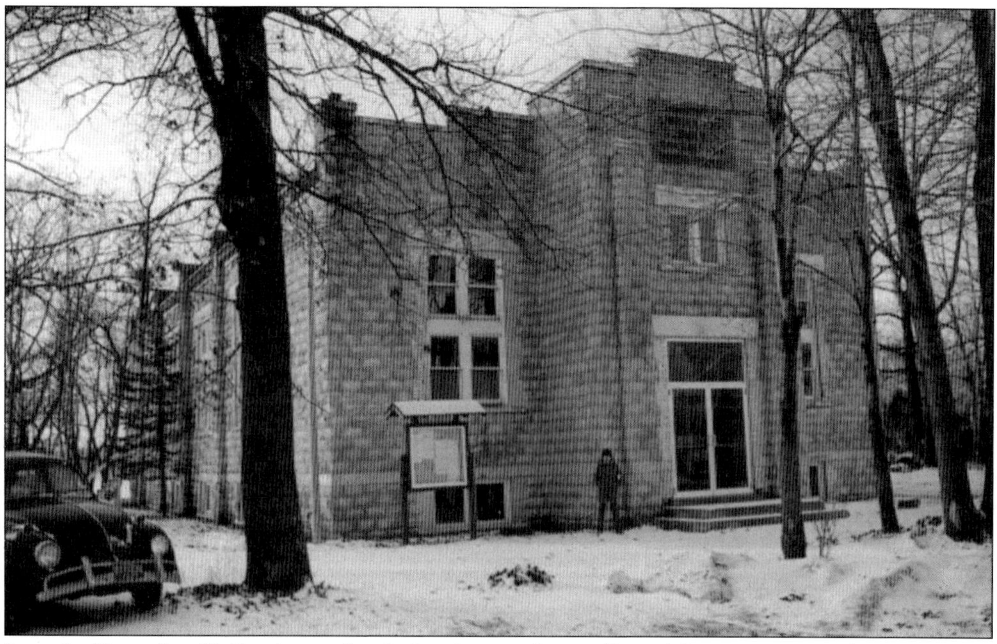

Lincoln Township Hall is located in Lake George. It is still used for meetings and serves as the Lake George Senior Center. The first supervisor of Lincoln Township was William Packard, in 1903. In addition to being a resort area, Lincoln Township has a large natural gas storage and transmission facility. (Meek.)

In 1913, as northern Michigan was gaining in popularity as a resort destination, the Fairview subdivision near Lake George in Lincoln Township was created. The original plat shows 24 lots. (CCHS.)

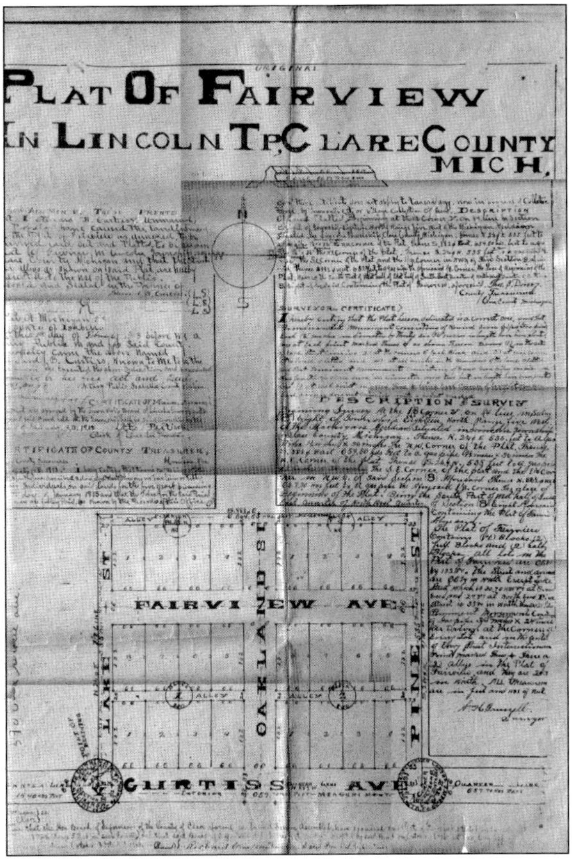

The Lincoln Township hall is pictured here with its namesake President Lincoln painted on the front. By the 1970s, the painting was barely visible. The Welty family is pictured attending Sunday school in August 1928. The building still stands today, though it is not used as the township hall. (Courtesy of the Welty family.)

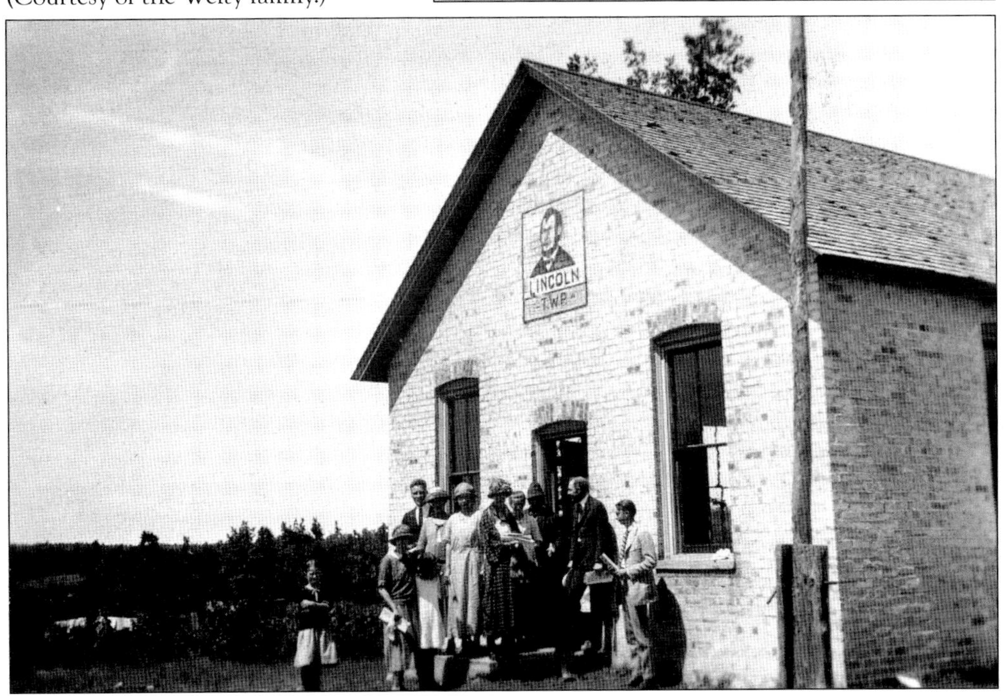

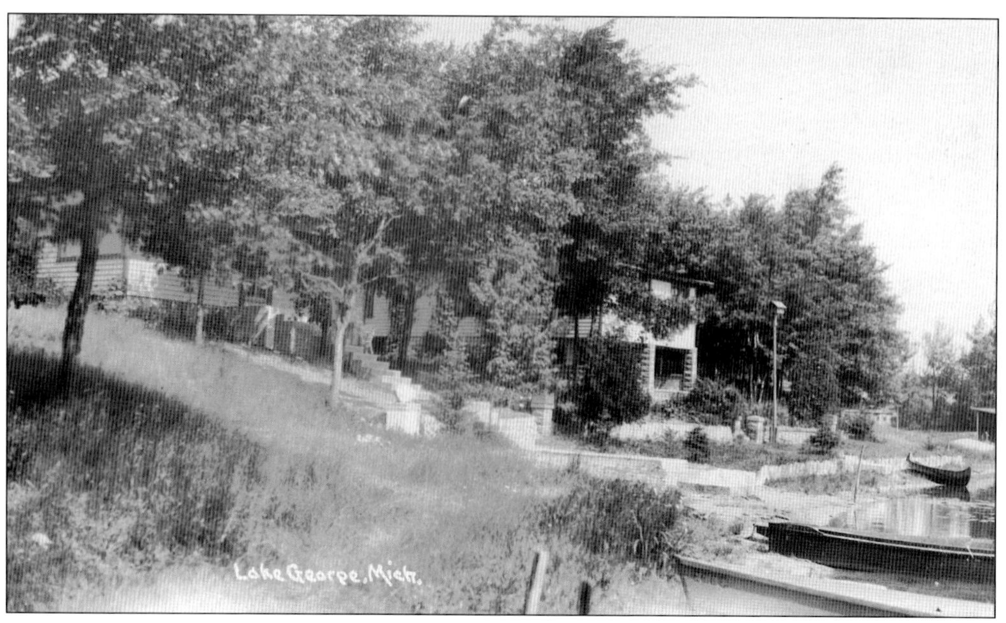

Lake George is three miles long and covers 134 acres. During the lumber era, a channel was dug from Lake George to Shingle Lake so logs could be floated and flooding of the area could move more logs. The Lake George area had the finest stands of virgin white pine in the entire state, as well as cedar, Norway pine, hemlock, and spruce. Shown here are two views of the same cottage on the lake in 1913.

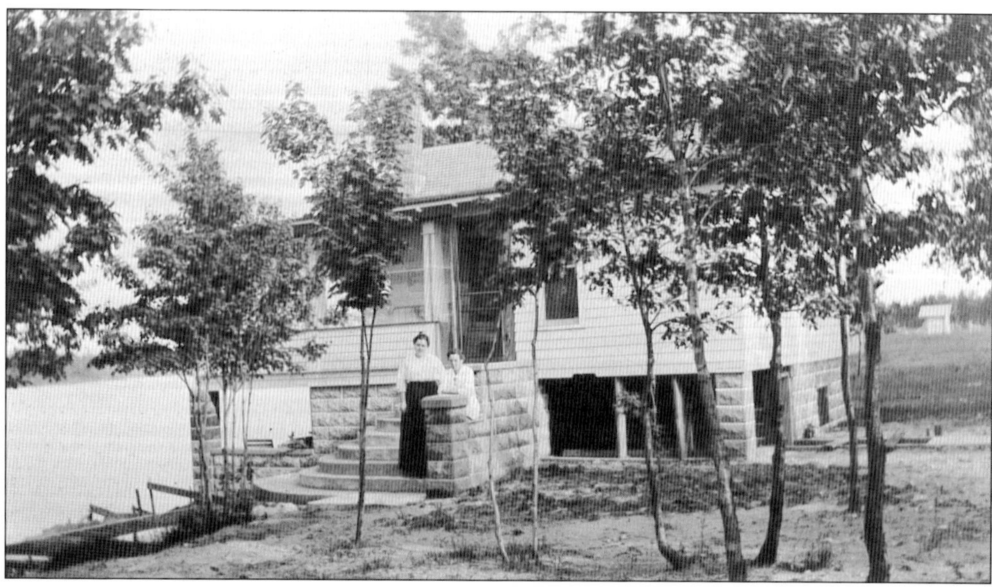

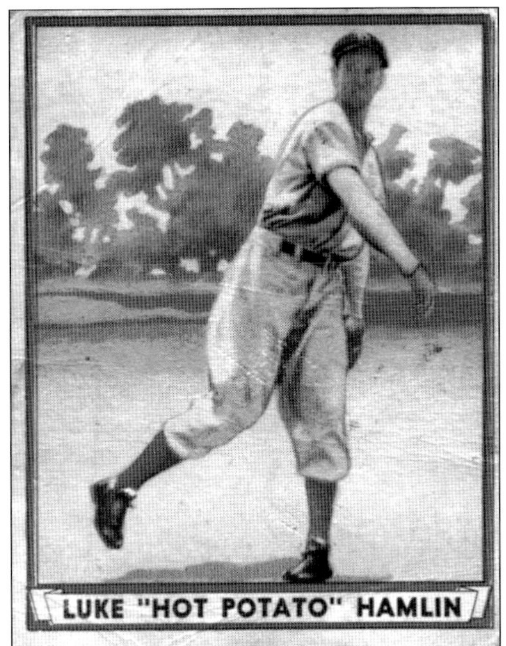

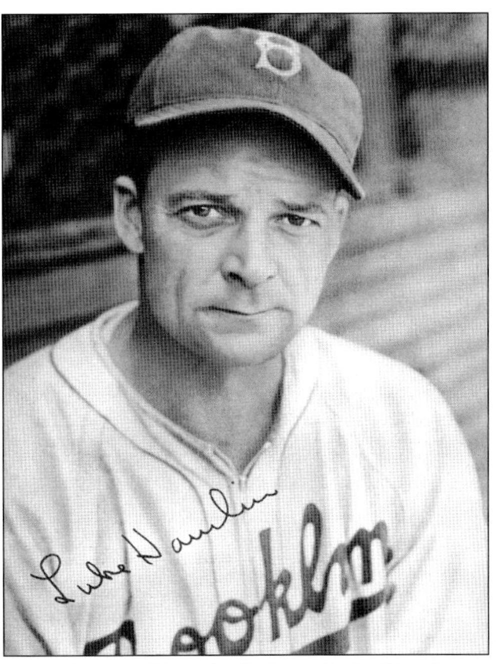

The baseball field in Lake George was dedicated to professional baseball player Luke Hamlin in 1972. Hamlin was nicknamed "Hot Potato" because of his tendency to juggle the ball before he pitched. He played for the Detroit Tigers, Brooklyn Dodgers, Pittsburgh Pirates, and the Philadelphia Athletics. Although he was born in Montcalm County, he called Clare County home. He died in 1978 and is buried at the Lincoln Township Cemetery.

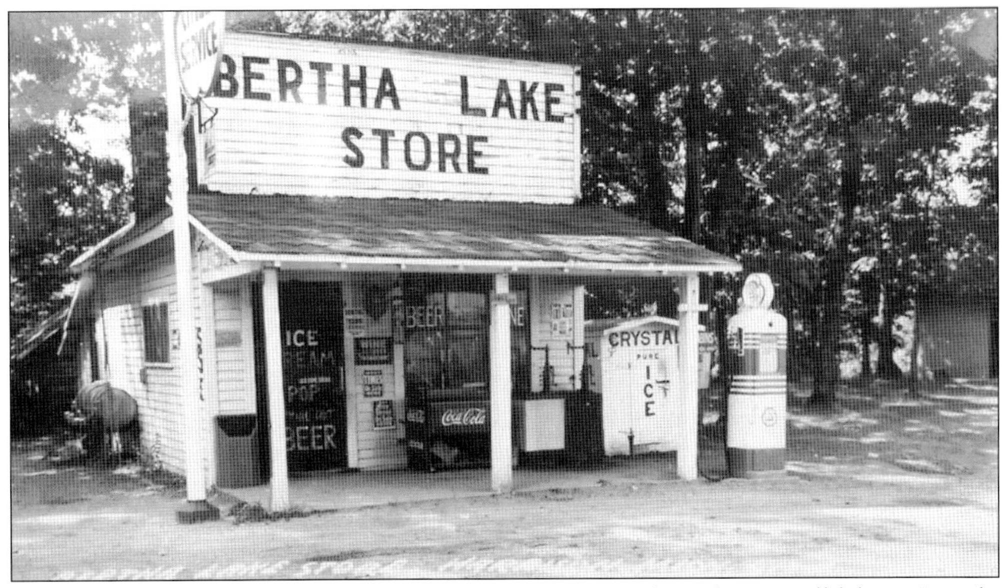

The Bertha Lake Store building still stands today near Bertha Lake, a small lake in Lincoln Township. A small community has always been present there, and in the 1960s, it had a 4-H Club. Today, it is a quiet, no-wake lake near White Birch Lakes, a private gated community.

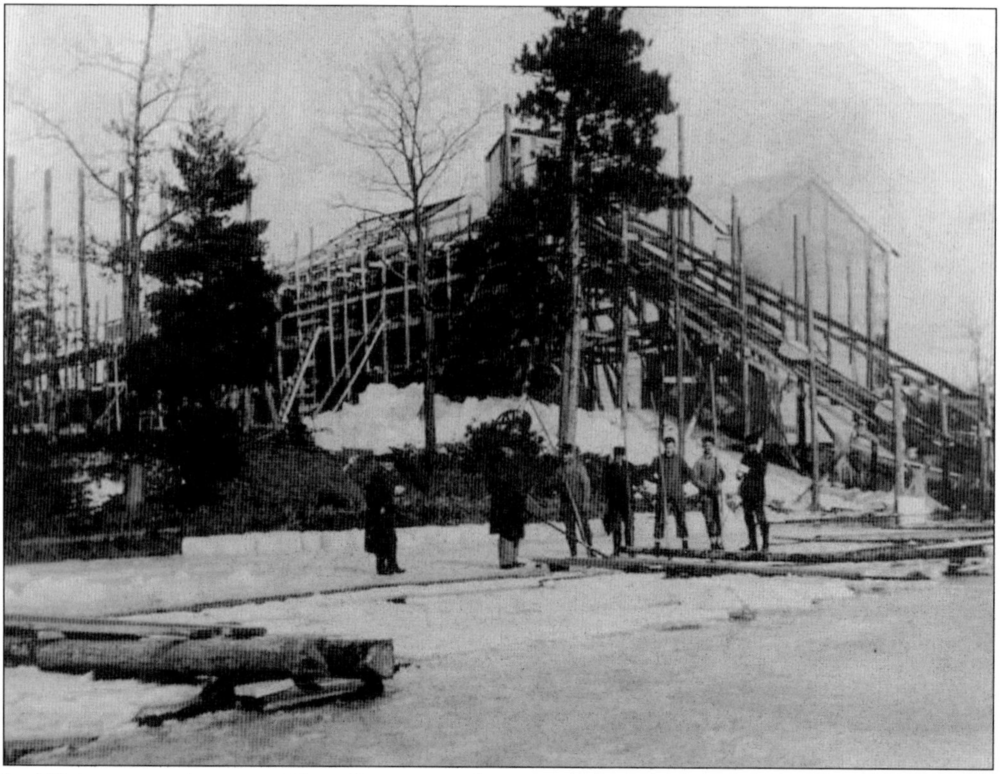

In 1890, every icehouse in Clare County was busy, including this one at Lake George, pictured during its construction. Saginaw companies ordered ice for shipment south to cities like Cleveland and Cincinnati, where the weather was mild that winter and demand for ice was high. (Meek.)

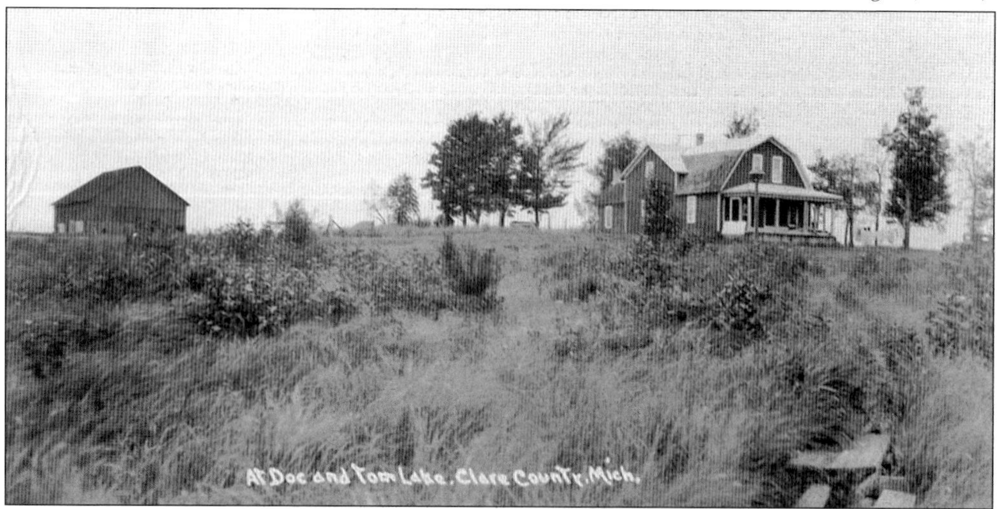

In local lore, Doc and Tom Lake and stream were named for Sam Sias's horses that fell through the ice and drowned while pulling logs. Sam Sias and his brother John came to the Midland area to log in the 1860s and later came to Clare County. The lake is more likely named for Doc Blodgett and Thomas Stimson, who logged in the area before most lumber operations began and sent their logs down the Muskegon River. Today, the area around the 187-acre lake is a community known as Lake of the Pines. Stimson Lumber still operates in the western United States.

Three

Lake

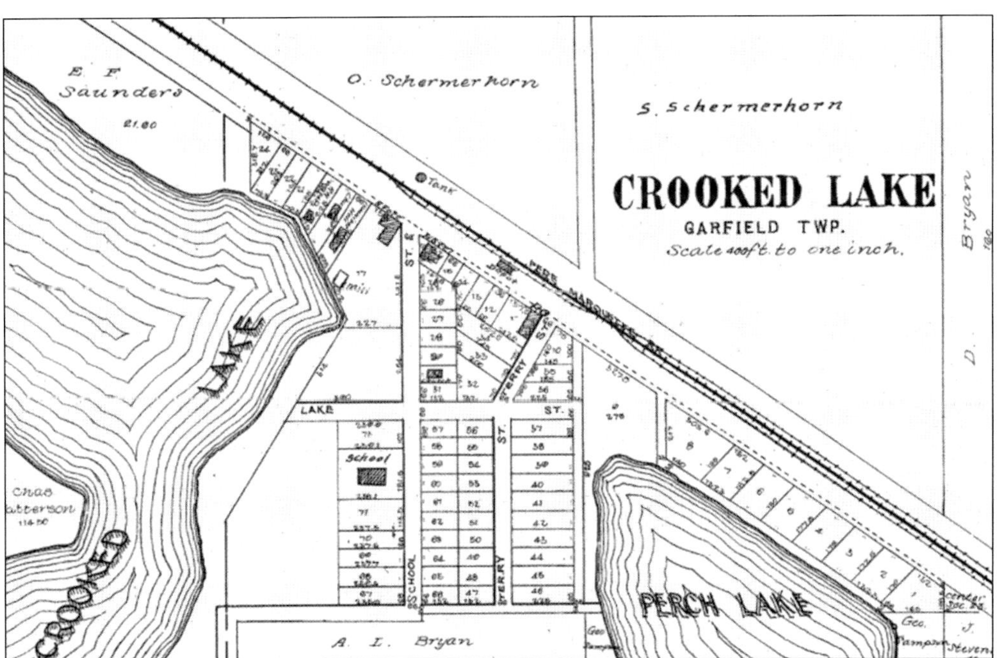

The area known as Lake, Lake Station, or Crooked Lake began as a depot on the Flint & Pere Marquette Railroad named Lake Station in 1877. The first post office was named Crooked Lake after the nearby lake. The railroad agent, Charles Bates, was the first postmaster. The large property owners to the north are brothers Oscar and Sam Schermerhorn, farmers and longtime residents. (HDL.)

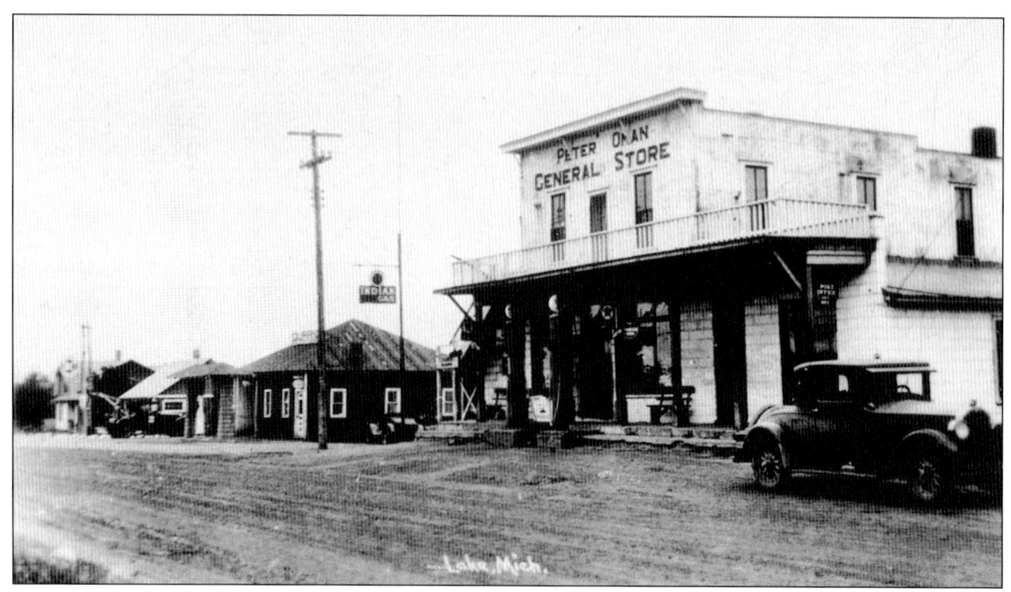

Peter Oman was born in 1886 in Sweden and came to Lake Station at age two. He attended Ferris State to become a teacher and taught in Clare County and worked for a time in Saginaw as well. He married Blanche Lansing in 1915. He ran this general store in Lake, catering to the growing tourism population. He served as treasurer of Clare County and was active in county government and the Republican Party. Peter Oman died in 1979 and is buried in Cherry Grove Cemetery in Clare.

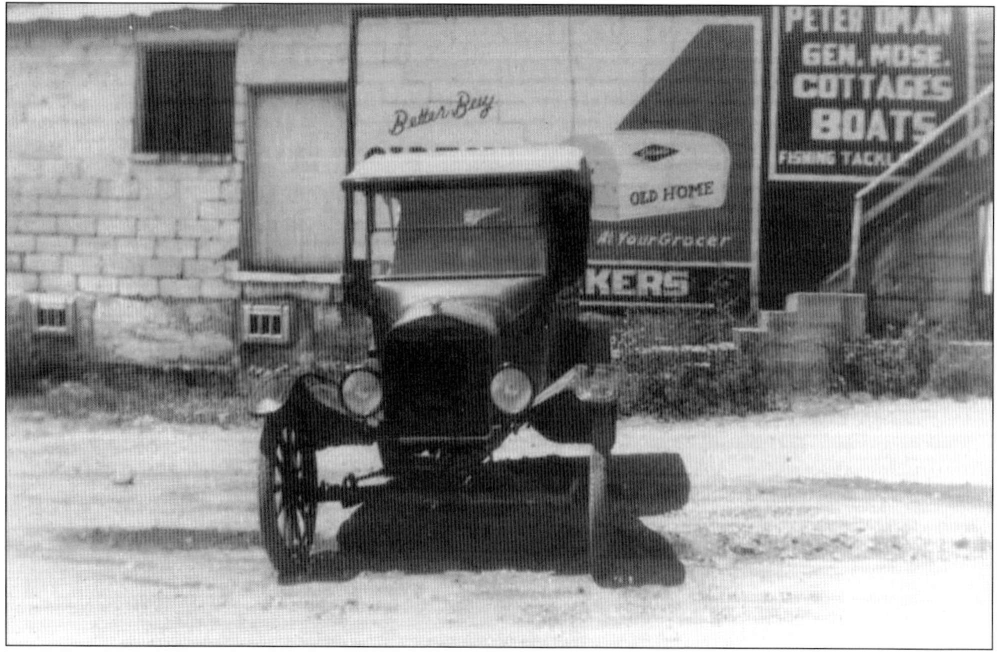

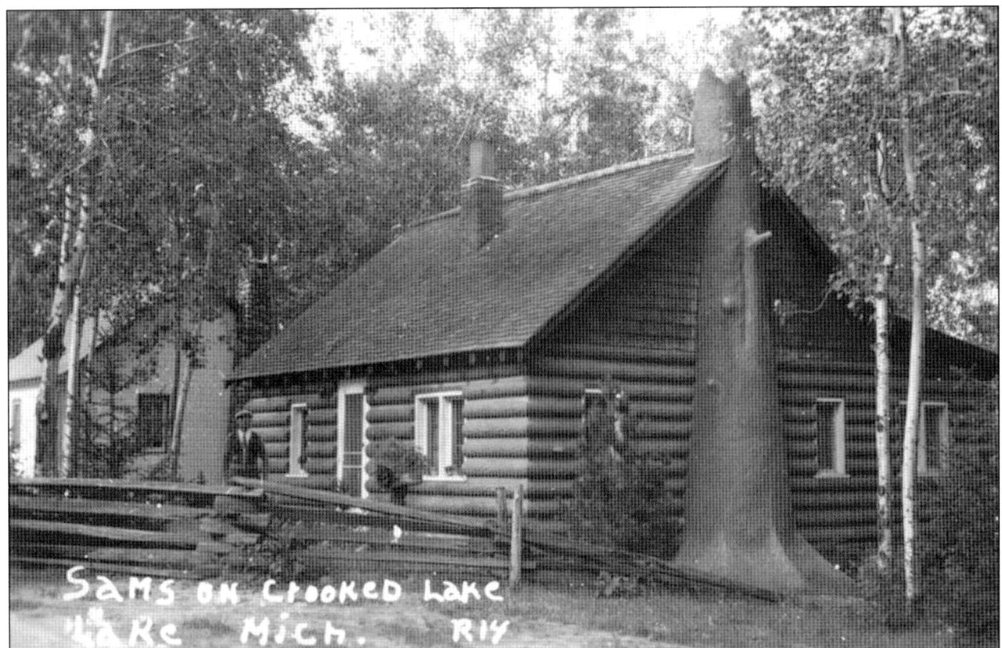

Crooked Lake was first popular for those "tenting out," known as camping today, in the early 1900s. Resort-goers later began building cabins and cottages and using the lakes for boating, swimming, and fishing. Fish were stocked as early as 1938. This cabin with its unique chimney on Crooked Lake was noted as Sam's place.

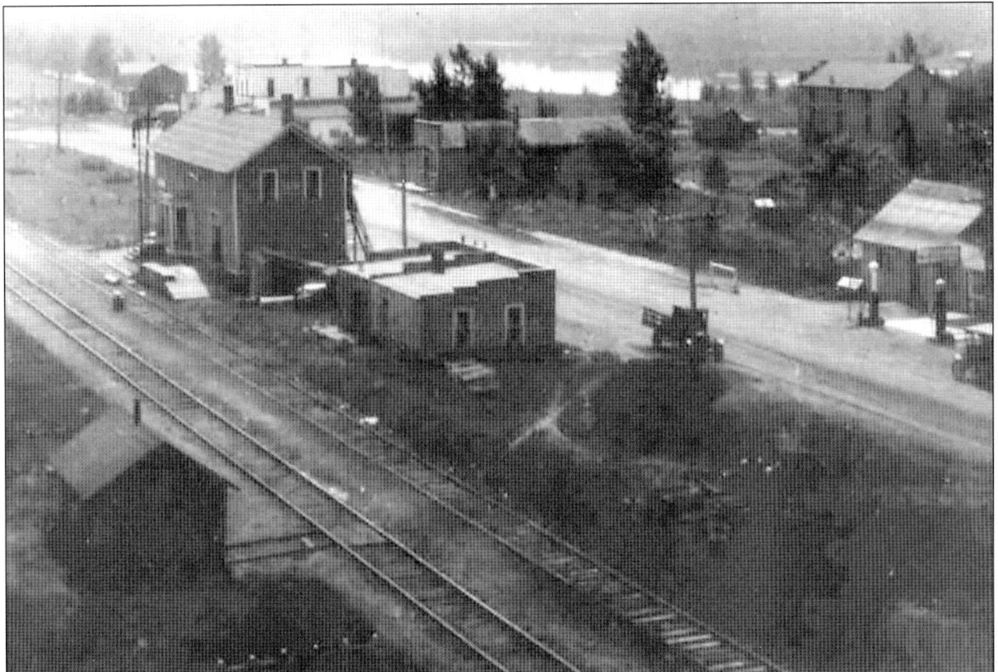

The road through Crooked Lake runs parallel to the railroad tracks. Peter Oman's general store is the white building past the depot on the corner. The now antique-style gas pumps (far right) are just beginning to serve the increasing number of cars and trucks.

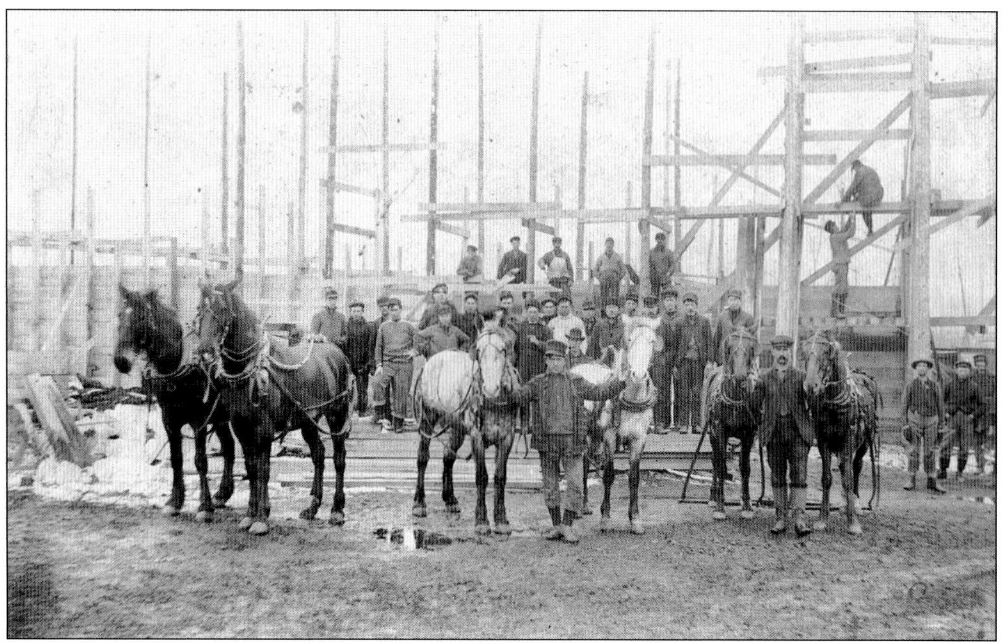

Some men are posing for the camera while others demonstrate their tools for building the icehouse. Winter work cutting and packing ice provided valuable jobs for farmers and other men.

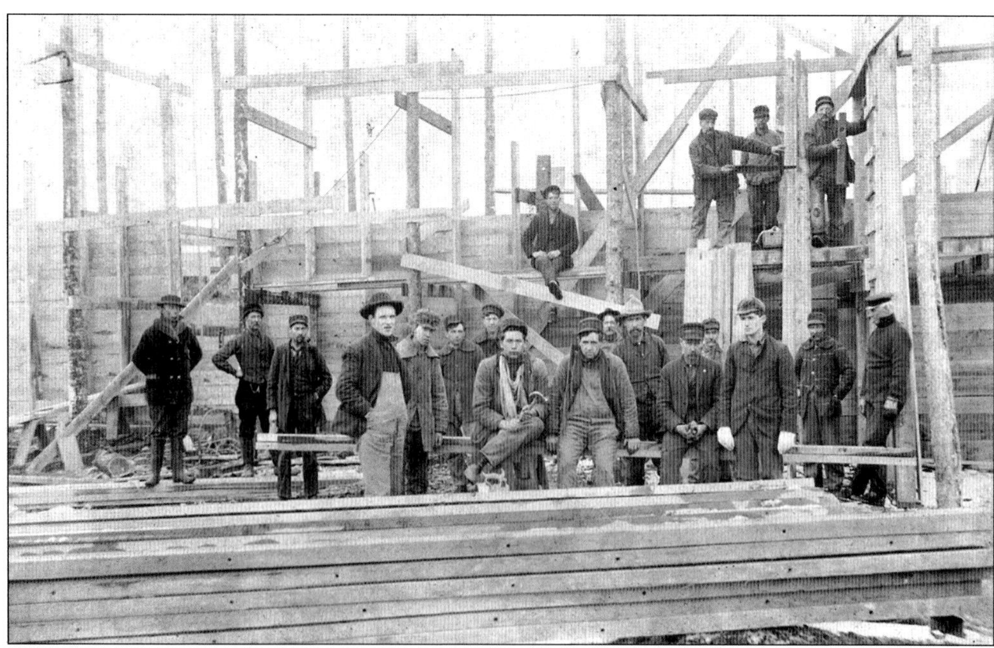

The icehouse was built in Lake in 1915. It was most likely at the south end of Big Cranberry Lake near the railroad tracks. Cutting ice was a very large business in all the northern states before refrigeration and artificial ice making was widely available. Ice was cut, packed in sawdust, and stored for local sale for the coming year, as well as packed onto trains to be transported and sold to southern states.

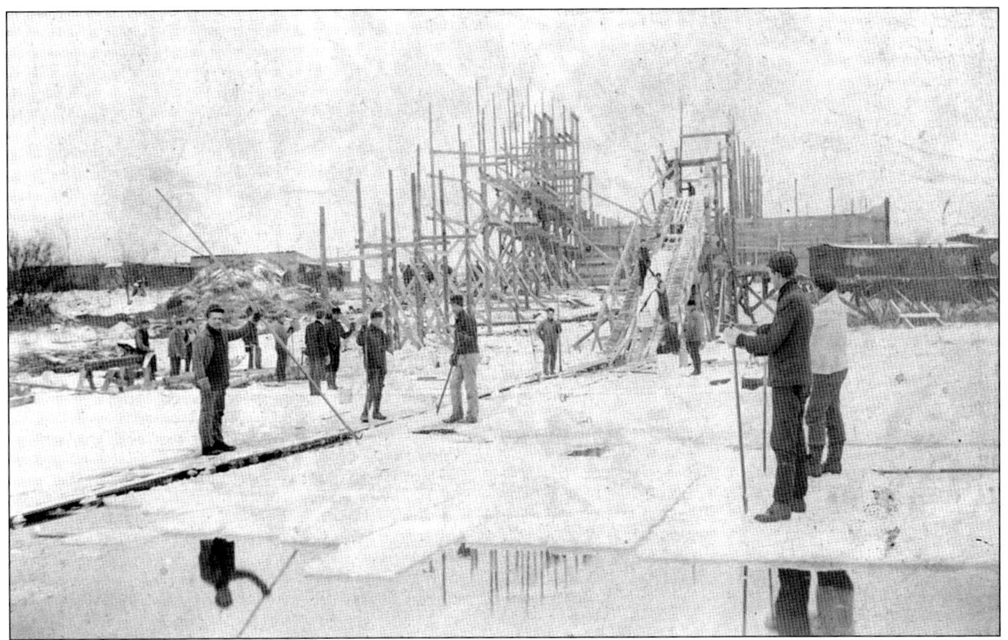

The men would cut out the huge blocks of ice, slide them up chutes, and then deposit them in the icehouse for storage or directly onto freight cars for shipping. In the very early days, most of the men harvesting ice were also lumberjacks and used many of the same tools, such as crosscut saws and cant hooks.

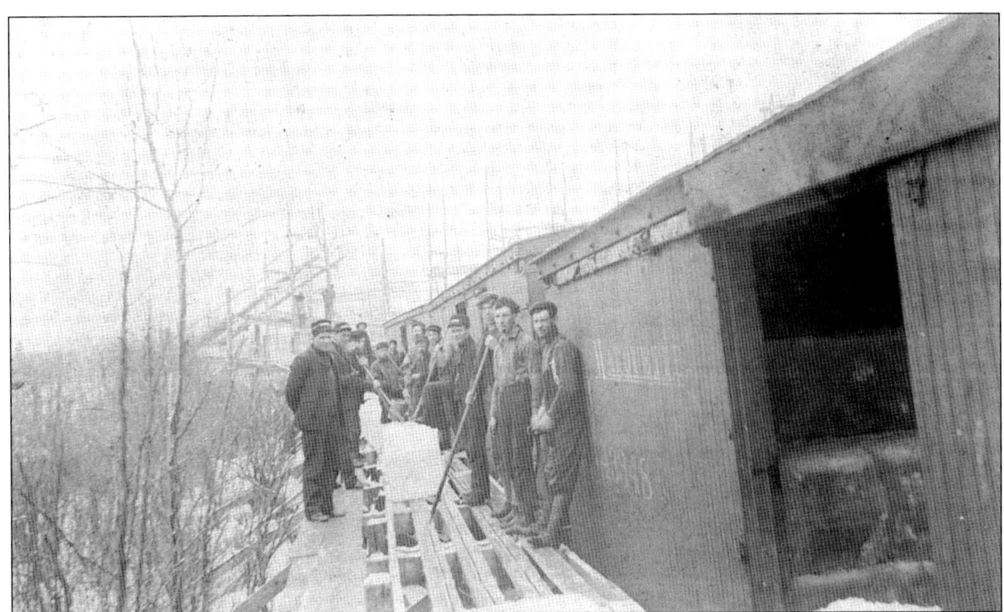

The blocks of ice are being loaded onto freight cars of the Flint & Pere Marquette Railroad. Ice was used for public consumption, and railroads also began to refrigerate cars to transport food. Refrigerated cars at the end of the 19th century revolutionized the meat, fruit, and vegetable industries in the United States by allowing fresh foods to be transported long distances.

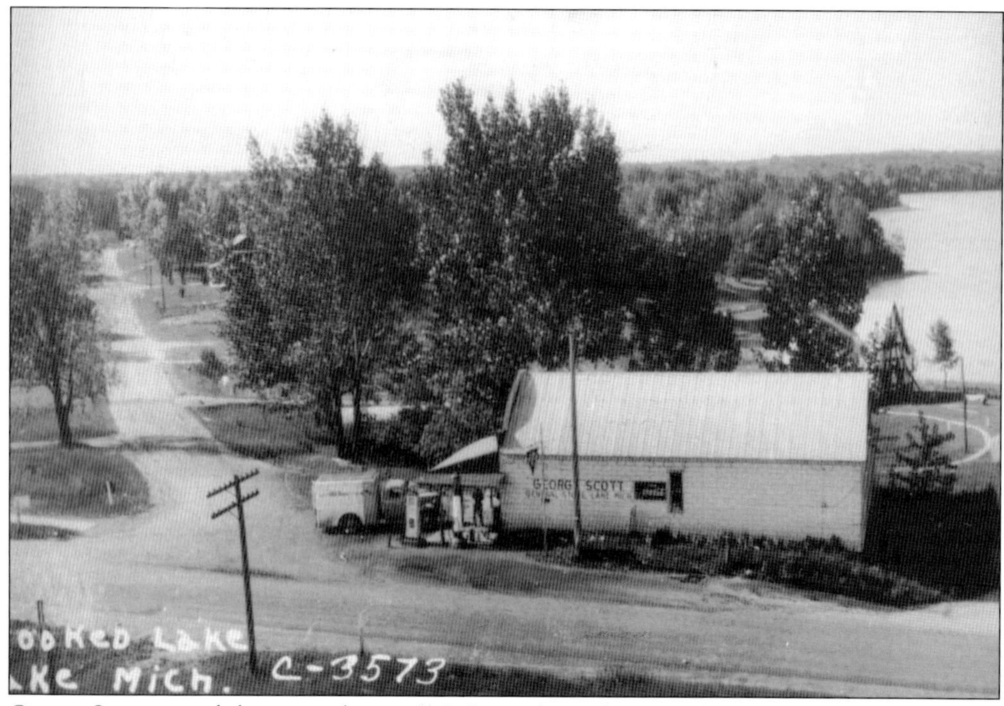

George Scott owned this general store in Lake in the early 1900s through the 1940s. Scott was married to Margaret Spence, who died in 1919. He later married Hilda Jane Smalley. He installed the first gas pump in Lake.

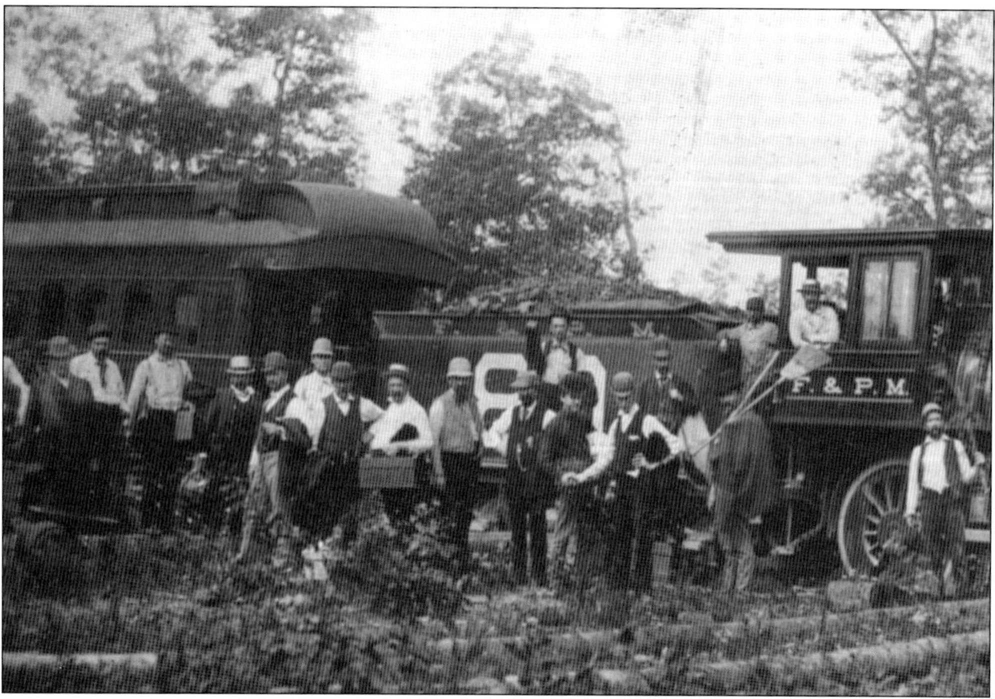

An 1890s pleasure outing to Crooked Lake on the Flint & Pere Marquette Railroad line is shown here. (Meek.)

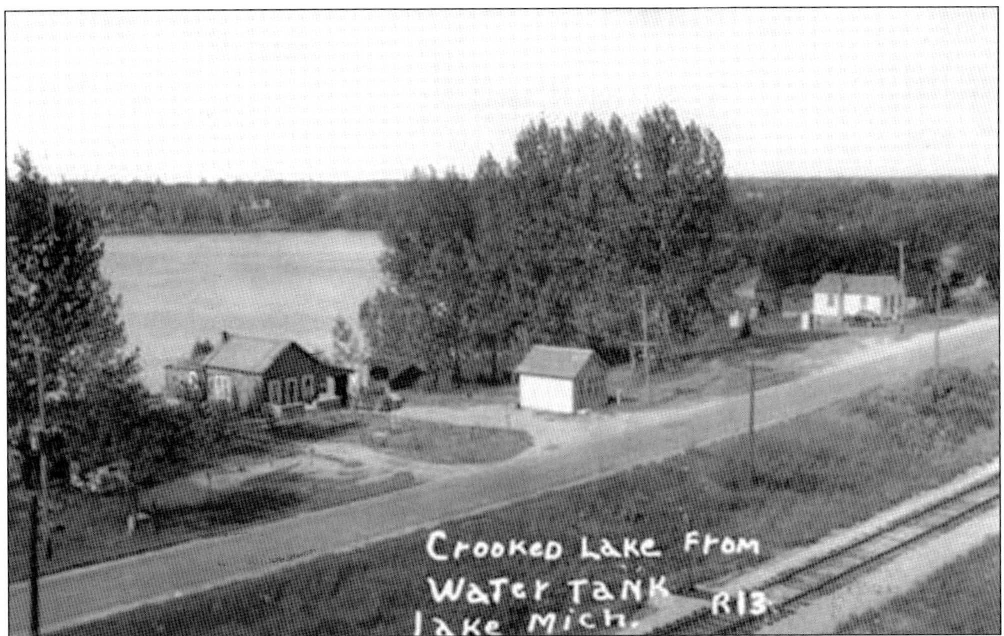

Early cabins are shown here on Crooked Lake. This picture postcard view of Crooked lake was taken from the water tank.

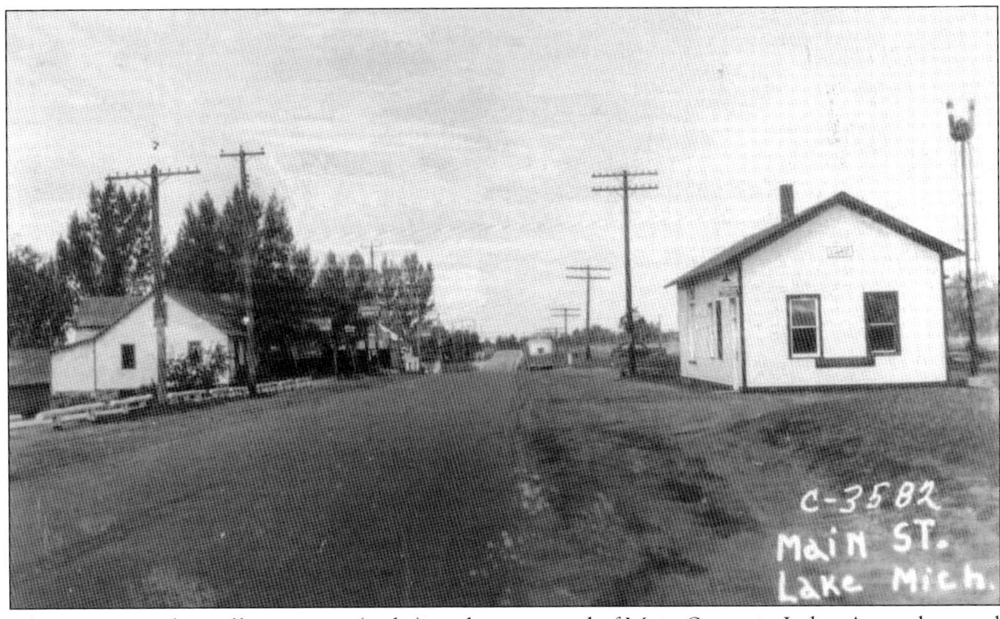

The train signal is still operating (right) in this postcard of Main Street in Lake. An early travel camper is parked at center. Americans began to travel more often and farther from home in the 1950s. The lakes attracted auto workers and other southern Michigan residents to come up north.

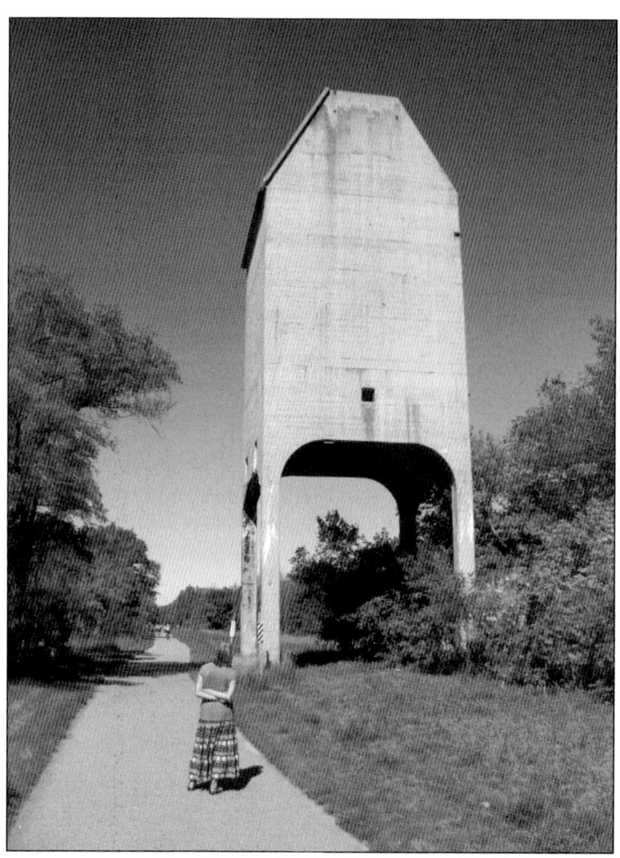

Early steam trains in northern Michigan fed their fires with wood as it was readily available. Later coal, a safer fuel, replaced wood, and trains would have stopped at this coal tower near Lake to refuel. Lake was a halfway point between Saginaw and Ludington and the ideal location for providing trains with coal and water. This coal tower was built in 1929. The railroad tracks are now a rail trail, and the coal tower is a popular stop for photographers. (Courtesy of Martin Johnson.)

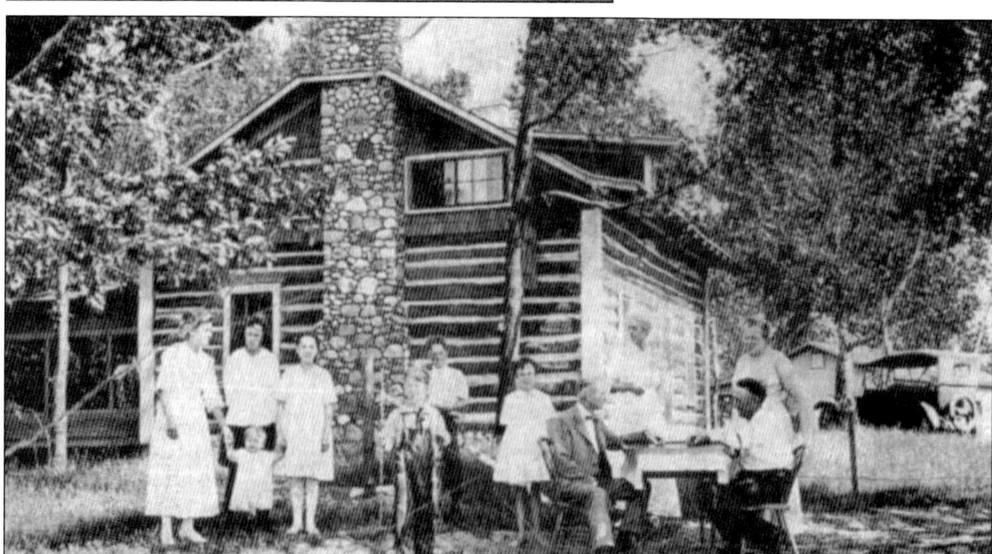

The first home in Farwell was made of logs and later moved to Crooked Lake. Built by George Hitchcock and his wife, Martha, they welcomed early travelers to the area in this home. Their daughter Alice Hitchcock married William Fuller and their family is shown here in 1918. From left to right are Edna Fuller, Martha Fuller, Marjory Fuller, Merrit Fuller, Wilton Powell, George Fuller, Marion Fuller, Frank Babcock, Alice, Effie Fuller Babcock, and William Fuller.

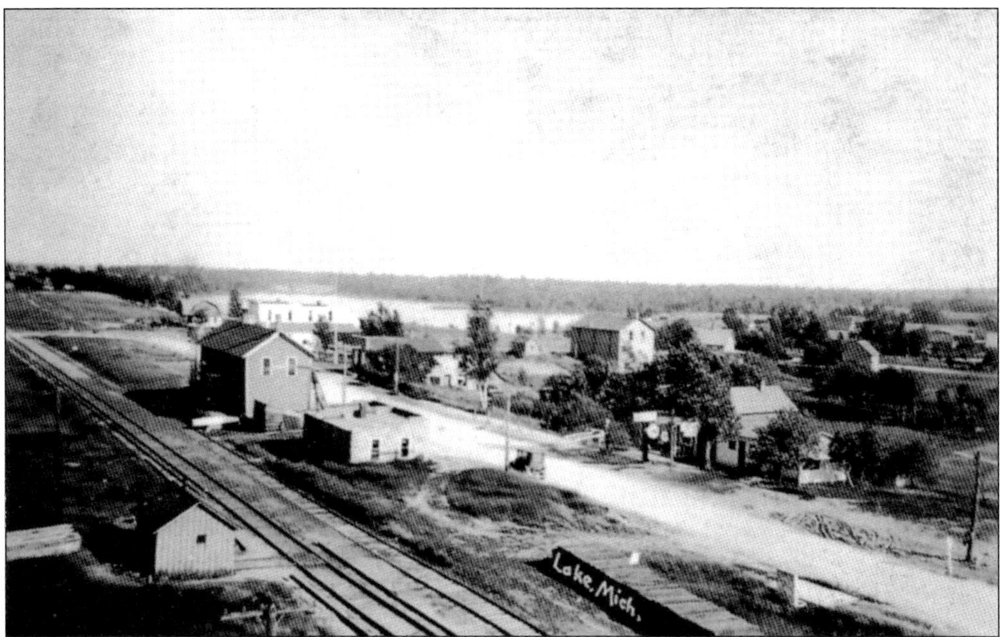

The Flint & Pere Marquette Railroad depot (left) is shown here in the 1920s. The depot building is still standing today accompanied by a decommissioned caboose. Crooked Lake is in the background.

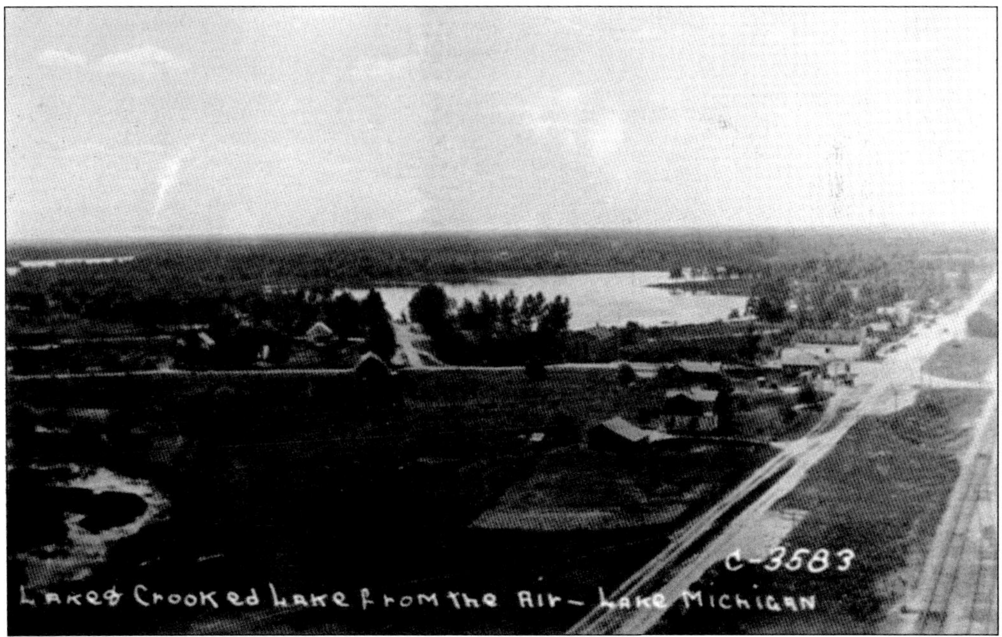

Crooked Lake (top center) is a 264 acre spring-fed, all sports lake. Perch Lake, which is close by, is 50 acres. The lakes, with their boat launches and beautiful waters, make the area a vacation paradise for generations of people from the cities of Southern Michigan. Notice the railroad tracks and siding at lower left. Railroad sidings were used to store rolling stock or allow trains to pass each other on the same track.

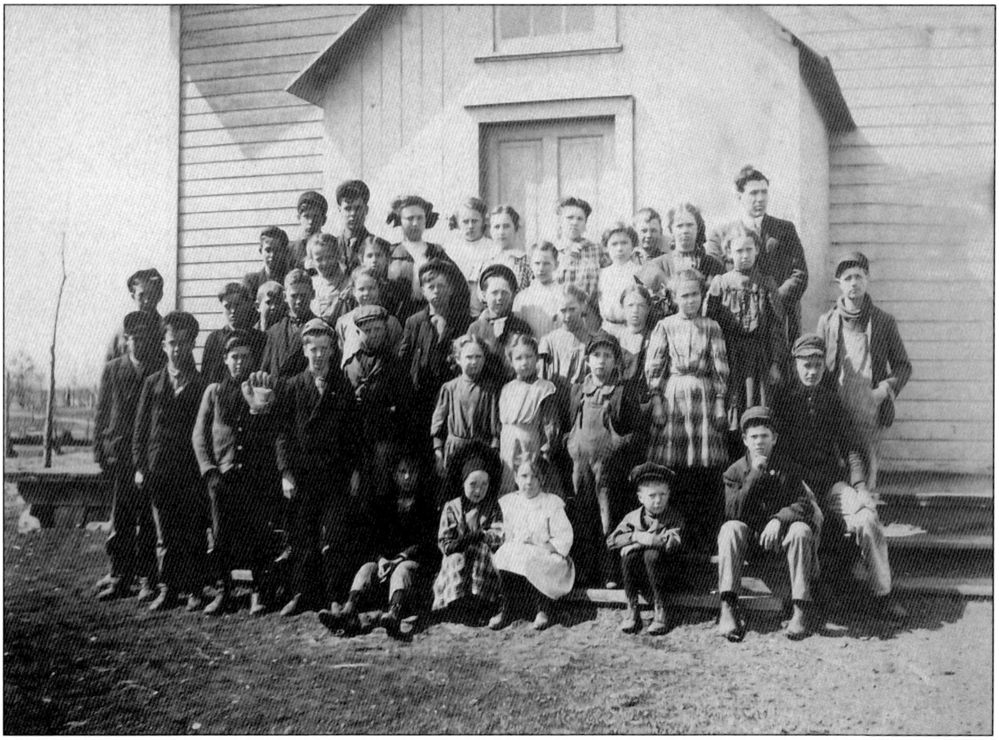

Students stand in front of the Lake school in the mid-1910s. Clark Sanborn (standing far right) and his sister Lela Sanborn (back row, second from right) were two of the 10 Sanborn children raised on a nearby farm. (CCHS.)

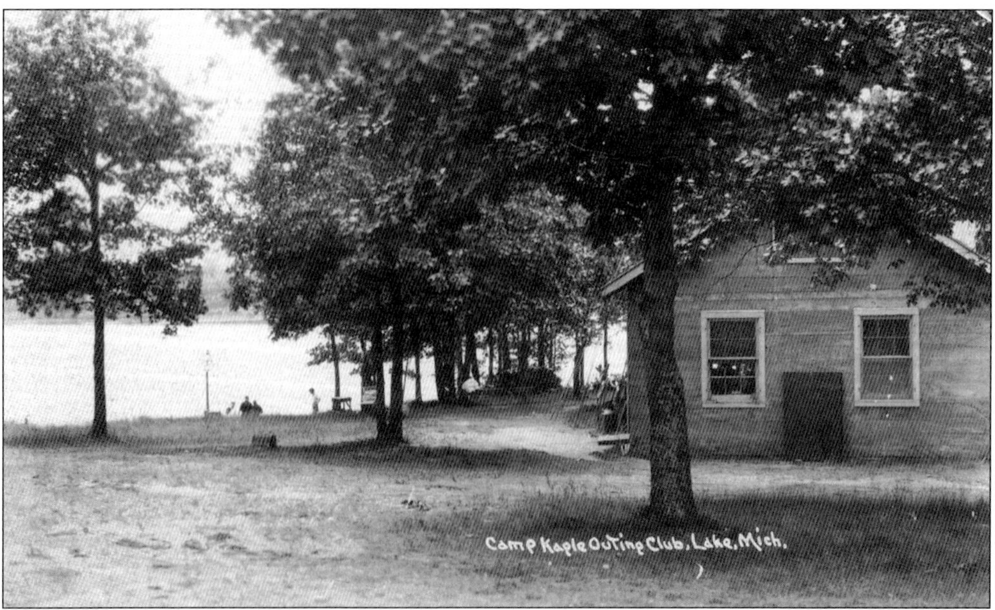

Pictured is one of many cabins on Crooked Lake enjoyed by vacationers. Properties and cabins were often given whimsical names or named after the family who owned it. This cabin was called the Camp Kagle Outing Club.

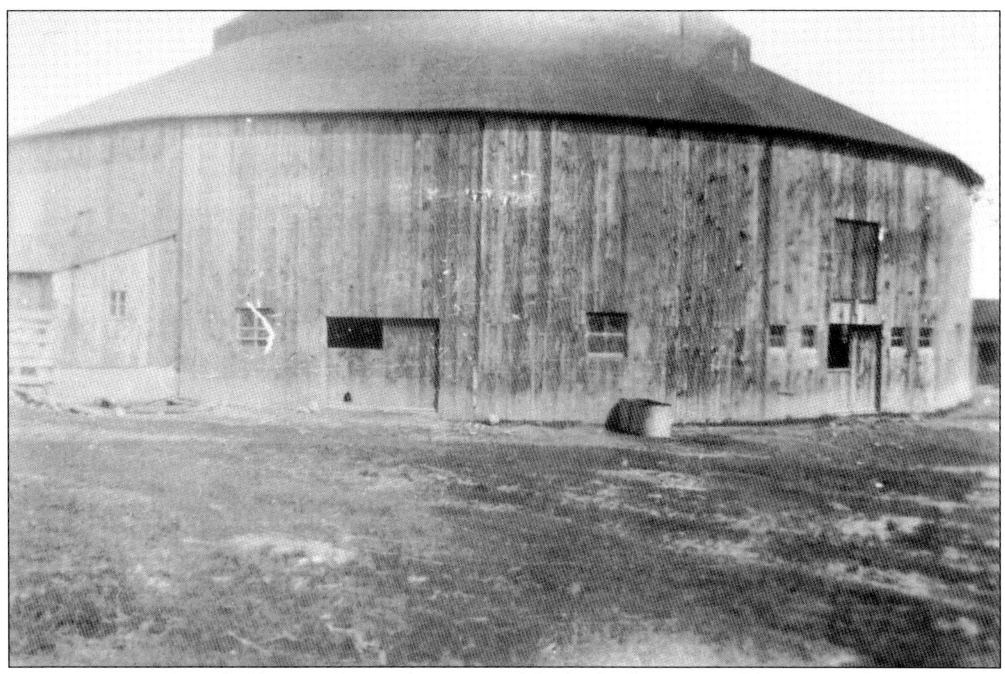

In section 26 of Garfield Township, Thomas Maltby built this unusual barn in 1914. It appears round, but is actually 12-sided. It was still standing in the 1970s, but unfortunately, it is not standing now. Maltby was born in England. He owned a general store in Crooked Lake and at one time was also the postmaster. (Meek.)

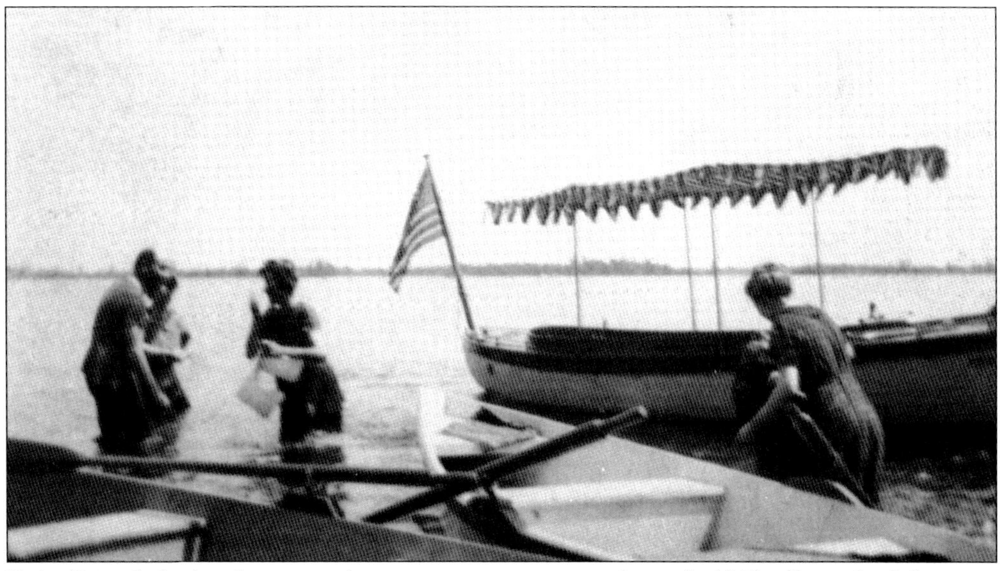

Eight Point Lake has been popular as a resort area since the early 1900s. Several subdivisions dot Eight Point Lake, such as the VanWelt and Raevena Shores areas. The 388-acre lake had a small marina by the 1950s. The boat shown here is most likely gasoline powered, which became popular in the 1910s. (Meek.)

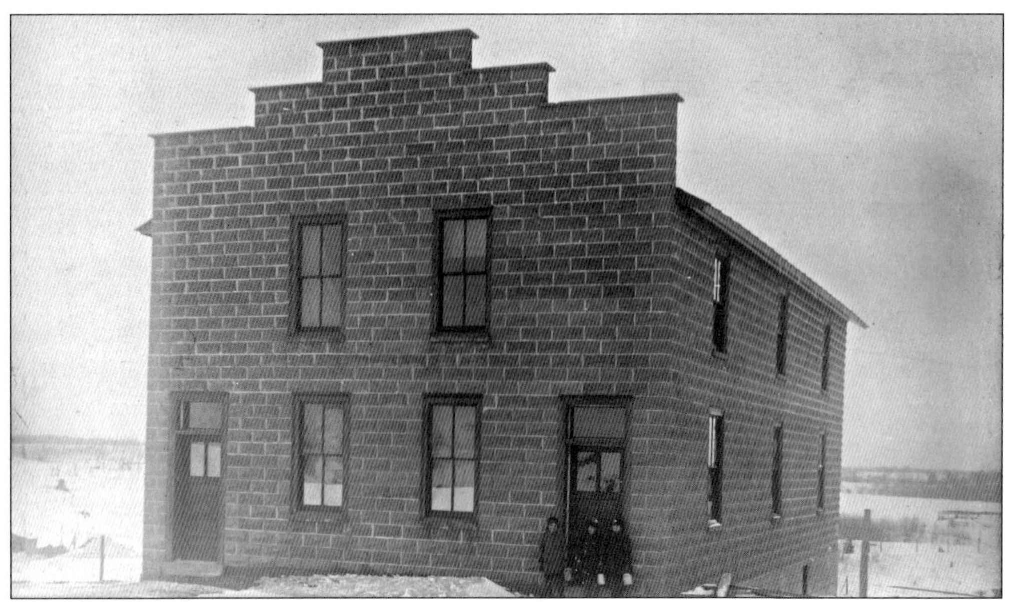

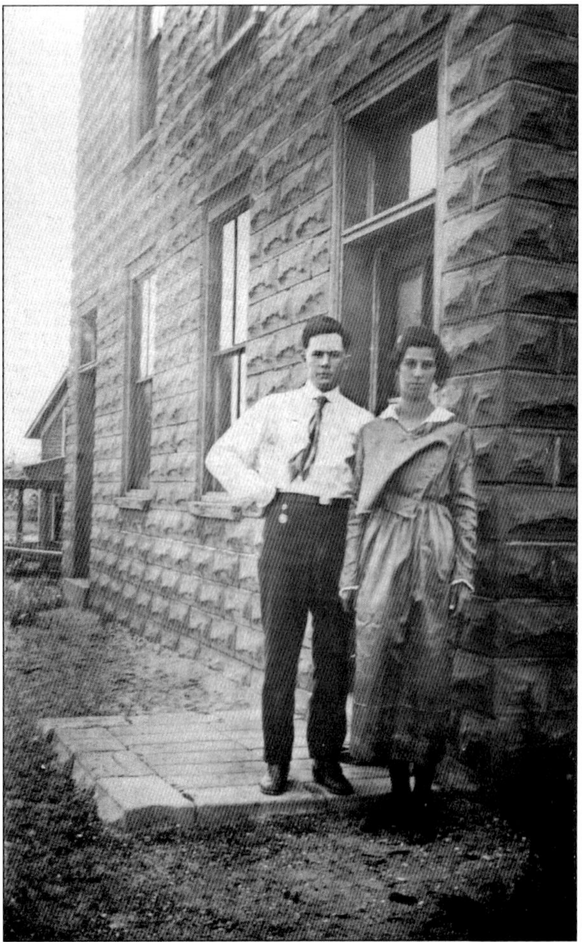

At left, Glen and Orpha (Martin) Amy stand in their wedding attire in front of the Gleaner Hall in Lake. They were married in 1918. Gleaner Hall was later the Garfield Township hall near Crooked Lake. Motion pictures were shown in the hall in the 1940s, and it was used for funeral services, reunions, and other gatherings. (Above, courtesy of Farwell Area Historical Society; left, courtesy of Nancy Bell Graham.)

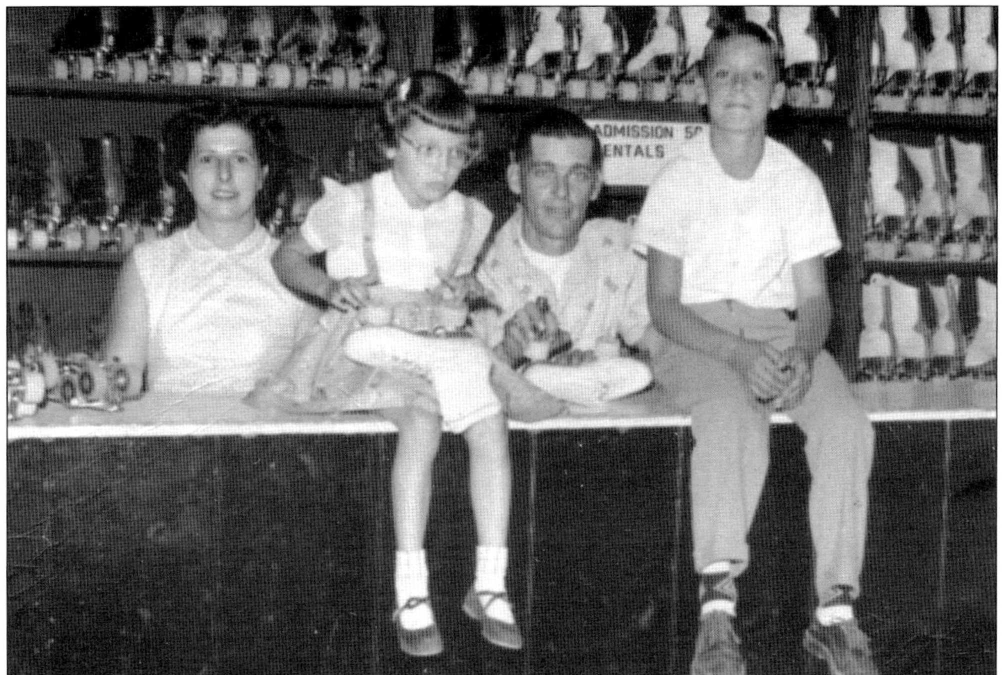

In the 1950s, the Lake Roller Rink opened and was owned by Richard and Mildred (Amy) Bell. Admission was 50¢ and skate rental was 25¢. The Bells are shown here with their children, Nancy and Neil. On Saturday nights, Mildred and Richard would skate and perform a beautiful waltz together. They would end the night with the Grand March, which they led and other couples followed. Each Christmas, the rink was decorated and two Christmas parties were held, one for the family and the other open to the public. (Courtesy of Nancy Bell Graham.)

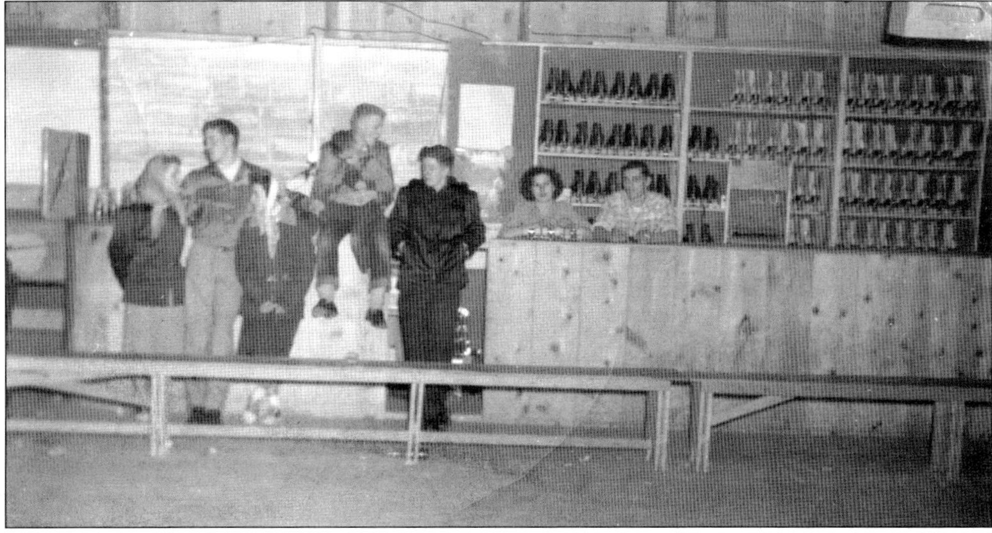

Generations of young people enjoyed the Lake Roller Rink before it closed in 2013. In the 1950s, people skated to organ music of waltzes, two steps, and popular songs of the day. The roller rink was for sale when the roof collapsed in March 2014 from a heavy snow load. The building was a total loss. Lloyd and Roberta Irwin owned the rink from 1978 to 1984. The last owners were Tom and Diane Gyulveszi, who owned it for 28 years. (Courtesy of Nancy Bell Graham.)

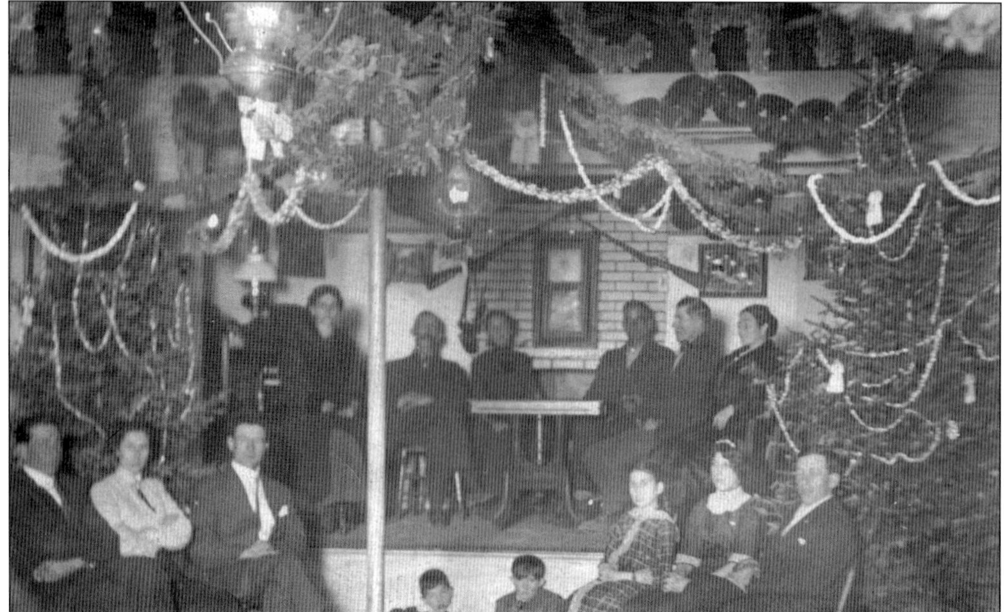

Grange Hall in Lake was the site of many parties, reunions, and weddings. This Christmas gathering includes, from left to right, (first row) Paul Finch, Eva Tryon, Pearl Tryon, Johnnie Martin, ? Tryon, Marguerite Martin, Orpha Martin, and Godfrey Beck; (second row) Arnett Martin sitting on piano bench, Lorenzo Martin, Calista Scott, Jacks Sutts, Al Tryon, and Jennie Tryon. (Courtesy of Nancy Bell Graham.)

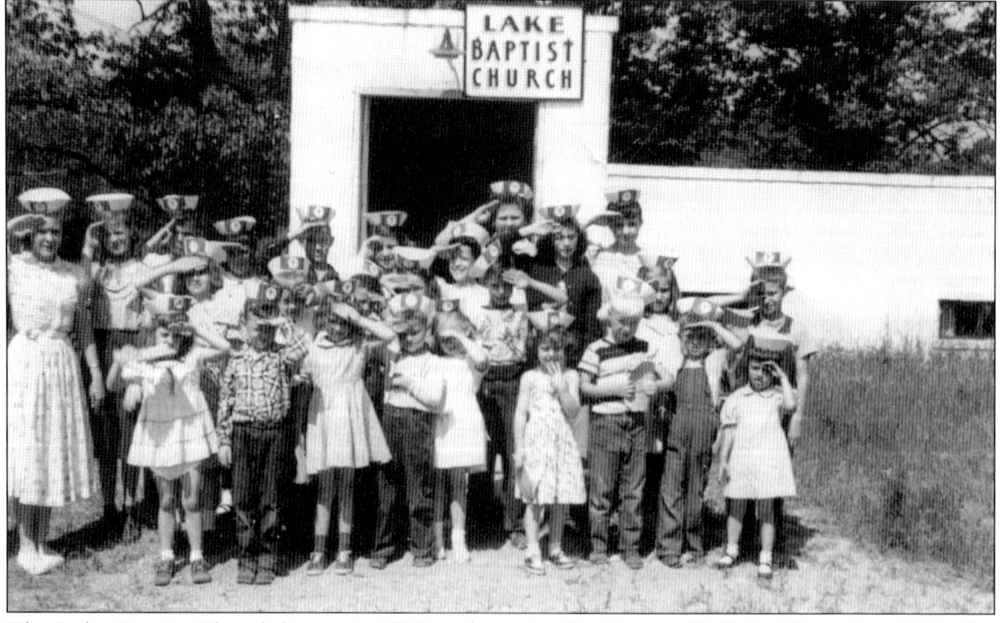

The Lake Baptist Church began in 1938 and met in the Grange Hall. In November 1946, the church had a new building constructed. Church papers and the first Bible the pastor used in his ministry were sealed in the cornerstone. Children are shown here in front of the church in the mid-1950s. It has had several additions, including a parsonage, since then. (Courtesy of Nancy Bell Graham.)

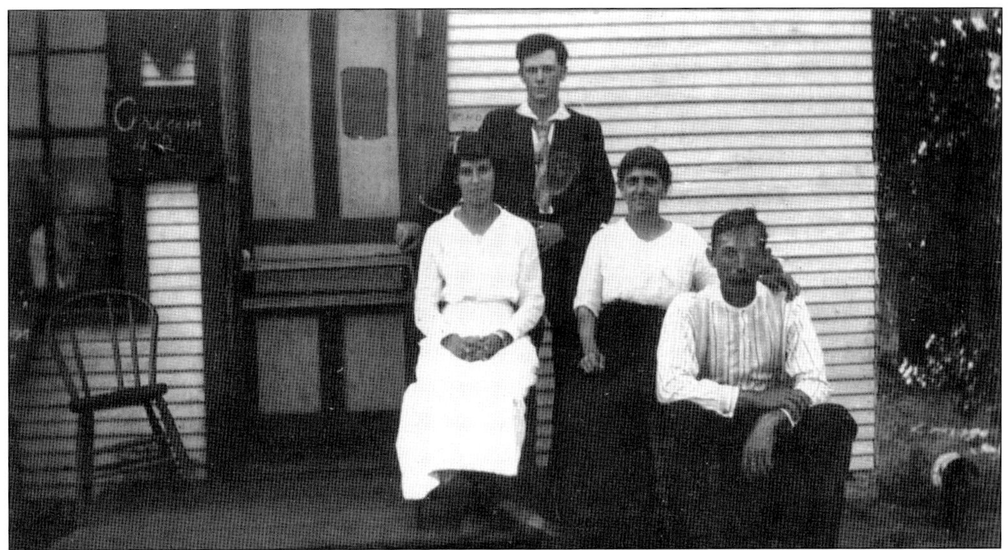

The Martin family poses in front of their creamery about 1918. The Lake creamery had a small bar with three stools and sold large portions of homemade ice cream. From left to right are Orpha Martin, her husband Glen Amy, Arnett Barton Martin, and Lorenzo Martin.

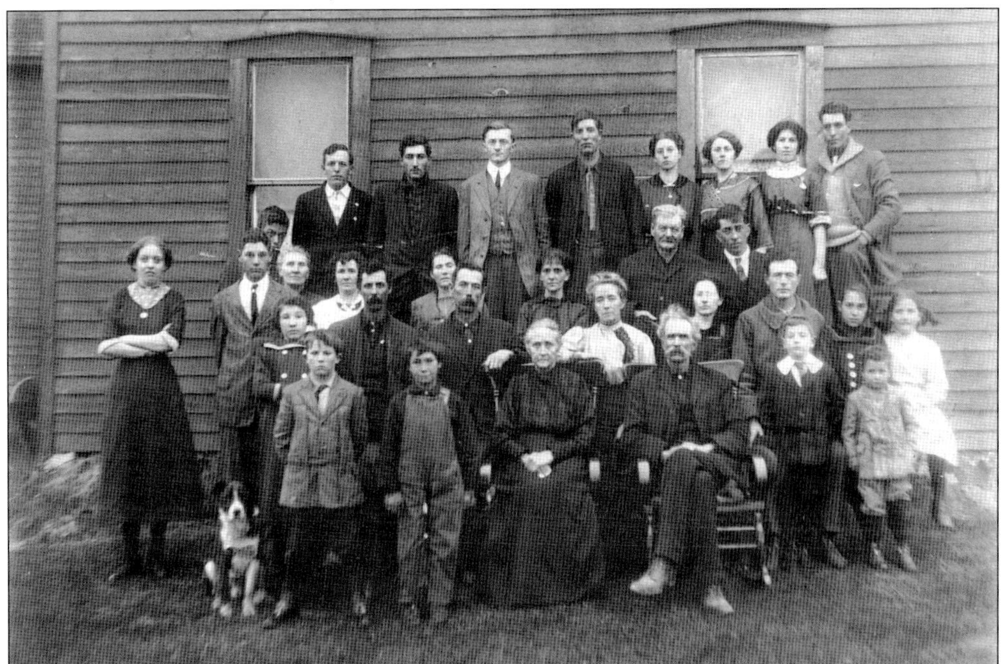

A gathering of friends and family is shown here at the Tryon home in Lake. Pictured are, from left to right, (first row) Calvin Tryon, Stanley Tryon, Barbarba Mills Martin-Tryon (sitting), Alfred Tryon, Sr. (sitting), John Martin, and Lewis Colton; (second row) Myra Pringle, Frank Pringle, Nina Martin, Frederick Martin, Lorenzo "Ren" Martin, Laura Martin Pringle, Eve Finch, Perl Tryon, Undine Tryon, and Marguerite Martin; (third row) Stephen Lorenzo Martin, Anna Oman, Effie Martin, Jennie Tryon, Amrett Barton Martin, Ulysses Pringle, and Paul Finch; (fourth row) Godfrey Beck, Grant McLane, Peter Oman, Alfred Tryon Jr., Edna Pringle, Anna Phipps, Orpha Martin, and Bill Pringle. (Courtesy of Nancy Bell Graham.)